W9-AFM-795

Student Workbook

for Ronald J. Comer's

Abnormal Psychology

third edition

Katherine M. Nicolai
Rockhurst College

W. H. Freeman and Company
New York

SUPPLEMENTS EDITOR: *Patrick Shriner*
ASSOCIATE EDITOR: *Robert Christie*
PROJECT EDITOR: *Erica Seifert*
ADMINISTRATIVE ASSISTANT: *Ceserina Pugliese*
COMPOSITION AND DESIGN: *Christopher Wieczerzak*
COVER DESIGN: *Blake Logan*
PRODUCTION COORDINATOR: *Maura Studley*

ISBN 0-7167-3205-X

© 1998 by W. H. Freeman and Company

No part of this book may be reproduced by any mechanical, photographic, or electronic process, or in the form of a photographic recording, nor may it be stored in a retrieval system, transmitted, or otherwise copied for public or private use, without written permission from the publisher.

Printed in the United States of America

First Printing, 1998

Contents

Preface

To the Student

This *Workbook* has been designed to help you excel in the study of abnormal psychology. While abnormal psychology is a fascinating course that should become one of the most memorable classes of your college experience, it is also one that is filled with detailed terms, topics, and concepts—so much so that you may find it a little intimidating at times. A key purpose of this workbook is to help you organize your study in this course so that you will have the time and the knowledge to delve more deeply into the disorders and the ideas presented.

The utility of the *Workbook* goes beyond simply being a concise way to organize the raw topic coverage of the textbook. A great deal of effort was put into designing exercises that call upon you to apply rote information in a way that gets you thinking about the underlying meaning of the ideas. In addition to fill-in-the-blank and short-answer questions, many exercises present a hypothetical set of facts relating to a patient or a psychological disorder. Applying your knowledge to hypothetical situations helps to bring the information to life. I have tried to "mix up" exercise types wherever possible, in order to keep things more engaging for you.

Ways to Use the Workbook

There are at least a couple of ways that you can use this *Workbook*. I recommend that my students first read the textbook a section at a time, and then attempt the corresponding section of exercises in the *Workbook*. Exercises explicitly follow the textbook's order of coverage, and each section (and usually each subsection as well) is clearly delineated in the *Workbook*. Many of the exercises call for a detailed knowledge of the material in the textbook. If you take a week, or even a day, between reading the textbook and attempting the exercises, you may be surprised at how little you remember. Completing the exercises in the manner I have suggested has an additional benefit—it provides you with an excellent set of study notes.

An alternative way to use the *Workbook* is to try to complete the exercises after you have read the book and attended your instructor's lectures. This is a way to identify areas where you need to concentrate your remaining study time before a test. The risk is that you may discover that you don't understand the material as well as you believed, and that you haven't left yourself enough time to learn it.

I hope that your studies with the *Workbook* will be a rewarding experience that truly helps you to understand, appreciate, and profit from the study of abnormal psychology.

To the Instructor

During a class term, time is a valuable commodity—especially with a topic-filled course like abnormal psychology. As an instructor, you probably already know that there never seems to be sufficient time to cover everything you would like in a term. Just imparting the strictly factual information can take so much time that you are left with little time to go into greater depth. If your students are using this *Workbook*, it can mean that you will have more time to devote to the conceptual and applied aspects of the factual material of abnormal psychology.

The *Workbook* is structured to enable you to assign it to your students in sections that correspond to the topic headings in the textbook. Each *Workbook* chapter begins with an outline of the chapter presentation, which facilitates assigning parts to students, and also helps your students keep their studies better organized.

My experience has been that the students who apply themselves to the kinds of exercises you will find in this *Workbook* are usually the ones who are the most prepared and the most engaged. They are also the ones who tend to perform better on exams.

I have recommended ideas based on my own experiences, but please use the *Workbook* in the manner that will serve you best. It could easily be used for homework to check that your students have completed and understood their reading assignments, especially in smaller classes. Also, if you have the opportunity for class involvement in your lectures, the *Workbook* can help your students come to class better prepared to discuss specific issues.

Chapter 1

Abnormal Psychology Past and Present

Chapter Organization

Chapter 1 is divided into three broad sections. The first section explores four features commonly used to define abnormal patterns of psychological functioning as well as difficulties in defining psychological abnormality. Section II comprises the bulk of the chapter, and thus gets the lion's share of coverage in the *Workbook.* It is divided into five subsections, each of which looks at the treatment of psychological problems in a distinct historical period. The final section deals with new treatments and treatment settings, the role of practitioners in psychology and emerging theoretical perspectives (to be covered in depth in the next chapter).

Be sure to read through each section before completing the exercises for that section.

Exercises

I: Defining Psychological Abnormality

Although no single definition of abnormal mental functioning is universally accepted, most definitions share four common features: the notions of deviance, distress, dysfunction, and danger. You can think of these as the "four D's" of defining abnormal functioning. All four are covered in this part of the Workbook.

1. Complete the table below by first identifying the feature (or the "D") associated with each definition listed and then giving a hypothetical example of a behavior that illustrates the defining feature. (The first one is done for you.)

	Feature	Definition	Example
a.	*danger*	Patterns of behavior, thoughts, and emotions that pose a risk to one's own or others' well-being and safety are considered abnormal.	*a young woman abuses cocaine and alcohol on a daily basis, drives recklessly when high, endangering herself and others*
b.		For patterns of behaviors, thoughts, and emotions to be labeled abnormal, the individual must experience them as unpleasant and adverse.	
c.		Behaviors, thoughts, and emotions that violate cultural norms are considered abnormal.	
d.		Patterns of behaviors, thoughts, and emotions that interfere with an individual's ability to maintain important aspects of life are considered abnormal.	

2. The major difficulty in defining abnormality is that the concept of "abnormality" is relative. Write a paragraph explaining what this means.

____

____

____

____

3. The term __________ is reserved for special __________ processes for helping people overcome psychological difficulties.

4. Briefly describe the 3 features common to all forms of therapy.

   1. ______________________________

   2. ______________________________

   3. ______________________________

II: Past Views and Treatments

1. Given that more than 25 percent of the people in the U.S. display psychological dysfunction serious enough to warrant treatment, some speculate that certain aspects of our modern world foster emotional maladjustment. List three recent societal developments that may contribute to psychological dysfunctioning.

a. ______________________________

b. ______________________________

c. ______________________________

A: Ancient Views and Treatments

1. It is believed that people in prehistoric societies viewed the human body and mind as sites of battle by __________________ forces, and they viewed both normal and abnormal behavior as the outcome of battles between good and evil spirits.

2. List and briefly describe two treatments for abnormality that may have occurred in prehistoric societies.

a. trephination ;

____

____

b. ______________ ; ______________________________

____

B: Greek and Roman Views and Treatments

Match the numbers 1–6 below with the appropriate option from the list a–f below the numbers.

1. ____ Greek and Roman physicians' treatment of mental illnesses
2. ____ Galen
3. ____ Hippocrates' treatment for melancholia
4. ____ Dementia
5. ____ Hippocrates
6. ____ Hysteria

a. Systematically distinguished emotional causes of abnormal behavior from medical ones

b. A mixture of medical and psychological techniques

c. Vegetable diet, temperance, exercise, celibacy, and bleeding

d. A general intellectual decline

e. Taught that illnesses had natural causes rather than metaphysical ones

f. Physical ailment with no apparent physical cause

C: Europe in the Middle Ages: Demonology Returns

1. What was the primary reason for the return of demonological views of psychological abnormality in the Middle Ages?

____

____

2. Large outbreaks of ___________ ____________________ in which large numbers of people shared similar delusions or hallucinations are an example of abnormal behavior present during the Middle Ages, a time of great societal stress and unrest.

3. List and briefly describe two prevalent forms of these shared delusions.

a. ______________ ; ____

____

b. ______________ ; people thought they were possessed by wolves or other wild animals, and acted as though they were these animals

D: The Renaissance and the Rise of the Asylums

1. The German physician Johann ________________, thought to be the first medical practitioner to specialize in mental illness, believed that the mind was as susceptible to illness as the body.

2. What was the purpose of the Gheel Shrine?

____

____

3. In the sixteenth century, the idea of asylums grew. Though usually founded with excellent intentions, such institutions as London's Bethlehem Hospital, the Lunatics' Tower in Vienna, and La Bicêtre in Paris degenerated into sites of degrading conditions where treatments of unspeakable cruelty flourished.

a. List some of these horrible conditions.

____

____

b. One reason behind these horrible conditions was the inability of municipalities to pay for large numbers of inmates. What was another reason?

____

E: The Nineteenth Century: Reform and Moral Treatment

1. What was the initial site of asylum reform (around 1793) and who was the man most responsible for the reform?

____

2. Describe an overall theme of the reforms in the treatment of patients during this period.

____

____

3. In addition to Pinel, there are others who are associated with the rise of moral treatment in Europe. Complete these statements regarding two of them.

a. Jean ________________ was Pinel's student and successor, who went on to establish ten new mental hospitals that operated by the same principles.

b. In England, William ________________ founded a "retreat" where rest, talk, prayer, and manual work replaced mechanical restraints and unfounded medical interventions as treatments for mental patients.

4. Benjamin Rush was the person who is credited with bringing moral treatment to the U.S. List two of his major innovations and accomplishments.

a. ______________________________

b. ______________________________

5. In 1841, a Boston schoolteacher named Dorothea Dix was shocked by the conditions she witnessed at a local prison. Dix began a 40-year campaign of reform that she broadened to include the plight of the mentally ill. Write a paragraph describing her remarkable effort.

____

____

____

____

6. Complete these statements describing how each of the following three factors contributed to the decline of moral treatment.

a. Moral treatment had advanced so quickly that many hospitals were built in a short period of time, leading to shortages of funding and ________________.

b. The basic assumptions of moral treatment—that patients would begin to function normally if they were treated with ________________ and if their ________________ needs were met—proved too optimistic.

c. Many people reacted to the trend of patients being removed to large, distant mental hospitals with a new wave of ________________ against the mentally ill.

7. In the late nineteenth century, the somatogenic perspective—the idea that abnormal psychological functioning has physical causes—once again gained acceptance and support. Explain how (a) the work of Emil Kraepelin, and (b) the discovery that general paresis is caused by syphilis were important to the resurgence of the somatogenic perspective.

a. ______________________________

____

b. ______________________________

____

8. The psychogenic perspective has the view that the primary causes of abnormal behavior are ________________ in nature.

9. Some scientists believed that the successes of the treatment called mesmerism in treating patients with ________________ disorders resulted from patients being induced into a trance-like stat

10. By the late nineteenth century, two competing views of the nature of hysterical disorders had emerged. One was that they were caused by the mind. What was the other?

____

____

____

11. Two French physicians, Bernheim and Liebault, settled the debate over the cause of hysterical disorders by showing that they could be induced and then removed in otherwise normal subjects by means of ____________________.

12. ____________________, a Viennese doctor who later worked with Freud, discovered that his hypnotized patients sometimes awoke free of hysterical symptoms after speaking freely about past traumas under hypnosis.

III: Current Trends

1. The current era of abnormal psychology can be said to have begun in what decade? ____________________

2. The discovery and use of psychotropic drugs resulted in the nearly immediate discharge of many severely disturbed patients. This policy is now known as ____________________.

3. ____________________ care has become the primary mode of treatment for people with severe psychological disturbances as well as for those with more moderate problems.

4. In the last 45 years there has been a dramatic increase in the number of persons seeking outpatient treatment for psychological problems. Complete this list of factors that have contributed to the growth.

a. The discovery of psychotropic medications.

b. ____________________

c. ____________________

One of the most significant developments in the understanding and treatment of abnormal psychological functioning has been the emergence of numerous, often competing theoretical perspectives. This will become more evident to you as you work your way through this course starting with Chapter 2.

5. At present, no single theoretical perspective dominates the clinical field. Many theories have influenced the current understanding and treatment of abnormal functioning. Complete the following statements about some of the perspectives.

a. Before the 1950s, the ______________________________ perspective, with its emphasis on ______________________ conflicts as the cause of psychopathology was dominant.

b. The somatogenic, or ____________________ view of abnormality grew in stature in the 1950s with the discovery of effective ____________________ drugs.

c. Some of the influential perspectives that have emerged since the 1950s include the behavioral, cognitive, humanistic-existential, and sociocultural schools. They explain and treat abnormality in very ____________________ ways.

6. Complete the following statements regarding professional careers in psychology.

a. Psychotherapy was the exclusive province of ________________________ before the 1950s. These people are physicians who have completed _____ to _____ years of training after medical school in the treatment of abnormal mental functioning.

b. Clinical psychologists are professionals who earn a doctorate by completing four years of graduate training in abnormal functioning and its treatment and also complete a one-year internship at a ______________________________________.

c. Counseling psychologists, educational psychologists, psychiatric nurses, marriage therapists, family therapists, and—the largest group—_______________ _______________ _______________ fall into a category of professionals who have completed a _______________ _______________ program in their specialty area.

Practice multiple-choice questions for this chapter begin on page 271.

Chapter 2

Research in Abnormal Psychology

Chapter Organization

The methods used by clinical researchers to discover and understand the central features and processes of abnormal behavior and its treatment are the focus of Chapter 2. The *Workbook* chapter will help you to review the basic principles and procedures of research in the field of psychology. The first of the chapter's five sections introduces details of the scientific method, a central concept to all the forms of research. The second section discusses the case study; and the third discusses the correlation method of research. Study the fourth section closely. It explores the many issues involved in the experimental method. The chapter concludes with a look at the limitations of these forms of research.

Be sure to read through each section before completing the exercises for that section.

Exercises

I: The Task of Clinical Researchers

The scientific method is the process of systematically acquiring and evaluating information by observation to gain an understanding of the phenomena being studied. It is a key concept to modern science. This section's exercises relate to this important basis for research.

1. Clinical research looks for general, or ____________________, truths about the nature, causes and treatments of abnormalities, while clinical practitioners search for truths regarding the abnormalities in individuals, which are called ____________________ truths.

2. To formulate a nomothetic explanation of abnormal psychology, scientists try to identify and explain relationships between **variables.** Any characteristic or event that can vary, whether from time to time, place to place, or person to person, is a variable.

a. List some of the variables that are of particular interest to clinical researchers.

____

3. Clinical researchers seek to determine whether two or more variables change together and whether ____.

4. The three primary methods of investigation—the case study, the correlation method, and the experimental method—enable clinical researchers to formulate and test **hypotheses.** Define the term hypothesis.

____

____

II: The Case Study

A: Contributions of the Case Study

1. Fill in the missing words in the this list of nomothetic roles case studies serve.

a. They are a source of ideas about universal psychological ____________________ and principles of ____________________.

b. They provide tentative support for a ____________________.

c. They may serve to challenge theoretical ____________________.

d. They serve as a source of ideas for new therapeutic ____________________.

e. They offer opportunities to study unusual problems that ____________________

____

B: Limitations of the Case Study

1. Case studies are reported by biased observers. Why does this limit the usefulness of the research method?

____

____

2. A study is said to have internal accuracy, **or internal validity**, when an investigator can show that only one possible ____________________

____

3. Why do case studies have limited internal validity?

____

____

4. The case study of the Genain quadruplets suggested that their schizophrenic disorders may have been genetically transmitted. What did further investigation reveal regarding other possible causal factors?

____

____

____

5. Although case studies provide rich detail about single individuals, they do not provide nomothetic insights, or information about large groups of people. Only **correlational** and **experimental** methods can accomplish this. Below, summarize (in your own words!) the three important characteristics of correlational and experimental research methods that allow investigators to gain nomothetic insights.

1. ______________________________

____

2. ______________________________

____

3. ______________________________

____

III: The Correlation Method

The following exercises, 1–8, cover material in subsections A, B, C, and D of Section III—"The Direction of Correlation," "The Magnitude of Correlation," "The Correlation Coefficient," and "Statistical Analysis of Correlation Data." Subsection E and F will be covered in separate successive parts.

1a. Define Correlation:

____

b. Formulate a question that might be asked by a researcher using the correlational method that includes the variables "procrastination" and "test anxiety." (Hint: make sure the word "cause" is not used in your question—you'll discover why later!)

____

____

2a. Define operationalization:

____

b. You are a researcher studying the relationship between marital satisfaction and number of pre-marriage sexual partners. List some of the ways that you could **operationalize** marital satisfaction

____

____

____

3. On the following graphs, draw in the "**lines of best fit**" which illustrate the labeled relationships between marital satisfaction and the number of pre-marriage sexual partners. (Be sure to examine the figures on p. 35 of the text)

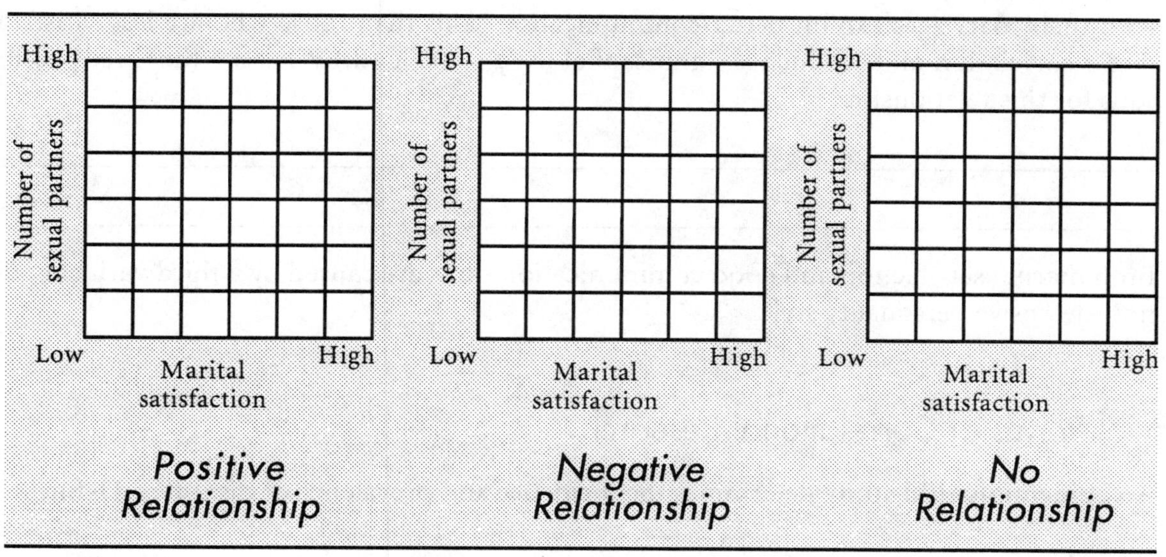

4. Other than knowing whether a correlation is positive or negative, it is also important to know the magnitude, or ________________, of the relationship between variables.

5. The statistical term known as the ________________ ________________, symbolized by the letter **r**, expresses the direction and the magnitude of the relationship between two variables.

6. Put the following list of coefficients in order of their strength of correlation:

.61 –.01 .50 –.58 –.82

________ ________ ________ ________ ________

Strongest correlation *Weakest correlation*

7. Statistical analyses of data are performed in order to discover how likely it is that a given correlation has been found by ________________.

8. What does the statistical notation $p < .05$ mean?

____

____

E: Strengths and Limitations of the Correlation Method

1. Correlational studies typically exhibit more ________________ validity than case studies because findings can be ________________ to people beyond those in the study.

2. Correlational studies lack ______________ validity because they do not explain the ______________ between variables.

3. Let's say that in your study of marital satisfaction you also discover that couples who are satisfied with their marriages exhibit better communication skills than those who are less satisfied. (You find a correlation of .65, which is significant at the $p < .05$ level.) What are the three possible reasons for this relationship?

a. ______________________________

b. ______________________________

c. Both marital satisfaction and good communication skills are caused by a third variable, such as a non-defensive personality style.

F: Special Forms of Correlational Research

1. An **epidemiological study** determines the incidence and prevalence of disorders. Define:

Incidence:

____

Prevalence:

____

2. List two findings of the epidemiological studies reported in your text.

____

____

3. Longitudinal research methods provide information about the ______________ of certain events, so they are more likely than conventional correlation studies to shed light on which events may be ______________ and which may be consequences. However, they still do not pinpoint ______________.

IV: The Experimental Method

1. Fill in the missing words in the following list of descriptions of the functions of researchers using the experimental method.

a. They formulate and test a ______________.

b. They manipulate the ______________ variable that is thought to cause some effect.

c. They observe the effect of the manipulated variable on the ______________ variable of interest.

2. Complete the following exercise by identifying the independent and the dependent variables of each fictional "study."

Hypothesis	Independent variable	Dependent variable
Drinking warm milk causes people to be sleepy		*sleepiness*
Using shampoo "X" causes hair loss		
Group therapy is more effective than individual therapy in the treatment of depression	*type of therapy*	

The following exercises, 3–15, cover material in subsections A–E of Section IV. They are: "Confounds," "The Control Group," "Random Assignment," and "Blind Design." Next, "Variations in Experimental Design" is covered.

3. Give a thorough definition of the term **confound**.

____

____

4. Why do the presence of confounds make it difficult to establish cause and effect relationships in experimental studies?

____

____

____

Read through the following "study," paying careful attention to its design and method. Then answer the questions posed in exercises 5–10, which are based on the "study."

Study

Study:	Classical Music Therapy
Hypothesis:	People experience mood elevation after listening to classical music.
Subjects:	Subjects were identified and recruited at a "Mozart by Moonlight" concert. Researchers told potential subjects "We think listening to classical music will make you feel better. Will you help us?"
Method:	Subjects filled out a questionnaire designed to assess mood prior to engaging in experiment. They were then asked to sit in comfortable recliners in the research lab. Subjects were given headphones and told by an attractive, pleasant research assistant to relax and listen to thirty minutes of classical music. After listening to the music, subjects removed their headphones and filled out the same mood questionnaires in order to assess pre- and post-music differences. A selection of sandwiches and soft drinks were provided to the subjects as they filled out the post-music questionnaire.
Results:	Pre- and post-music scores were significantly different in the hypothesized direction. The experimenter concluded that classical music therapy results in people feeling happier.

5. There are numerous confounds present in the "Classical Music Therapy" study. List as many as you can that could explain the results of the experiment.

____

____

____

____

6. What are the three features that researchers incorporate into their experiments in order to control potential confounds?

a. control groups

b. ____________________

c. ____________________

7. Ideally, what is the only difference between the control group and the experimental group?

____

8. In the "Classical Music Therapy" study, what might be an appropriate control group?

____

9. Was **self-selection** present in the "Classical Music Therapy" study? Explain your answer.

__________, ______________________________________

____

10. Explain why **random assignments of subjects to groups** minimizes the effects of potential confounds in an experiment.

____

____

Box 2-1

The term "artifact" describes a research finding that is shown to be a result of something the experimenter did (or didn't do) rather than a result of experimental manipulation. Thus, researchers may mistakenly conclude that an experimental hypothesis was supported by their findings, when in fact the findings are "artifactual" due to an unrecognized confound in the experiment. Read through Box 2-1 and be sure you understand why researchers in the "executive monkey" study reached just this kind of mistaken conclusion.

11. Subjects may bias the results of an experiment because they have attempted to please or ______________ the experimenter to get the findings he or she wants.

12. Another type of subject bias is called the **placebo effect**, in which subjects' ______________ of a positive outcome may affect the way that they respond to a particular manipulation or treatment.

13. How might experimenter bias, also known as the **Rosenthal effect**, occur in an experiment?

____

____

14. Give thorough definitions of the terms (a) **blind design**, (b) **double-blind design**, and (c) **triple-blind design**.

a. A study in which the subjects are unaware if they are in the experimental group or the control group.

b. ____

____

c. ____

____

F: Variations in Experimental Design

Workbook coverage of subsection F is divided into four parts—one for each of the variations of experimental design discussed in the textbook. They are: "Quasi-experimental Design," "Natural Experiment," "Analogue Experiment," and "Single-subject Experiments."

1. Quasi-experimental Design

1. Quasi-experimental designs make use of groups that already exist in the real world as opposed to experiments in which subjects are ________________ assigned to ________________ and ________________ groups.

2. Because quasi-experimental designs are technically correlation, they are sometimes called ________________ designs.

3. What is the benefit of using the quasi-experimental design of **matched control groups**?

____

____

2. Natural Experiments

1. Natural experiments are those in which nature rather than the experimenter manipulates a(n) ________________ variable, and the experimenter systematically ________________ the effects.

2. The natural experiment conducted by Gleser et al. (1981) on the psychological effects of a flood showed that survivors were significantly more depressed and anxious than control subjects. List some other results of the experiment.

a. ____

b. ____

c. ____

3. Limitations of the natural experimental method include the facts that natural experiments cannot be ________________, and broad ________________ drawn from from a single study could be incorrect.

3. Analogue Experiments

1. A major strength of analogue designs is that researchers can manipulate the ________________ variables, while avoiding some of the ________________ and practical limitations of other research designs.

2. How do analogue studies provide information about real-life abnormal behavior?

____

____

____

3. **Martin Seligman's** hypothesis about the cause of human depression says that people become depressed when they believe that they no longer have any _______________ over their lives—that they are helpless.

4. In his study of dogs that were unable to predict or escape electric shocks, Seligman created a pattern of behavior called _______________ _______________ which he believes is an analogue of human depression.

5. Describe (a) the method, and (b) the findings of Seligman's analogue research with humans.

a. _______________

____

b. _______________

____

4. Single-Subject Experiments

1. In simple-subject experiments, **baseline data** is information gathered during an observation period before any _______________ or interventions, which establish a standard with which to compare later change.

2. Why is it so important to collect baseline data in single-subject designs?

____

____

3. Subjects serve as their own _______________ in ABAB, or reversal designs.

4. When are researchers most likely to use an ABAB design?

____

____

The information in the following sample case will be used in exercises covering each of the two most commonly used single-subject experimental designs: the ABAB design and the multiple-baseline design.

Sample Case

Nathan is an eight-year-old boy who is in a classroom for severely disturbed children. He has been diagnosed with autism, a pervasive developmental disorder whose central features are a profound unresponsiveness to others, poor or absent communication, and a range of unusual—even bizarre—responses to the environment. Recently, Nathan's teachers have grown very concerned about his safety in the classroom. He has begun to repeatedly bang his head on his desktop, resulting in bruises and abrasions on his forehead. Autistic children who demonstrate this behavior are frequently equipped with helmets to prevent serious injury. However, Nathan became extremely upset when his teachers attempted to use this form of intervention. In fact, he became almost uncontrollable when the helmet was placed on his head.

Because Nathan has responded favorably to being rewarded with fruit juice for positive behavior in the classroom, his teachers would like to find out if this method of reinforcement would be effective in reducing or eliminating his head-banging behavior. They would like you, a clinical researcher, to design a single-subject experiment to test their hypothesis.

5. Use the preceding information to complete the following chart of an ABAB design for this sample case.

Reinforcement Program (The Independent Variable)

Nathan will be rewarded with friut juice for every 10 minute period of time that he does not bang his head on the desk.

A The frequency of Nathan's head-banging is measured before the introduction of the independent variable (in the baseline period).

(Think of each of the following steps as the test of a separate hypothesis.)

B
Step Taken: Nathan is given a reward of juice for not banging his head
Expectation:

A
Step Taken:
Expectation: Head-banging behavior will increase

B
Step Taken:
Expectation:

6. If your predictions are supported in this ABAB design, what conclusion can be drawn about the reintroduction of the independent variable?

____

7. Like the ABAB design, the **multiple-baseline design** is also a single-subject experimental design. Complete the following statements addressing two important differences between the ABAB design and the multiple baseline design.

a. The multiple baseline design does not contain the ____________ found in the ABAB design (i.e., the alternating introduction and removal of the reinforcer).

b. In the multiple baseline design, at least ____________ distict behaviors are identified, and the ____________ variable (the reinforcer) is manipulated to examine its effect on those behaviors.

8. By examining more than one behavioral ____________, the researcher can eliminate ____________ variables from his/her interpretation of findings.

V: The Limits of Clinical Investigation

1. Describe the factors that complicate or limit what we can learn about abnormal behavior and its treatment through clinical research. Try using your own words. That is, see how well you can explain these five scientific ideas without using the textbook's exact wording.

a. ____

____

b. ____

____

c. ____

____

d. ____

____

e. ____

____

Practice multiple-choice questions for this chapter begin on page 272.

Chapter 3

The Psychological Models of Abnormality

Chapter Organization

Psychologists explain abnormal behavior within the framework of a particular paradigm, or model, that provides a set of assumptions and conclusions regarding how and why people develop psychological problems. Chapter 3 guides you through the four models of abnormal behavior most prominent among psychologists today.

Be sure to read through each section before completing the exercises for that section.

Exercises

I: The Psychodynamic Model

1. One belief of psychodynamic theorists is that our behavior is determined by interacting, dynamic psychological forces outside of our awareness. Complete the following list of additional assumptions of the psychodynamic model of abnormal behavior.

a. Abnormal behaviors are the result of ________________ between psychological forces.

b. These conflicts are linked to people's early relationships with people's __________ and to ______________ experiences that occurred during early stages of development.

c. Psychodynamic theories rest on the ____________________ assumption that no symptom or behavior is "accidental."

2. In the development of his psychodynamic theory, Freud was influenced by many people. Complete the descriptions of how these individuals affected Freud's work.

a. Jean Charcot: Freud went to Paris in 1885 to study hypnosis under Charcot, who was a famous neurologist.

b. Josef Breuer: Freud followed up his studies with Charcot by working with Breuer, a physician experimenting with hypnosis and ____________________.

c. Anna O.:____

____

A: Freudian Explanations of Normal and Abnormal Functioning

Exercises covering this portion of the text are broken down in the same manner as the textbook's discussions. Coverage of the id, the ego, and the superego are followed by coverage of the Freudian developmental stages.

Freud believed that the "personality" is comprised of three forces: the id (instinctual needs), the ego (rational thinking), and the superego (moral standards). Complete the following list of characteristics that define each of these forces.

1. The Id

1. The id operates according to the __________ principle, which means that it always seeks __________.

2. The id can be gratified through reflexive activity, or through __________ __________ thinking, in which mental images of a desired object (such as food) are activated. When the id is gratified in this way, it is called __________ __________.

3. Id instincts are primarily __________ in nature. __________ is the term that describes the person's dynamic, intrapsychic sexual energy.

2. The Ego

1. The ego operates according to the reality principle. What does this mean?

____

____

2. The ego's mode of operation is called __________ process. Complete the following list of functions that this sort of thinking process serves.

a. assessment of new situations

b. __________

c. __________

d. __________

3. The Superego

1. The superego is developed when we realize that many of our id impulses are unacceptable. This realization comes as we unconsciously incorporate, or __________, our parent's moral values and standards.

2. List and describe the two components of the superego.

a. __________, __________

____

b. __________ __________, a composite image of the values we have acquired —the kind of person we think we should strive to become.

4. Developmental Stages

1. Certain demands or pressures are so threatening to a growing child that the id, ego, and superego do not mature properly, and result in the child becoming ________________ at a particular developmental stage.

2. Three of Freud's five stages of development are differentiated by a(n) ________________ zone that corresponds to the part of the body that represents the child's sexual drives and conflict

3. Complete the following table summarizing the key aspects of each of the five stages of psychosexual development.

Stage	Age	Erogenous zone	Gratification achieved through
Oral			
Anal			
Phallic			
Latency		*none*	
Genital		*none*	

B: Other Psychodynamic Explanations

1. Ego Theory

1. What is the primary difference between Freud's psychoanalytic theory and the ego theory?

____

____

____

2. Self Theory

1. What is the primary difference between Freud's psychoanalytic theory and the self theory?

____

2. Kohut asserted that the self (the unified personality) is developed when a child's basic needs are satisfied through relationships with ____________________, which are people that help the self define itself and grow.

3. Object Relations Theory

1. What is the primary difference between Freud's psychoanalytic theory and the object relations theory?

____

____

2. Complete the following list of themes in the object relations theory.

a. Focus on ____________________ and ____________________ as the central processes in personality development and psychopathology.

b. The motivating force in human behavior is the desire for ____________________ with objects (other people).

C: Psychodynamic Therapies

1. In the form of psychotherapy called __________ __________, the patient describes any thoughts or feelings that come to mind.

2. Therapists allow the patient to generate the discussion, while they are constantly interpreting the patients thoughts and feelings.

a. Patients demonstrate __________ when they change the subject to avoid painful discussion.

b. Patients often __________ their feelings for parent or significant other to their relationship with the therapist.

D: Assessing the Psychodynamic Model

. A reason why this model has received little research support is that processes such as id drives and ego defenses are abstract and operate at an ____________________ level, making it often impossible to determine if they are occurring.

2. Why is it difficult to predict abnormality based on the psychodynamic model?

____

____

II: The Behavioral Model

1. The behavioral model was the first perspective to be developed in ________________ laboratories. Psychologists in these laboratories conducted experiments on learning that takes place through ________________.

2. Behavioral principles established by research psychologists were applied to clinical problems in part because clinicians were becoming frustrated with

____

A: Classical Conditioning

1. The textbook states that "Classical conditioning is a process of learning by temporal association." Briefly explain what this means.

____

____

Read the following sample case relating to classical conditioning.

Sample Case

Thirteen-year-old Diane was riding her bicycle home one day after school while listening to her favorite *Nine Inch Nails* song on her headphones. She was thinking about what to wear to a party her friend Jackie was having that night and paid more attention to the song than to the traffic around her. She glided through a red light at a busy intersection. Her preoccupation was suddenly interrupted by the sounds of a car screeching to a halt and blaring its horn. Diane swerved around the car, narrowly avoiding a collision. As she walked her bike home, Diane's entire body trembled with fear—she thought she might vomit. Later, when Diane arrived at the party, her friend Jackie put on the CD of the same *Nine Inch Nails* song, which she knew Diane liked. Jackie was surprised to see Diane turn pale and rush to the bathroom. "I guess she doesn't like this song," thought Jackie as she went to check on her friend.

2. Complete this diagram by providing the unconditioned stimulus and the conditioned stimulus in the preceding sample case.

	fear, nausea
Unconditioned Stimulus	Unconditioned Response
	nausea
Conditioned Stimulus	Conditioned Response

3. Diane's conditioned fear response would undergo ______________________ if she repeatedly listened to her *Nine Inch Nails* tape and nothing terrible happened. (But she might never get the same thrill from listening to it again.)

B: Operant Conditioning

1. ______________ is the rewarding successive approximations of desired behavior.

2. Describe how the following maladaptive behaviors could be maintained through operant conditioning (reinforcement).

a. A four-year-old child consistently throws tantrums in the store check-out line.

____

____

b. Your boyfriend/girlfriend is chronically late for pre-arranged meetings and dates.

____

____

C: Assessing the Behavioral Model

1. Complete the following list of strengths and limitations of the behavioral model as described in the textbook.

Strengths:

a. behavioral explanations can be tested in the laboratory and predicted effects can be observed and measured

b. ____

Limitations:

c. it is not certain that abnormalities are ordinarily acquired in the same way as clinically-induced symptoms

d. ____________________

2. Some behaviorists believe that the traditional focus on overt (observable) behaviors does not adequately capture the complexities of human behavior. For example, Albert Bandura argues that one's behavior is affected by one's sense of ____________________, an assessment of whether one can master and perform necessary behaviors.

3. Behaviorists who take into account covert (unobservable) behaviors such as thoughts and beliefs represent the ____________________ model.

III: The Cognitive Model

The cognitive model suggests that in order to understand human behavior we must investigate WHAT and HOW people think—the CONTENT and PROCESS of human thought.

1. In the 1950s, research in social psychology was focused on cognitive phenomena known as attributions. Define the term attributions.

____

A: Cognitive Explanations of Abnormal Behavior

According to cognitive psychologists, we create representations of the world in our minds that dictate the way we perceive and understand events in our lives. "Errors" or inaccuracies in these mental representations can lead to maladaptive functioning. These inaccuracies include maladaptive assumptions, specific upsetting thoughts, and illogical thinking processes. Exercises covering each of these follows.

1. Maladaptive Assumptions

1. The well-known cognitive psychologist Albert Ellis believes that people who hold basic ____________________ ____________________ are led to behave in ways that are inappropriate and can result in unhappiness and distress.

2. Pages 73-74 of the textbook list several common irrational assumptions as identified by Ellis in 1962. These are reprinted below. Read through each assumption and assign it a rating based on the extent to which you hold the assumption using the following scale:

1 = *I do not hold this assumption.*
2 = *I hold this assumption, but not to a great degree.*
3 = *I hold this assumption to a great degree.*

Rating	Irrational assumption
	One is an abject failure if he or she is not loved or approved of by virtually every person one knows.
	One should be thoroughly competent, adequate, and achieving in all possible respects if one is to consider oneself worthwhile.
	It is awful and catastrophic when things are not the way one would very much like them to be.
	Human unhappiness is externally caused and people have little or no ability to control their sorrows and disturbances.
	One should be dependent on others and need someone stronger than oneself on whom to rely.
	One's past history is an all-important determiner of one's present behavior and that because something once strongly affected one's life, it should indefinitely have a similar effect.
	There is invariably a right, precise, and perfect solution to human problems and it is catastrophic if this perfect solution is not found.

2. Specific Upsetting Thoughts

1. As we confront the many challenging situations of life, numerous uninvited thoughts come to mind, which Beck has called automatic thoughts. How does Beck think these automatic thoughts relate to depression?

____

____

2. Donald Meichenbaum suggests that people who experience anxiety generate negative ______________________ during stressful situations.

3. Illogical Thinking Processes

1. Complete the following exercise by identifying and describing the illogical thinking processes demonstrated by a hypothetical man called "Gary" during a disappointing dinner party. The sample case is divided into lettered parts. The contents of each part correspond to the lettered exercises.

Sample Case

(a) Gary spends the entire day preparing a lavish six-course meal for his friends. When Gary discovers that the beans are slightly overcooked, he becomes very upset, despite the fact that the rest of the food is delicious.

(b) After his guests leave, Gary vows that he will never again prepare food for others because he is a horrible cook.

a. This is an example of ________________ ________________, which means that Gary saw only the negative features of the dinner he had prepared.

b. This is an example of ______________________________, which means that Gary:

____

____

B: Cognitive Therapy

1. In Ellis' ______________________________ therapy, therapists help clients discover the irrational assumptions that govern their ________________ responses, and to change these faulty thinking processes.

2. Beck's cognitive therapy has been successfully applied to which disorders?

____

3. Meichenbaum's ______________________________ training helps clients make positive ________________ statements, and apply them to difficult situations.

C: Assessing the Cognitive Model

1. Describe two research findings that support the cognitive model's prediction that maladaptive assumptions, thoughts, and thinking processes play a role in psychological distress.

a. When experimental subjects are manipulated into adopting unpleasant thoughts or assumptions they become more ________________ and ________________.

b. ______________________________

____

IV: The Humanistic-Existential Model

1. Humanistic and existential perspectives of behavior both focus on:

____

2. Humanistic models assert that human beings are born with a natural drive to fulfill their innate potential for goodness and growth. This is know as the drive to ______________.

3. Which perspective (humanistic or existential) is considered to be more pessimistic, and why?

__________, ______________________________

____

A: Rogers Humanistic Theory and Therapy

1. Rogers called his humanistic approach ______________ therapy.

2. Therapists focuses on displaying the qualities of ________ ________ ________, accurate ________, and genuineness.

B: Gestalt Theory and Therapy

1. Gestalt therapists attempt to challenge and ______________ their clients in order to move them toward self-awareness and self-______________.

2. Describe the following gestalt techniques: (a) skillful frustration, (b) role plays, (c) exaggeration game.

a. ______________________________

____

b. ______________________________

____

c. ______________________________

____

C: Existential Theory and Therapy

1. Complete the following flow chart that illustrates the existential explanation of psychological distress and abnormal behavior.

A person hides from personal responsibility and choice when he or she becomes engulfed in constant change, confusion, and the emotional strain of present-day society, as well as the particular stress of his/her immediate environment

leading to either

he or she overlooks his or her personal freedom of choice and won't take responsibility for his or her own life. This abdication can be a form of refuge, but can

either way

excessive ________________ or a building ________________ towards society

lead to

the person being left with an empty, inauthentic life and experiencing

- anxiety
- ________________
- ________________
- ________________

D: Assessing the Humanistic-Existential Model

1. Among the strengths of the humanistic-existential model of abnormal behavior are that it is optimistic and that it places emphasis on health rather than illness. Complete these questions regarding other strengths of this model.

a. It focuses on broad human issues rather than on a single aspect of functioning.

b. Unlike some other models, it recognizes the special features and challenges of ________________ ________________.

c. Factors that the model identifies as key to effective psychological functioning are clearly lacking in many with psychological disturbances. List some of these.

____

____

2. Complete this list of limitations of the humanistic-existential model

a. It has limited ________________ support.

b. ____

V: The Sociocultural Model

1. Sociocultural theorists are particularly interested in answering questions about a person's social and cultural environment in order to understand their abnormal behavior. Complete the following list of questions that are posed by the sociocultural model.

a. What are the ______________ and ______________ of the person's society?

b. What roles does the person play in the social environment?

c. What kind of ______________ structure is the person exposed to?

d. How do other people ______________ and react to the person?

A: Origins of the Sociocultural Model

The sociocultural perspective is rooted in the fields of sociology and anthropology. For exercises 1 and 2, complete the lists of important ideas contributed from these fields to the sociocultural model.

1. *Sociology:*

a. In order to adapt to a disorganized community's norms and standards, members may have to engage in odd behavior just to "fit in."

b. Stable societies may produce and maintain abnormal behavior by identifying certain members as ______________, reacting to them in special ways, and encouraging them to take on the ______________ assigned to "abnormal people."

2. The emergence of the sociocultural model was marked by three events. Complete the descriptions of why each of these events was important.

a. Publication of *Social Class and Mental Illness* by Hollingshead and Redlich: It found that psychotic, ________________, and rebellious behavior was much more common in the lower socioeconomic classes than in the upper classes.

b. Development of family theory and therapy:

____

____

c. The work of Thomas Szasz:

____

____

B: Sociocultural Explanations of Behavior

Sociocultural explanations of abnormal behavior focus on three areas: family structure and communication, societal stress, and societal labels and reactions. The following exercises mimic the textbook's structure of coverage of these three areas.

1. Family Structure and Communication

1. How, according to family systems theorists, do some families force individual members to behave in ways that society at large would deem abnormal?

____

____

2. Families that are resistant to almost all external influences are often called _____________________ by family therapists

3. Families whose members are grossly overinvolved in each other's lives have a(n) _____________________ structure, while families with overly rigid boundaries between members are said to display a structure of _____________________.

2. Societal Stress

1. The total number of cases of something occurring in a population over a given period of time is its _____________________; while _____________________ is the total number of new cases occurring over a given period.

2. Research has shown evidence that abnormal functioning is related to factors involving societal stress. Complete the following table by explaining how each listed factor might be related to psychological dysfunction and abnormal behavior.

Societal factor	*How factor is related to abnormal behavior and psychological problems*
Social change	
Social class	
Ethnic, religious, and national background	
Racial and sexual prejudice	
Cultural values and institutions	

3. Societal Labels and Reactions

1. Complete the following diagram that depicts the "vicious cycle" that ensures the development of mental illness according to sociocultural theorists.

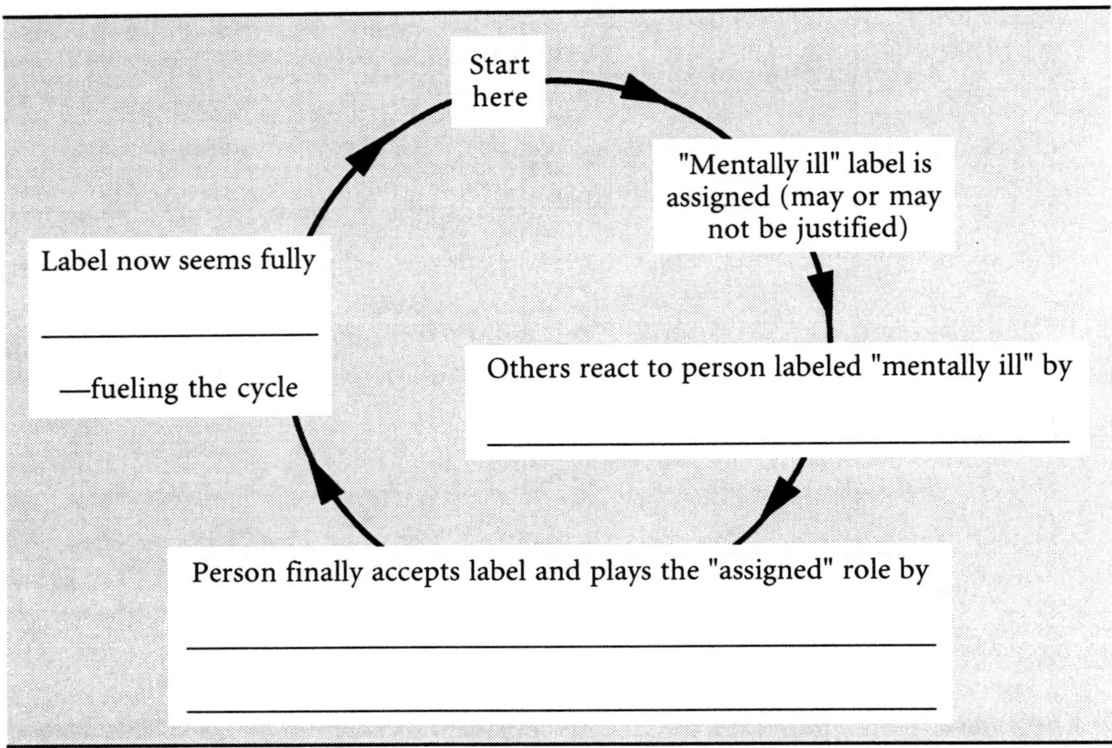

2. What were the key findings of the controversial Rosenhan (1973) study of schizophrenic pseudopatients? (Complete the list.)

a. it was very difficult to get rid of the "schizophrenic" label once it was assigned

b. ______________________________

c. ______________________________

d. overall, the pseudopatients felt powerless, depersonalized, and bored

C: Assessing the Sociocultural Model

1. Complete this exercise by summarizing the primary limitations of the sociocultural model and filling in the missing word(s). After filling in the missing information, give an example that supports the statement. The first is given.

a. Research used to support the model is sometimes inaccurate.
Example:
prevalence rates are based on mental health clinic admissions, so they may not reflect a disorder's incidence within the general public

b. Studies have failed to support key ____________________ of the model.

Example:

____

____

c. Research findings are difficult to ________________.

Example:

____

____

d. Model is unable to predict ____________________ in specific individuals.

Example:

____

____

VI: Relationships Between the Models

1. Although the models presented in this chapter differ in many ways, their conclusions are often ____________________.

2. Models presented in this chapter may focus on different kinds of causal factors. Complete the following table by matching each causal factor with the best illustration from the list of examples following the table, then write a definition for each.

Casual factor	Example	Definition
Predisposing factor		
Precipitating factor		
Maintaining factor		

Examples:

a. Lee discovers his wife is having an affair, and becomes depressed and suicidal.

b. Claire's family has struggled to survive financially for several years, fueling her sense of anxiety and hopelessness.

c. Stan's parents were killed in a plane crash when he was six years old. At the age of 37, Stan develops an intense fear of traveling by air.

3. An increasingly popular view is ______________________________—an explanation of certain forms of abnormal behavior that says a person must have a predisposition to a disorder and then be subjected to an immediate form of psychological stress.

Practice multiple-choice questions for this chapter begin on page 274.

Chapter 4

The Biological and Sociocultural Models of Abnormality

Chapter Organization

The methods used by clinical researchers to discover and understand the central features and processes of abnormal behavior and its treatment are the focus of Chapter 4. The first of the chapter's two sections focuses on the biological model of explanation for abnormal behavior. The second section presents the sociocultural model for abnormal behavior. Both sections include their associated therapy techniques and model assessment.

Be sure to read through each section before completing the exercises for that section.

Exercises

I: The Biological Model

A: Biological Explanations of the Biological Model

1. ____________________ are the nerve cells in the brain, and ____________________ are the supporting brain cells.

Make sure you have studied and can identify the various regions of the brain described and illustrated on page 90 of the textbook.

2. Biological theorists believe that mental disorders are linked to problems in ____________________ functioning. The problems may be ____________________ or biochemical.

3. Brain dysfunction resulting in abnormal behavior may be caused by numerous factors, including excessive stress and physical trauma. List three others.

   ____

   ____

4. Describe the distinction that was traditionally drawn between organic mental disorders and functional mental disorders.

   ____

   ____

5. In this exercise, give the names of the six terms relating to a typical neuron that are being described.

a. Found at the axon's terminus: ____________________

b. Neuronal chemicals: ____________________

c. Extensions (or antennae) located at the end of the neuron: ____________________

d. Proteins located on dendrite: ____________________

e. A long fiber which electrical impulses travel down: ____________________

f. A tiny space separating one neuron from the next: ____________________

Study the following diagram which depicts how messages get from the nerve endings of one neuron to the dendrites of another neuron.

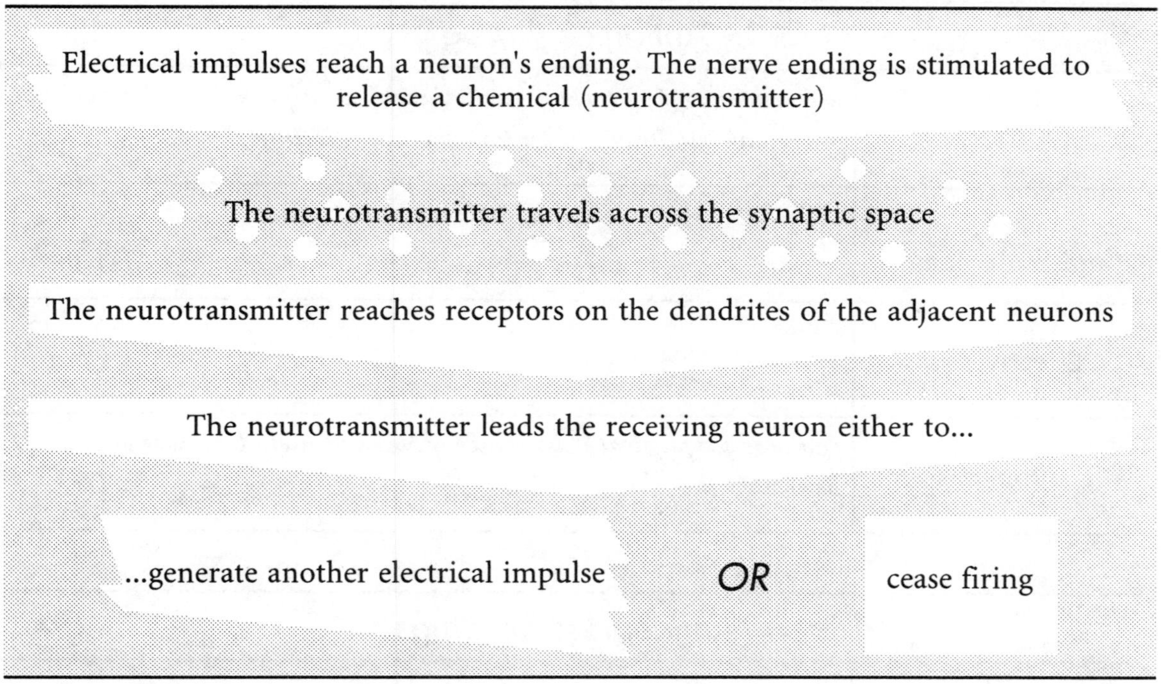

Electrical impulses reach a neuron's ending. The nerve ending is stimulated to release a chemical (neurotransmitter)

The neurotransmitter travels across the synaptic space

The neurotransmitter reaches receptors on the dendrites of the adjacent neurons

The neurotransmitter leads the receiving neuron either to...

...generate another electrical impulse **OR** cease firing

6. What determines if a neurotransmitter will lead a receiving neuron to generate another electrical impulse or to cease firing?

____

7. Abnormal neurotransmitter activity has been implicated in several mental disorders. Complete the following statements regarding these activities.

a. ____________________ disorders have been linked to low GABA activity.

b. Schizophrenia has been linked to excessive ____________________ activity.

c. ____________________ has been linked to low activity of both norepenephrine and ____________________.

B. Biological Therapies

1. Describe three problems accompanying the "psychotropic drug revolution."

a. ____

b. ____

c. ____

2. Complete the following tables of characteristics of drug therapies. *Organizing information from the textbook in this manner should help with studying.*

Antianxiety drugs	
Purpose	*meprobamate (Miltown); benzodiazepines: alpraxolam (Xanax), diazepam (Valium), chlordiazepoxide (Librium)*
Type (and trade names)	
Effectiveness	
Problems	*can produce physical dependence if taken in high doses over a long period of time*

Antidepressant drugs	
Purpose	
Type (and trade names)	
Effectiveness	*tricylics success rate is 65%; MAO inhibitors success rate is 50%*
Problems	

Antipolar drugs	
Purpose	*help stabilize mood of person diagnosed with bipolar disorder (manic-depression)*
Type (and trade names)	
Effectiveness	
Problems	

Antipsychotic drugs or neuroleptic drugs	
Purpose	
Type (and trade names)	
Effectiveness	
Problems	

3. Give two reasons why electroconvulsive therapy (ECT) is used to treat depression less often today than it was in the past.

a. ______________________________

b. ______________________________

4. In a lobotomy procedure, the connections between the cortex of the brain's ________________ ________________ and its lower centers are severed.

C: Assessing the Biological Model

1. The textbook lists two major criticisms of the biological model. Complete the summary of the first one, and then give a summary of the second one.

a. Although biological processes certainly do affect our behavior, thoughts, and emotions, they are just as certainly affected *by* our behavior, thoughts, and emotions. Our mental life is a(n) ______________________ of biological and nonbiological factors.

b. ____

____

II: The Sociocultural Model

1. Sociocultural theorists are particularly interested in answering questions about a person's social and cultural environment in order to understand their abnormal behavior. Complete the following list of questions that are posed by the sociocultural model.

a. What are the _______________ and _______________ of the person's society?

b. What roles does the person play in the social environment?

c. What kind of _______________ structure is the person exposed to?

d. How do other people _______________ and react to the person?

A: Sociocultural Explanation of Abnormal Behavior

Sociocultural explanations of abnormal behavior focus on three areas: family structure and communication, societal stress, and societal labels and reactions. The following exercises mimic the textbook's structure of coverage of these three areas.

1. Family Structure and Communication

1. How, according to family systems theorists, do some families force individual members to behave in ways that society at large would deem abnormal?

____

____

2. If a person in a "dysfunctional" family system began to behave normally, what would happen according to family theorists?

____

3. Families that are resistant to almost all external influences are often called _______________ by family therapists

4. Families whose members are grossly overinvolved in each other's lives have a(n) _______________ structure, while families with overly rigid boundaries between members are said to display a structure of _______________.

5. Even if only one member of the family is identified as "sick," family therapists treat the family system as a whole. Why?

____

____

2. Societal Stress

1. The total number of cases of something occurring in a population over a given period of time is its _______________; while _______________ is the total number of new cases occurring over a given period.

2. Research has shown evidence that abnormal functioning is related to factors involving societal stress. Complete this table by explaining how each listed factor might be related to psychological dysfunction and abnormal behavior.

Societal factor	*How factor is related to abnormal behavior and psychological problems*
Social change	
Social class	
Ethnic, religious, and national background	
Racial and sexual prejudice	
Cultural values and institutions	

3. Societal Labels and Reactions

1. What were the key findings of the controversial Rosenhan (1973) study of schizophrenic pseudopatients? (Complete the list.)

a. it was very difficult to get rid of the "schizophrenic" label once it was assigned

b. ______________________________

c. ______________________________

d. overall, the pseudopatients felt powerless, depersonalized, and bored

B: Sociocultural Therapy

1: Individual Therapy

1. What are some of the factors that might determine the length of individual therapy sessions?

____

____

2: Group Therapy

The following case study relates to group therapy. It consists of a statement made by "Jerry," who is a 19-year-old college student. Jerry participated in a multiple-issue therapy group held on his campus for one semester. He joined the group because he felt depressed to such an extent that is was affecting his concentration and motivation, and ultimately his grades. His other reason for going into group therapy was that, like a lot of students who leave home for college, Jerry felt that he didn't really "belong" or fit in anywhere. At the end of the semester of therapy, each group member was asked by the therapist to write about his or her experience in group.

As you read the case study, ignore the numbers in brackets. They have to do with the exercise that follows the case study.

Case Study

I know I got a lot out of being in the group. First of all, I realized that I wasn't the only one who felt down and out—it reassured me to know that I wasn't weird because I felt depressed [1]. I really got to know and trust the other group members, too. Even though I was nervous, I was able to talk about what I was feeling instead of keeping those feelings inside [2]. The fact that we were so close made it easier to hear feedback about my tendency to blame others for a lot of my problems [3]. Also, group made me aware of some things I unintentionally do that turn people off. Instead I learned how to "turn people on" in social situations [4]. I know that I learned a great deal by simply watching other people in the group work on their problems and get results [5]. I felt especially good when someone in the group would tell me that something I said helped them out [6]. Finally, both the therapist and the other members gave me good, specific ideas on how to be more motivated and how to expand my social network [7].

1. Page 106 of the textbook lists Yalom's (1985) "curative" features of group therapy. Make sure you understand them. Using the following abbreviations, match the numbered statements in Jerry's case to the appropriate curative feature.

G	Guidance	*U*	Universality
I	Identification	*A*	Altruism
GC	Group cohesiveness	*C*	Catharsis
SB	Skill building		

[1] ____ [2] ____ [3] GC [4] ____ [5] ____ [6] ____ [7] G

2. Describe the following techniques used in psychodrama: (a) auxiliary ego, (b) role reversal, (c) magic shop.

a. ______________________________

b. ______________________________

c. ______________________________

3. List some of the reasons for the popularity of self-help groups.

a. ______________________________

b. perceived ineffectiveness of traditional treatments

c. ______________________________

d. ______________________________

3: Family Therapy

1. Regardless of their orientation, family therapists adhere to the principles of family system theory. Describe the principles of this theory.

____

____

2. Structural family therapists focus on the family ______________ structure, the role each family member plays, and the ______________ between family members.

3. What is the goal of structured family therapy?

____

____

4. Therapists pay special attention to family communication patterns in the ______________ family approach.

4: Couple Therapy

1. Couple therapy is usually used when a relationship is unsatisfying or in conflict. What is another situation where it may be employed?

____

2. Complete the following lists of the most common complaints of men and women entering couple therapy.

Women's complaints:	*Men's complains:*
1. feeling unloved	1. being neglected
2. ______________	2. ______________
3. ______________	3. ______________
4. sexual depravation	4. sexual depravation
5. ______________	5. ______________

3. ______________ marital therapists attempt to replace detrimental marital behavior with more productive behavior.

4. According to behavioral marital therapists what is meant by a "core symbol" ?

____

____

5. Can you give an example of a core symbol of either a relationship you have in (romantic, friendship, family, etc.) or a relationship you have witnessed?

____

6. ____________________ behavioral couple therapy tries to help partners accept marital behaviors they cannot change and adopt the view that such behaviors are an understandable consequence of basic differences between them. ____________________ strategies, as well as behavioral strategies are used to achieve this.

7. List some of the goals of the type of therapy referred to in exercise #6.

a. partners will learn to empathize with each other

b. ____

c. ____

d. ____

e. partners will learn to see the positive aspects of "problem" behaviors

C: Assessing the Sociocultural Model

1. Complete this exercise by summarizing the primary limitations of the sociocultural model and filling in the missing word(s). After filling in the missing information, give an example that supports the statement. The first is given.

a. Research used to support the model is sometimes inaccurate.

Example: prevalence rates are based on mental health clinic admissions, so they may not reflect a disorder's incidence within the general public

b. Studies have failed to support key ____________________ of the model.

Example: ____

____

c. Research findings are difficult to ____________________.

Example: ____

____

d. Model is unable to predict ________________________ in specific individuals.

Example: ____

____

Practice multiple-choice questions for this chapter begin on page 275.

Chapter 5

Clinical Assessment, Diagnosis, and Treatment

Chapter Organization

One of the primary roles of the clinical practitioner is to develop a comprehensive understanding of the nature and origin of a client's problems. Chapter 5 covers ways that clinicians *assess* a client's problems, and *diagnose* a particular disorder. The effectiveness of treatment approaches is also discussed.

Be sure to read through each section before completing the exercises for that section.

Exercises

I: Clinical Assessment

1. Complete the following list of the uses of clinical assessment techniques.

a. *to determine how and why someone behaves abnormally*

b. ______________________________

c. ______________________________

d. *to select appropriate, representative subjects for research*

2. A clinician's ______________ orientation will influence his or her decision about what type of assessment technique to use.

3. Re-write the question, "Have you used cocaine in the past 24 hours?" to improve its test-retest reliability:

____

4. A clinical test's validity is the ______________ with which it measures what it is intended to measure.

5. Concurrent validity is the degree to which test scores agree with:

____

A: Clinical Interviews

1. What pieces of information are typically gained through clinical interviewing?

____

____

____

2. The textbook describes how clinicians give special attention to topics that are important to their particular theoretical orientation. Complete the following box by providing the name of the orientation that fits each description of topics.

Interview topics	*Orientation*
Try to discover assumptions, interpretations, and cognitive coping skills that influence the way a person acts and feels	
Pinpoint signs of any biochemical or neurological dysfunction	
Relevant information about the Stimuli that trigger the abnormal functioning, the Organism or person, the precise nature of the abnormal Responses, and about the Consequences of the responses	
The person's needs and fantasies, relevant memories about past events and relationships, and observation of how the person molds the interview	
The person's self-concept and unique perceptions	

(Once you have mastered identifying the theoretical orientations based on their descriptions, you might try providing the descriptions based on a list of orientations.)

3. Unstructured interviews are comprised of open-ended questions (questions that cannot be answered with a simple "yes" or "no"). The textbook gives the example of "Would you tell me about yourself?" Try to think of two more open-ended questions that might be asked in a clinical interview.

a. ______________________________

b. ______________________________

4. Clinicians who use ______________ interview strategies sometimes rely on published interview ______________ that provide a standard set of questions.

5. The different theoretical orientations tend to favor either structured or unstructured interviews. Complete the listing of each of the five theoretical orientations according to the type of interview its adherents tend to favor.

Structured:

____

Unstructured:

psychodynamic, ______________________________

6. Complete the description of four of the limitations of clinical interviewing.

a. Information gathered at the interview is—to some extent—preselected by the client and may be self-serving and less than accurate.

b. Some clients are simply unable to provide ________________ information in an interview.

c. ____

____

d. Clients respond differently to different interviewers. List some characteristics of clinicians that clients may respond to in one way or another.

____

B: Clinical Tests

Make sure you understand the coverage of reliability and validity, as they serve as a basis for "testing" each type of test.

1. Projective Tests

1. The primary assumption of projective tests is that clients will "project" aspects of their own ________________ onto the ________________.

2. Complete the following flow chart relating to the questions a clinician using the Thematic Apperception Test would ask.

People who take the TAT are shown one picture at a time and asked to make up a dramatic story about it stating...

1. What is happening?

2. ________________

3. What are the characters ________________ and ________________

4. ________________________

An inquiry phase follows to

____

3. The assumption behind the TAT is that the test-taker identifies with a character, called a ________________, on each card. In their ________________ people are thought to be expressing their own circumstances, needs, pressures, emotions, and perceptions of reality and fantasy.

4. Other projective tests include the ____________________-completion test and the Draw-a-________________ Test, which is the most prevalent drawing test.

2. Personality Inventories

Note that for all practical purposes, the text uses the terms personality inventory and self-test inventory interchangeably.

1. Complete the following table by matching the MMPI clinical scales with the letter corresponding to the content description from the list following the scales.

Number	Scale	Content description
1 or HS	Hypochondriasis	
2 or D	Depression	
3 or Hy	Hysteria	
4 or PD	Psychopathic deviate	
5 or Mf	Masculinity-femininity	
6 or Pa	Paranoia	
7 or Pt	Psychasthenia	
8 or Sc	Schizophrenia	
9 or Ma	Hypomania	
0 or Si	Social introversion	

Content descriptions:

a. Obsessions, compulsions, fears, and guilt

b. Suspicion, delusions of grandeur, persecutory delusions

c. Excessive concern with bodily functions

d. Shyness, insecurity, little interest in people

e. Conventional masculine and feminine styles

f. Emotional shallowness, disregard for social norms

g. Pessimism, hopelessness, lethargy

h. Bizarre thoughts and behavior, hallucinations

i. Use of symptoms to avoid conflicts and responsibilities

j. Excitement, overactivity, racing thoughts

2. People can score from 0 to _______ on each MMPI scale, with scores of _______ or above indicating clinical significance or deviance.

3. List and describe two sets of responses people may exhibit when completing an inventory such as the MMPI.

a. ____

____

b. ____

____

4. List three problems that the MMPI-2 assesses that were not included in the original MMPI.

____

____

____

5. Complete the following table by describing the purposes of the listed "response" inventories.

Inventory	*Purpose*
Affective inventories	
Social skills inventories	
Cognitive inventories	

3. Psychophysiological Tests

1. Two psychophysiological tests used in the assessment and treatment of sexual disorders are the ________________ plethysmograph and the ________________ plethysmograph (also called the ____________ gauge) used to measure sexual arousal in women and men, respectively.

2. In a paragraph, describe how biofeedback is used to help with tension headaches.

____

____

____

____

3. One limitation of psychophysiological assessment methods is that the equipment is expensive, and must be expertly maintained. List two more limitations.

a. ____

b. ____

4. Neuropsychological Tests

1. List several causes of neurological damage in the brain that can result in psychological or behavioral problems.

____

____

2. Describe the procedure used to detect neurological impairment by the Bender Visual-Motor Gestalt Test.

____

____

3. Because no single neuropsychological test can distinguish between specific kinds of impairment, clinicians often use a ________________ of tests which measures multiple skill areas.

5. Intelligence Tests

1. The overall score on an intelligence test is called the ________________ ________________ or ________.

2. List the three most widely used measures of intelligence.

3. Intelligence tests generally demonstrate high validity and reliability, but they do have several shortcomings. Describe two of these important limitations.

a.

b.

C: Clinical Observations

1. Describe how clinicians use the following strategies to observe behavior.

a. Naturalistic observations:

b. Structured observations:

2. Describe how the following factors can limit the validity of clinical observations.

a. Observer overload

b. Observer drift

c. Observer bias

d. Subject reactivity

3. Imagine that you are a clinician and a 26-year-old man suffering from obesity comes into you clinic for help. You would like him to begin self-monitoring immediately. What are some of th things that you would like him to record?

II: Diagnosis

A: Classification Systems

1. A clinician makes a diagnosis when he or she determines that a person's pattern of symptoms constitutes a particular ______________________.

2. Define (a) ICD-10, and (b) DSM-IV.

a. ____

____

b. ____

____

B: DSM-IV

1. The DSM-IV includes descriptions of about ___________ mental disorders.

2. Describe the primary difference between the DSM-IV and its earliest predecessors, the DSM-I and the DSM-II.

____

____

____

3. The following table relates to the five axes (branches of information) of DSM-IV. Match each of the first four axes with the appropriate examples (there are none for Axis V) from the list of entries following the table, and then by giving a short description for each axis. The numbers in parentheses under "Examples" are the number of examples you should choose for that particular axis.

Axis	Examples	Description
Axis I	(5)	*an extensive list of clinical syndrome that typically cause significant impairment*
Axis II	(4)	
Axis III	(3)	
Axis IV	(3)	
Axis V	(none)	

Examples:

a. Major depression

b. Recent death of a spouse

c. Alcohol dependence

d. Antisocial personality disorder

e. Leukemia

f. Sexual sadism

g. Mental retardation

h. Autism

i. Ongoing sexual abuse

j. Schizophrenia

k. Dependent personality disorder

l. AIDS

m. Anorexia nervosa

n. Epilepsy

o. Chronic unemployment

C: Reliability and Validity of Classification

1. What does "reliability" mean in the context of a diagnostic classification system?

____

____

2. A diagnostic classification system that is most useful to clinicians is one that demonstrates ________________ validity in that it helps predict future symptoms.

D: Problems of Clinical Misinterpretation

1. List some examples of how clinicians, in interpreting assessment data, may be "flawed information processors."

____

____

____

E: Dangers of Diagnosing and Mislabeling

. Some theorists believe that diagnostic labels may be ________________ prophecies.

. Explain the reasoning behind this belief.

____

____

____

II: Treatment

A: Investigating the Effectiveness of Treatment

. One of the problems with answering the question, "Is treatment 'X' effective?" is that researchers and clinicians could define "successful" in many different ways. What are two other problems with answering this question?

. ____

. ____

: Is Therapy Generally Effective?

. Describe the method and results of the statistical technique called a "meta-analysis" employed by Smith, et al., to examine treatment effectiveness.

Method: ____________________________________

____

b. *Results:* ______________________________

____

2. What kind of "deterioration effects" appear to occur in 5–10 percent of those in therapy?

____

____

____

C: Are Particular Therapies Effective?

1. The ______________ ______________ describes the false belief that all therapies are the same despite differences in therapists' theoretical orientation, personality, etc.

2. Answer the following questions relating to the results of the Sloane et al., (1975) comparative study.

a. What were the findings after four months regarding the effectiveness of psychodynamic therapy vs. the effectiveness of behavioral therapy?

____

b. What were the findings after four months in regards to the question of receiving therapy vs. not receiving therapy?

____

3. List some of the "basic ingredients" or "common therapeutic strategies" that seem to characterize all effective therapies.

____

____

D: Are Particular Therapies Effective for Particular disorders?

1. Complete the following table by identifying the most effective treatment approach(es) for the listed psychological problems/disorders.

Disorder	Effective treatment approach(es)
Schizophrenia	
Phobic disorders	
Depression	

Practice multiple-choice questions for this chapter begin on page 277.

Chapter 6

Generalized Anxiety Disorder and Phobias

Chapter Organization

Chapter 6 is divided into the three major sections delineated below. The first section discusses the nature of stress, how we cope with stressors, and the anxiety response. The next two sections cover Generalized Anxiety Disorder and Phobias. Within each of these sections, characteristics of each type of disorder are presented first, followed by theoretical perspectives on the origins of the disorders, and finally treatment strategies.

Be sure to read through each section before completing the exercises for that section.

Exercises

I: Stress, Coping, and the Anxiety Response

1. Complete the following statements which are paraphrased from the textbook:

a. Our reactions to stressors are influenced by ______________ ______________, in which we decide if a situation is harmless, and ______________ ______________, in which we weigh what kind of response is needed and assess whether we have the resources to cope with it.

b. Fear responses are generated by the ______________ ______________ ______________ (ANS) which connects the ______________ ______________ ______________ (the brain and the spinal cord) to all the other organs of the body.

c. The special group of ANS fibers that are responsible for "fight or flight" responses are known collectively as the nervous system.

d. The ______________________ nervous system is a second group of ANS fibers that returns body processes to a normal resting state following arousal.

2. One of the most important channels through which the ANS regulates our fear reactions is the endocrine system. Complete the following statements relating to this important system.

a. The ANS triggers the __________ glands to secrete hormones called __________ when we are confronted by stressors.

b. These hormones stimulate body organs and various parts of the brain, including the __________, which appears to regulate emotional memories and helps "turn off" the body's anxiety reaction.

3. Define (a) trait anxiety, and (b) state anxiety.

a. ____

____

b. ____

____

II: Generalized Anxiety Disorder

1. People with generalized anxiety disorders are often described as having ______________________________ anxiety because they experience worries about so many things in their lives.

2. To meet the DSM-IV criteria for a diagnosis of generalized anxiety disorder, individuals must experience anxiety about numerous activities, situation, or events, and they must have symptoms that are present for at least how long?

____

3. It appears that most people with generalized anxiety disorder also develop another anxiety disorder and/or ____________________.

The following subsections examine six perspectives on how and why people develop generalized anxiety disorder. Within each subsections, treatment strategies are based on each of the perspectives are discussed.

A. Sociocultural Perspective

1. Sociocultural theorists suggest that people who are confronted with societal situations that represent __________ __________ are more likely to develop generalized anxiety disorders.

2. Several important studies have provided evidence that the increased prevalence of generalized anxiety disorders are related to societal changes, poverty, and race. Complete the following table by briefly summarizing these findings.

Social force	Evidence
Societal changes	
Poverty	
Race*	

B. The Psychodynamic Perspective

1. Psychodynamic Explanations

1. Freud suggested that people can develop generalized anxiety disorders when their defense mechanisms break down. The textbook lists two ways that this break down can occur and result in generalized anxiety disorders. Give one.

____

____

2. Describe the views of two more contemporary psychodynamic theoretical perspectives on the causes of generalized anxiety disorder: (a) object-relations theorists, and (b) self-theorists.

____

____

b. ______________________________

____

3. List two major criticisms of research on psychodynamic explanations of generalized anxiety disorders.

a. ______________________________

____

b. ______________________________

____

2. Psychodynamic Therapies

1. Write a description of how practitioners of the following psychodynamic therapies treat with anxiety disorders.

a. Classic psychodynamic therapists: *try to help clients become less afraid of their id impulses and more able to control them successfully.*

b. Object-relations therapists: ______________________________

____

c. Self therapists: ______________________________

____

2. Describe research findings on the effectiveness of psychodynamic approaches in the treatment of anxiety disorders.

____

____

C. Humanistic and Existential Perspectives

1. Humanistic and existential theorists suggest that generalized anxiety disorder can result from a "defensive posture" that creates anxiety. What are some characteristics of this posture?

____

____

2. What are the characteristics of the "inauthentic life," according to existential therapists?

____

____

1. Humanistic Explanations and Treatments

1. Because they do not receive unconditional positive regard from their parents, some children go on to develop conditions of worth. Why might attempts to live up to these conditions of worth eventually lead to intense anxiety?

____

____

2. Carl Rogers developed a form of treatment called __________ - __________ therapy, which is characterized by the therapist's provision of unconditional positive regard, empathy, and genuine acceptance to the client.

3. What is the central goal of the Rogerian therapist?

____

____

2. Existential Explanations and Treatments

1. **Existential anxiety** is the universal human fear of the limits of one's existence. Complete the list of reasons given by existentialists of why people experience it.

a. *we know that life is finite and we fear death*

b. ____

c. ____

2. What are the characteristics of the "inauthentic life," according to existential therapists?

____

____

D. The Cognitive Perspective

1. Cognitive Explanations

1. Cognitive theorists believe that generalized anxiety disorders are caused by __________________ __________________.

2. The letters a–e represent a jumbled set of steps in the process of how a person could develop a generalized anxiety disorder according to the work of cognitive theorist Albert Ellis. Demonstrate that you understand this process by numbering the steps 1–5 in the correct order to fit Ellis' explanation.

___ a. Maladaptive assumptions are applied to more and more life situations.

___ b. A stressful event such as an exam or a date occurs.

___ c. A person holds a maladaptive assumption such as, "It is catastrophic when things are not the way one would very much like them to be."

___ d. The person develops generalized anxiety disorder.

___ e. An event is interpreted as highly dangerous and threatening leading a person to overreact and experience fear.

3. Another prominent cognitive theorist, Aaron Beck, has a similar cognitive theory which is illustrated in the following diagram. Fill in more examples of unrealistic silent assumptions and automatic thoughts.

People with generalized anxiety disorder make unrealistic silent assumptions that imply they are in imminent danger.	Silent assumptions lead people to experience narrow and persistent anxiety-provoking images and thoughts called automatic thoughts.
Examples:	**Examples:**
"a situation or a person is unsafe until proven to be safe"	"people will laugh at me"
	"what if I fail?"

2. Cognitive Therapies

1. Briefly describe the techniques of (a) Albert Ellis and (b) Aaron Beck that are designed to change the maladaptive assumptions at the root of generalized anxiety disorder.

a. Albert Ellis: ____________________

____

b. Aaron Beck: ____________________

____

2. Donald Meichenbaum's self-instruction training, or __________ training, attempts to replace anxious people's negative __________ with more positive ones.

E. The Biological Perspective

1. Research has indicated that _____% of the relatives of people with generalized anxiety disorder also have the disorder, compared to the 4% prevalence rate in the general population.

2. Findings such as the one above can be used to support either a biological or an environmental explanation of generalized anxiety disorder. Briefly, make a statement supporting each of these perspectives.

a. *Findings support biological explanation:*

____

____

b. *Findings support environmental explanation:*

____

____

1. Biological Explanations

Coverage of the biological treatments are divided into three parts: antianxiety drugs, relaxation training, and biofeedback.

Antianxiety Drugs

1. Until the 1950s, ____________________ drugs—especially ______________—were the primary drug treatment for anxiety disorders.

a. What were some of the problems associated with these drugs?

____

2. Chlordiazepoxide (trade name ________________________) and diazepam (trade name ________________) are antianxiety drugs from the ____________________ family of drugs.

3. While benzodiazepines are effective in reducing symptoms of generalized anxiety disorders, they are not helpful in the treatment of some specific anxiety disorders. Which ones?

____

4. Buspirone appears to be as effective as benzodiazepines and is ______________ addictive.

• Relaxation Training

1. In relaxation training, clients learn to __________ individual muscle groups, tense and __________ these muscle groups, and __________ the whole body at will.

2. List some of the ways that clinicians might induce anxiety in their clients (so that they can practice relaxing under stress).

____

____

3. Relaxation training appears to be most beneficial to people with generalized anxiety disorders when it is combined with what other technique?

____

• Biofeedback

1. The ________________________ (EMG) device provides visual and/or auditory feedback that informs the client when their ______________________ are more or less tense.

2. The goal of biofeedback training is for people to become skilled at voluntarily ____________________ muscle tension through a process of trial and error.

3. Why is the use of the electroencephalograph (EEG) biofeedback technique only minimally effective in the treatment of generalized anxiety disorders?

____

____

III. Phobias

1. A phobia is defined as a persistent and ______________________ fear of a particular ________________, ________________, or ________________.

2. What were the most important findings of the Burlington, Vermont, study of the relationship between fears and stage of life?

____

____

____

3. Complete the following statements. They relate to the characteristics, which according to the DSM-IV, differentiate normal fears from phobic fears.

a. Fear experienced in a phobic disorder is more intense and ________________.

b. The phobic person's desire to ________________ the object or situation is more compelling.

c. People with phobias experience such distress that their fears often interfere dramatically with their personal, social, or occupational functioning.

A. Types of Phobias

1. The three categories of phobias distinguished by the DSM-IV are agoraphobia, social phobias, and specific phobias. Complete the table below by defining characteristics of each of these disorders.

Phobias	*Characteristics*
Agoraphobia	
Social phobia	
Specific phobia	

B. Explanations of Phobias

1. Psychodynamic Explanations

1. Freud posited that people use ego defense mechanisms in order to protect themselves from experiencing anxiety associated with unacceptable id impulses. In particular, he believed that people with phobic disorders rely heavily on the defense mechanisms of repression and displacement. Complete the following statements regarding the use of these defenses in phobias.

a. People use repression in order to:

____

____

b. People use displacement in order to:

____

____

2. Behavioral Explanation

Read the following sample case.

Sample Case

It was 1:00 a.m. and Malcolm was driving home to North Dakota for his sister's wedding. It was snowing heavily, and the roads were icy; he was driving as fast as he safely could, but the trip had already taken two hours longer than it normally would. As Malcolm was fiddling with the radio dial, he looked up to see a huge semi trailer swerving dangerously in front of him. Malcolm pumped his breaks, but began to spin toward the truck, which was now facing him head-on. Malcolm leaned on the steering wheel, and swerved into the ditch. His small car crashed into a fence by the ditch, but fortunately he suffered no physical injuries. Malcolm's heart was pounding and he had never been so frightened in his life. Since his near-fatal accident, Malcolm cannot travel in a car. Simply contemplating a short drive fills him with panic and dread. In short, Malcolm has developed a phobia.

1. Using this case and adhering to the behavior explanation, complete this diagram.

	fear response
Unconditioned Stimulus	*Unconditioned Response*
Conditioned Stimulus	*Conditioned Response*

2. Behaviorists agree that fear will undergo ______________________ if a person is repeatedly exposed to the feared object or situation and nothing bad happens.

3. Why would one fear-provoking experience (such as Malcolm's accident) develop into a long-term phobia?

____

____

4. Describe how Malcolm's phobia could develop into a generalized anxiety disorder.

____

____

____

3. Behavioral-Biological Explanation

1. ______________________________ is the idea that human beings, as a species, are predisposed to develop some fears (e.g., of snakes, lightening, heights) rather than others (e.g. of trees, rabbits, candy).

2. Refer to the study conducted by Ohman and his colleagues on conditioned fears in humans, and describe (a) its methods, and (b) its findings.

a. ____

____

b. ____

____

3. The textbook describes two possible explanations of why humans might be predisposed to certain fears. Briefly, describe the underlying arguments of each.

a. Biological (evolutionary) predisposition: ____

____

b. Cultural predisposition: ____

____

C. Treatments for Phobias

1: Specific Phobias

1. ____________________ therapy appears to be the most effective form of treatment for phobic disorders.

2. Systematic desensitization, flooding, and modeling are known collectively as ____________________ treatments because clients are ____________________ to the object or situation they dread.

3. In the following table provide the name and a description of each of the three phases of systematic desensitization.

Phase name	Description
1.	
2.	
3.	

4. Behavioral therapists who use flooding techniques believe that when phobic clients are repeatedly ________________________ to feared stimuli, they will see that the stimuli are quite ____________________.

5. In modeling, or ____________________ conditioning procedures, the ______________ confronts the feared object or situation while the ____________________ watches.

2: Agoraphobia

1. List two behavioral techniques used to treat agoraphobia.

a. ____

b. ____

2. Describe some of the features of the support group approach in the treatment of agoraphobia.

____

____

3. Although between _____ and _____ percent of agoraphobic people who have received exposure treatment seem to improve markedly, relapses occur in as many as _____ percent of successfully treated clients.

3. Social Phobias

1. People with social phobias have incapacitating social fears. What is the second distinct component of the social phobias?

____

____

2. Why is group therapy an ideal setting for exposure-based treatment of social phobias?

____

____

3. Complete the following flow chart that depicts basic elements of social skills training.

Therapists	Clients	Therapists provide
______________	______________	______________
appropriate social behavior	social behaviors with the therapist or other clients	to clients regarding their "performance"

Practice multiple-choice questions for this chapter begin on page 278.

Chapter 7

Panic, Obsessive-Compulsive, and Stress Disorders

Chapter Organization

Chapter 7 is divided into five sections delineated below. Sections II–V cover the specific anxiety disorders. Characteristics of each disorder are presented along with case studies that will help you to see the "clinical picture" of each disorder. Next, theories that will offer explanations of the anxiety disorders are discussed, as are supporting research and criticisms of the theory.

Be sure to read through each section before completing the exercises for that section.

Exercises

I: Panic Disorders

1. Panic attacks are discrete bouts of panic that occur __________ and usually reach a peak within ________ minutes.

2. List some symptoms of panic attacks.

____

____

3. Describe the relationship between panic attacks and maturity.

____

____

4. The DSM-IV states that a diagnosis of panic disorder is warranted if, after having at least one unexpected panic attack, the person spends one month or more:

a. worrying persistently about ____,

b. worrying about the ____,

c. and changes his or her ____.

A: The Biological Perspective

1. Unexpectedly, it was found that people with panic disorders seem to respond most favorably to antidepressant drugs, rather than to ________________________.

1. Biological Explanations

1. Since it was known that antidepressant drugs can alter the activity of norepinephrine activity, a logical suggestion was that panic disorders and generalized anxiety may involve different biological processes. Complete the following list of additional evidence that supports this idea.

a. There are a large number of neurons that utilize norepinephrine in the area of the brain known as the _______________ ____________________. When this area is electronically stimulated in monkeys, the monkey displays a paniclike reaction.

b. When the norepinephrine-rich brain area is surgically damaged in monkeys, monkeys show no reaction at all in the face of unmistakable danger.

c. Researchers have induced panic attacks in humans by administering chemicals known to alter the activity of norepinephrine, such as the chemical compound ______________________.

d. Another drug, clonidine, has been shown to: ______________________________

____

2. Although the issue of a genetic predisposition to panic disorder is still debated, one study found that when one identical twin had panic disorder, _____ percent of the identical co-twins also had the disorder, whereas when on fraternal twin had panic disorder, only _____ percent of the fraternal co-twins had the disorder.

2. Drug Therapies

1. Panic attacks seem to be related to abnormal activity of the neurotransmitter ____________________.

2. ____________ percent of patients who experience panic attacks improve somewhat with drug treatment; about _____ percent improved markedly or fully.

B. The Cognitive Perspective

1. The Cognitive Explanation

Read the following sample case of Dave, a 34-year-old male suffering from panic attacks.

Sample Case

Dave woke up early one April morning feeling good. While eating his usual breakfast he noticed in the newspaper that a run was being held on Memorial Day to raise money for a charity. Although he hadn't run much in two years, he decided that he would participate in the event and that he would begin training for it that very morning. Dave felt really winded after three miles, but pushed himself to run two more. When he got home, he was sweating profusely, his heart was pounding, and his legs felt shaky and slightly numb. Fearing that he was having a heart attack, Dave began to hyperventilate and had a panic attack that lasted for approximately 20 minutes. Dave went to his doctor and was assured that his heart was very healthy. Two weeks later, he went to a new restaurant with a friend. They both ordered extra spicy dinners. Midway through the meal, Dave and his friend both complained of stomach pain and nausea. Dave became increasingly upset and told his friend that he had to leave right away because he was certain a panic attack was imminent.

1. Briefly describe how Dave's escalating anxiety and panic can be explained by the cognitive-biological perspective of panic disorders.

____

____

2. What are some of the factors that may be related to why some people are more prone to misinterpret bodily sensations?

____

____

2. Cognitive Therapy

1. Cognitive therapists teach clients about the nature of panic attacks, the actual causes of their bodily sensations, and their tendency to ______________ them.

2. Recent studies have shown that _____ percent of subjects with panic disorders significantly improved after receiving cognitive therapy (compared to only 13 percent of control subjects who improved).

3. How did cognitive therapy fare in research comparing it to drug therapies as a treatment for panic disorders?

____

II: Obsessive-Compulsive Disorders

A: Obsessions

1. What may happen when people try to resist their obsessions or compulsions?

____

Match the numbers 2–6, which list terms clinicians use to distinguish various kinds of obsessions, with the appropriate option from the list a–e, which are examples of these obsessions.

2. ____ obsessive thoughts and wishes

3. ____ obsessive impulses

4. ____ obsessive images

5. ____ obsessive ideas

6. ____ obsessive doubts

Examples:

a. A student sees himself starting an arson fire in his dormitory.

b. A man dwells on the notion that he should have stayed in the Navy in 1954.

c. A woman incessantly worries that the mosquitoes in her backyard will give her malaria.

d. A girl thinks about paying someone to kill her older sister.

e. A man worries that one day he will purposely spill hot coffee onto his co-worker's lap.

B: Compulsions

1. Complete the list of steps that are typically followed by a person with a compulsion.

a. He believes that something terrible will happen if he does not act on his compulsion.

b. He tries to resist, but gives in when ________________ overcomes him.

c. After giving in, he usually feels less anxious for a short while because of the release of ________________.

d. However, no ________________ is derived from the act of giving into the compulsion itself.

2. Complete the following table by listing and giving examples of the types of compulsive rituals.

Type	*Example*
cleaning cumpulsion	*washing hands 30 or 40 times a day*

C: Relationship Between Obsessions and Compulsions

1. Most people with an obsessive-compulsive disorder experience ________ obsessions and compulsions.

2. In one study, 61% of the subjects with obsessive-compulsive disorder indicated that their compulsions represented ________________________, while six percent had compulsions that served to ____________________ obsessions.

3. What is perhaps the greatest fear of people with obsessive-compulsive disorder?

____

D: Explanations and Treatments for Obsessive-Compulsive Disorder

Psychodynamic, behavioral, cognitive, and biological theories and treatments of obsessive-compulsive disorder are explored in this subsection.

1. The Psychodynamic Perspective

1. According to psychodynamic theorists, three ego defense mechanisms are commonly used by people with obsessive-compulsive disorder. Complete the table below by first defining each ego defense mechanism and then giving an example of each relevant to someone with obsessive-compulsive disorder.

Mechanism	Definition	Example
Isolation		
Undoing		
Reaction formation		

Freud explained obsessive-compulsive disorders within the framework of his theory of psychosexual development. Study this diagram of his conceptualization.

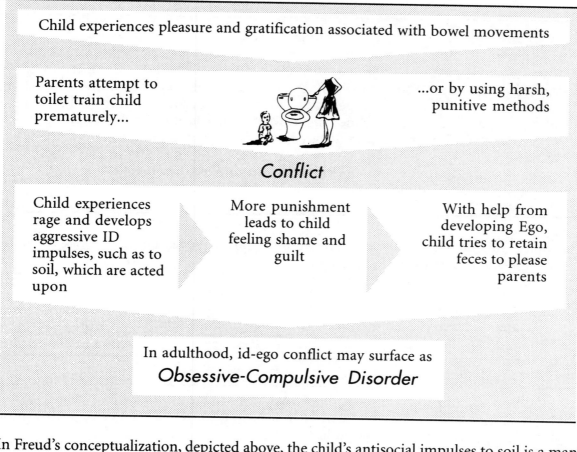

Child experiences pleasure and gratification associated with bowel movements

Parents attempt to toilet train child prematurely...

...or by using harsh, punitive methods

Conflict

Child experiences rage and develops aggressive ID impulses, such as to soil, which are acted upon

More punishment leads to child feeling shame and guilt

With help from developing Ego, child tries to retain feces to please parents

In adulthood, id-ego conflict may surface as

Obsessive-Compulsive Disorder

2. In Freud's conceptualization, depicted above, the child's antisocial impulses to soil is a manifestation of his ____________, while his desire to retain his feces is a manifestation of his ____________.

3. Some theorists in other psychodynamic schools disagree with Freud's explanation of obsessive-compulsive disorders. Give the explanation of (a) the object-relations theorists who disagree, and (b) the ego theorists who disagree.

a. ____

____

b. ____

____

2. The Behavioral Perspective

Read the following sample case.

Sample Case

Patricia is obsessed with counting rituals, and specifically with the number three. Although she is not distressed when, for example, her dishes sit unwashed on the counter, Patricia does feel compelled to order them in groups of three—three plates in a stack, three glasses lined in a row, etc. Patricia answers the telephone only after the third ring, and must buy three of any item on her grocery list. She also checks compulsively, always in increments of three. For instance, she is not satisfied that her front door is locked until she turns the key three times, counting "one-two-three" aloud.

1. Complete this exercise by writing three more response prevention homework assignments for Patricia in addition to the one already given.

a. buy only one of each item on the grocery list

b. ______________________________

c. ______________________________

d. ______________________________

2. Between _____ and _____ percent of obsessive-compulsive clients treated with exposure and response prevention show significant improvement.

a. List three signs of this improvement.

____

____

3. The Cognitive Perspective

1. Compared with most people, how do those with obsessive-compulsive disorder interpret their intrusive, unwanted thoughts?

____

____

2. "Neutralizing" is when a person seeks to eliminate unwanted, intrusive thoughts by thinking or behaving in a way meant to put matters "right" internally. Give three example of "neutralizing" behavior.

____

____

3. Researchers have discovered four factors that appear to explain why people with obsessive-compulsive disorders are so disturbed by their intrusive thoughts. Complete the table below by writing a statement summarizing the findings on each of the factors, and then matching each with the example that best fits it.

Factor	Summarization of findings	Example
Depressed mood		
Strict code of acceptability		
Dysfunctional beliefs about responsibility and harm		
Dysfunctional beliefs about the control of thoughts		

Examples:

a. I am afraid I will act on my thoughts and force myself sexually on someone.

b. My sexual thoughts about co-workers are dirty and despicable. God will surely punish me for being such an evil person.

c. It seems that the more down I feel, the more I have these awful thoughts about sex.

d. Other people are able to control their thoughts, so I must not be normal.

4: Cognitive Therapies

1. Habituation training is a cognitive approach in which obsessive clients are asked to think about their specific obsessions over and over. What is the goal of this procedure?

____

____

2. Under what circumstances might a therapist add covert-response prevention to a plan of treatment containing habituation training?

____

____

5. The Biological Perspective

1. Two sets of findings support the notion that biological factors play a role in obsessive-compulsive disorders. Complete the statements related to them.

a. Obsessive-compulsive symptoms are reduced with the ______________ drugs clomipramine (Anafranil) and fluoxetine (Prozac), which seem to increase ______________ activity in the brain. The implication of this finding is that obsessive-compulsive disorder is associated with ________ ______________ activity.

b. Two areas of the brain—the orbital region of the frontal cortex and the caudate nuclei—may be functioning abnormally. These parts of the brain control the conversion of ______________ input into cognitions and ______________.

Study the following diagram.

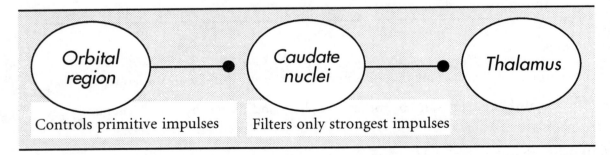

c. List two of the primitive impulses that appear to originate in the orbital region.

____

2. Complete the following statements regarding research support that the caudate nuclei and the occipital region are implicated in obsessive-compulsive disorders.

a. Obsessive-compulsive symptoms sometimes arise or subside after the orbital region or the caudate nuclei are ______________ by illness or accident.

b. PET scans of obsessive-compulsive patients indicate that the caudate nuclei and orbital region are more __________ in people with OCD, compared to control subjects.

c. Compared to obsessive-compulsive patients who do not improve, patients whose symptoms respond well to treatment show:

____

5: Drug Therapies

. Again, research and treatment seem to indicate that certain ____________________ drugs are much more effective in the treatment of obsessive-compulsive disorder; these drugs increase __________ activity and establish __________ activity in the orbital region and caudate nuclei.

. Antidepressant drugs that increase __________________ activity, as opposed to those which affect other neurotransmitters are the only antidepressant drugs that alleviate obsessive-compulsive disorders.

. Use of antidepressant drugs results in reduced, more normal __________________ activity in the orbital region and caudate nuclei of patients with obsessive-compulsive disorders.

I: *Acute Stress Disorders & Posttraumatic Stress Disorders*

. According to the DSM-IV, acute stress disorders and posttraumatic stress disorders differ primarily in onset and duration. Complete the following table to fit the DSM-IV.

	Acute stress disorders	Posttraumatic stress disorders
Onset	Symptoms begin within ______ weeks of the traumatic event.	Symptoms begin anywhere from shortly after to many ____________ after the event.
Duration	Symptoms last from 2 to ______ days.	Symptoms have continued for ______ days or more.

Read the following sample case.

Sample Case

Sarah is a 23-year-old female who works as a pediatric nurse. At 3 a.m. one night, Sarah finished her shift and walked to her car in the parking garage adjacent to the hospital. As Sarah approached her car, she heard footsteps behind her. Before she was able to react, she was thrown down and pinned to the cement floor by a man with a stocking mask over his face. Brandishing a knife, the attacker threatened to kill Sarah if she made any noise or attempted to fight or run. She was brutally raped and knocked unconscious. When she regained consciousness several minutes later, the perpetrator had fled the scene. Sarah drove home in a state of shock, and managed to call a close fried, who immediately drove her to the emergency room.

2. Four types of symptoms Sarah might manifest if she developed a stress disorder are listed belo as a–d. In the spaces provided list two examples of each symptom specific to Sarah's cas (Symptom "a" is provided.)

a. Re-experiencing the traumatic event:

- Sarah has nightmares in which she "relives" the rape
- Sarah often imagines that she hears the footsteps of her attacker when she goes outside

b. Avoidance:

- ______________________________
- ______________________________

c. Reduced responsiveness (also called psychic numbing or emotional anesthesia):

- ______________________________
- ______________________________

A: Stress Disorders Caused by Combat

1. This exercise refers to the syndrome involving symptoms of anxiety and depression in soldie *during* combat.

a. At the time of the American Civil War, it was thought that the syndrome was caused by extend absence from home. It was called ______________________.

b. During World War I, the syndrome was called ______________________________.Clinicia thought its cause was minute brain ______________________ or ______________________ caused by artillery explosions.

c. During World War II and the Korean War the syndrome was called ____________________ ____________________.

2. By the late 1970s, it was apparent that many Vietnam veterans were still experiencing psychological problems long after they came home to the U.S. from the war. List some of the signs of these disturbances.

a. ____

b. ____

c. ____

d. ____

B: Stress Disorders Caused by Disasters

. List two natural and/or accidental disasters that had an impact on you, your family, or your community in the last five years.

. ____

. ____

. What kinds of acute or posttraumatic stress symptoms were seen in people as a result of one or both of the events in the preceding exercise?

____

____

C. Stress Disorders Caused by Abuse and Victimization

Complete the following statements regarding statistic on sexual assault.

Although an estimated __________ persons in the U.S. are victims of rape each year, only about ______ of the assaults are reported to the authorities.

Between ______ and ______ percent of all women are the victims of sexual assault at some point in their lives.

Approximately 29% of rape victims are under age ______, 32% are between the ages of __________, and 29% are between the ages of __________.

A very important legal precedent was set in 1982 that led to changes in the way that at least half of the states deal with certain group of rapists. Describe the court's ruling and its relevance.

____

____

3. What do the Senate Judiciary Committee report and recent national surveys tell us about the inci- dence of rape in the U.S.?

____

____

____

D: Explanations of Acute and Posttraumatic Stress Disorders

Why do some people develop stress disorders following a traumatic even and others do not? Researchers hav focused on a number of factors that could distinguish these groups of people including biological/genetic fac tors, childhood experiences, personality, and social support, and the severity of the trauma.

1. Some researchers suggest that people who develop stress disorders may have inherited a geneti __________ to biologically respond to stressful events more strongly than others (e.g., experienc extreme changes in norepinephrine and/or hormonal activity).

2. After a traumatic event, people who lived in poverty as children seem to be more likely to devel op stress disorder. List three other childhood experiences that could leave a person more vulner able to stress disorders.

a. ______________________________

b. ______________________________

c. ______________________________

E: Treatments for Acute and Posttraumatic Stress Disorders

1. Describe the treatment strategy called "eye movement desensitization and reprocessing."

____

____

2. With respect to the families of people with stress disorders, what is the "conspiracy of silence"?

____

____

3. What are some of the skills that individuals and families coping with stress disorders develop ov the course of family therapy?

____

____

Practice multiple-choice questions for this chapter begin on page 280.

Chapter 8

Mood Disorders

Chapter Organization

This chapter presents an overview of the two major types of mood disorders: unipolar depression and bipolar disorders, or alternate periods of mania and depression. The first half of the chapter is much larger because far more is known about depression than about mania. The core of each half is the section describing explanations of the disorder that have been offered by various theoretical perspectives. Studying the research and views of all the perspectives should provide a deeper understanding of the innate nature of mood disorders. Another important fact to remember is that much of what is known about both major types of mood disorders has been discovered only in the last 25 years or so. Mood disorders are a burgeoning area of abnormal psychology, and much of this chapter is based on some of the most interesting and important psychological research that is going on today.

Be sure to read through each section before completing the exercises for that section.

Exercises

I: Unipolar Depression

A: The Prevalence of Unipolar Depression

1. Complete the following statements about the prevalence of unipolar depression.

a. Each year, five to ten percent of adults in the U.S. suffer from a severe unipolar pattern of depression and another three to five percent suffer mild forms.

b. As many as _____ percent of adults worldwide experience a sever depressive episode during their lifetime.

d. __________________ are two times more likely to suffer depression than the other gender.

e. Few differences in prevalence have been found among ethnic or age groups.

f. While _______________ of severely depressed people recover within six months, those who have been depressed are more likely to become depressed again.

B: The Clinical Picture of Depression

1. Complete the table below by giving three key words or phrases that describe the symptoms of depression in the listed areas of functioning.

Area of functioning	Key words or phrases
Emotional	*miserable, loss of pleasure, anxiety*
Motivational	
Behavioral	
Cognitive	
Physical	

C: Diagnosing Unipolar Patterns of Depression

People experiencing a major depressive episode are usually assigned a diagnosis of "major depressive disorder." A clinician may clarify this diagnosis by indicating the type of depression. This part of a diagnosis will use the following terms: single episode, recurrent, seasonal, catatonic, postpartum, and melancholic.

1. Complete this exercise by putting yourself in the place of a clinician clarifying a diagnosis of "major depressive disorder." Match each of the following examples with one of the terms listed in the preceding paragraph.

Example	*Diagnosis*
Although he feels fine most of the year, Clark feels extremely depressed from Thanksgiving until well past New Year's Day.	
Sherrie has been experiencing symptoms including excessive crying, loss of appetite, feelings of hopelessness, and insomnia since the birth of her son three weeks ago.	
Martin says he's been depressed for six weeks, but never like this before. He denies having any "manic" symptoms.	
Until recently, Richard loved to go to basketball games. Now he won't even watch them on TV. He feels very guilty and eats one meal a day. He is depressed, but particularly so at 4 a.m., when he usually wakes up.	
Marjorie's primary and most debilitating symptom is that she feels unable to move at all. She stays in bed for days on end.	
Over the last ten years, Debbie has experienced seven depressive episodes. She fears that she will never have a "normal" life.	

2. Complete the following statements regarding dysthymic disorder.

a. It is a more chronic but less ____________________ pattern of unipolar depression.

b. Typically, a depressed mood and only two or three other symptoms are present and the depression persists for at least ________________________ in adults.

c. Depression might alternate with periods of normal mood.

d. ____________________ depression is the term used when dysthymic disorder leads to a major depressive disorder.

D: Explanations of Unipolar Patterns of Depression

Explanations of unipolar patterns of depression from the perspectives of five theoretical orientations are discussed in the textbook. Each of their five views are covered separately in the following part of the Workbook.

1. The Biological View

1. Complete the following table summarizing research into biochemical factors and unipolar depression starting in the 1950s.

Neurotransmitter studied	norepinephrine	serotonin
Findings on reserpine		
Findings on MAO inhibitors	*works as an antidepressant; increases supplies of norepinephrine and/or serotonin*	
Tentative conclusion		
Name of theory		*indoleamine theory*

2. Complete the following statements regarding research on the various possible contributions of norepinephrine and seratonin to unipolar depression.

It may be the unipolar depression is related to...

a. ... low activity levels of __________ norepinephrine and seratonin

b. ... low activity levels of __________ norepinephrine or serotonin

c. ____

3. Elevated levels of the stress hormone known as __________ which is released by the __________ glands, has been implicated in depression.

2. The Psychodynamic View

Freud and Abraham's psychoanalytic theory of depression was based on the observation that people's grief reactions are very similar to symptoms of major depression.

1. Study and complete the following chart based on Freud and Abraham's formulation.

A loved one dies or is lost in some way, and a series of unconscious processes is set in motion

People regrss to the oral stage of development in order to fuse their own identity with that of the person they lost

That is, they introject the loved one and experience feelings toward the loved one as feelings toward themselves

The length of the reaction period differs among people

For some, the mourning perid lasts a relatively short time	For others, the reaction worsens and they feel empty and avoid social contact
These people re-establish a separate identity and resume social relationships	Introjected feelings of anger create self-hatred, self-blame, and DEPRESSION

The two kinds of people who are most susceptible to introjection and depression following the loss of a loved one are:

1.

2.

2. Which Freudian concept is illustrated in the following scenario?

A teenager fails to gain admittance to his father's college and becomes depressed because he unconsciously believes that his father will no longer love him.

____

3. Object relations theorists suggest that people whose parents pushed them toward excessive ____________________ or excessive ____________________ are more likely to become depressed when faced with the loss of a relationship.

3. The Behavioral View

Peter Lewisohn's behavioral explanation of unipolar depression suggests that some people engage in fewer positive behaviors when the reward for their positive behaviors start to diminish, and that this is the basis for the development of a depressed style of functioning. Read the following sample case relating to Lewisohn's theory of depression.

Sample Case

Saul is a 59-year-old grocery store owner, who through 40 years of hard work has made his store the biggest in town. He has accomplished this in spite of stiff competition from national chain stores. He has always taken great pride in beating them. Saul has earned the respect of his customers and employees alike. But profits have been down for a few years—a situation he blames on his advancing age. He decides to sell his store when one of the chains offers him a good price. He and his wife retire to the coast of Maine.

Saul enjoys retirement for about a week and then starts to complain of feeling "empty." He tries improving his golf game, but quits when he is consistently beaten at the sport by his wife and others. He finds himself drinking more alcohol than ever before. He had wanted to take up sailing, but decides not to, figuring he is too old. Within six months of retirement, he is doing little more than watching television, drinking, and going to bed early every night.

1. Apply Lewisohn's explanation of unipolar depression to the sample case.

a. List some of the rewards for positive behavior Saul received as a store owner.

____

b. Saul's eventual depressed style of functioning results from a spiral toward depression. Which of Saul's activities could be seen as evidence of a spiral?

____

2. A study by Lewisohn examining the number of reinforcers in the lives of depressed people compared to those in the lives of nondepressed people found that depressed people have more unpleasant life experiences related to health, finances, social interactions, and professional and academic pursuits. Give one more research finding consistent with this theory.

____

3. Lewisohn believes that social reinforcements are crucial to whether people develop depressive styles. Studies have found that depressed patients tend to make others angry, are avoided, have fewer friends, and more unpleasant social interactions with others. Based on your own experiences or observations, write a little about whether or not you think these studies are accurate.

____

____

4. The Cognitive View

You should recall from Chapter 2 that theorist Aaron Beck is closely associated with the cognitive perspective. His theory of depression rests on the notion that maladaptive attitudes, the cognitive triad, errors in thinking, and automatic thoughts combine to produce the negative thinking patterns that are characteristic of depression. In this part of the Workbook, each of these components, as well as a feedback system that abets them, will be covered in succession.

• Maladaptive Attitudes

1. Beck suggests that children's attitudes about themselves and the world are based primarily on what three sources of information?

    ____

2. Beck further posits that negative attitudes become templates, or ______________ through which all of a person's experiences are evaluated and interpreted.

• The Cognitive Triad

3. In this exercise, complete the following figure by supplying the missing "forms" in Beck's cognitive triad.

Negative view of self

The Cognitive Triad

Negative view of ______________

Negative view of ______________

• Errors in Thinking

4. Page 254 of the textbook lists five of the common errors in logic that depressed people habitually employ. Define the following terms:

a. Arbitrary Inference: ______________________________

b. Selective Abstraction: ______________________________

c. Overgeneralization: ______________________________

d. Magnification/Minimization: ______________________________

e. Personalization: ______________________________

• Automatic Thoughts

5. According to Beck, people experience (or manifest) the cognitive triad in the form of automatic thoughts, a steady train of unpleasant, "reflexive" type thoughts that remind depressed people of their assumed ____________________ and the ____________________ of their situation.

6. Complete the following table summarizing the empirical support for Beck's theory of depression. Provide one example of a research finding that provides evidence for each tenet of the theory listed.

Tenet	Supportive finding
Depressed people hold maladaptive attitudes	the number of maladaptive attitudes correlate strongly with the degree of depression
Depressed people exhibit the cognitive triad	
Depressed people show errors in logic	
Depressed people experience negative automatic thoughts	

5. The Cognitive-Behavioral View: Learned Helplessness

1. What are the two primary components of Martin Seligman's cognitive-behavioral view of depression? "People become depressed when they think that...

a. ______________________________

b. ______________________________

2. Complete the following table summarizing one of Seligman's studies of learned helplessness in people.

Subjects	Nondepressed people		
Conditions:	Group I: exposed to loud noise which subjects could stop by pushing a button	Group II:	Group III:
Procedure:	After subjects were "pretreated" in each condition, all subjects were given a control shuttle box and exposed to loud noise. The control box was "rigged" so that the noise would stop if subjects moved the handle from one side to another.		
Results:	Group I:	Group II:	Group III: subjects quickly learned to move the handle and stop the loud noise

3. Passivity is only one depressive-like reaction observed in humans and animals who were "taught" helplessness. List some other reactions observed in subjects who thought they could not control aversive events in the experiments.

____

____

According to the revised learned helplessness theory, when people make attributions for events in their lives that they cannot control, they are implicitly breaking down the causes in terms of internal vs. external, global vs. specific, and stable vs. unstable.

4. Complete the list of questions that people are implicitly asking themselves when they assign attribution for an event that they cannot control.

a. What question is being asked in the dimension of internal vs. external?

"Is the cause located within myself or is it elsewhere?"

b. What question is being asked in the dimension of global vs. specific?

____

c. What question is being asked in the dimension of stable vs. unstable?

____

5. The most recent refinement of the learned helplessness model of depression suggests that attributions cause depression when they result in a feeling of __________.

6. The combination of dimensions that seems to indicate a person is most likely to be depressed is internal, ____________________, and ____________________.

7. The most recent refinement of the learned helplessness model of depression suggests that attributions cause depression when the result in the feeling of __________.

6. The Sociocultural View

1. Although people in all cultures are at similar risk for depression, the fact that characteristics of depression vary from culture to culture is illustrated by the observation that depressive symptoms differ in Western vs. Non-Western countries. Describe the characteristics of depression in non-Western countries.

____

____

2. Sociocultural theorists note that although there appear to be few differences in overall __________ rates of depression among various ethnic populations, differences emerge when researchers examine __________ ethnic populations living in __________ circumstances.

3. A number of research finding highlight the fact that depression is linked to the immediate social environment (including relationship status and levels of social support). Below, list the three findings that you find mist interesting for compelling.

a. ____

b. ____

c. ____

II: Bipolar Disorders

A: The Clinical Picture of Mania

1. Rather than feeling down in the dumps, people in a state of mania experience dramatic ____________________, and disproportionate elevations in mood.

2. Complete the table below by giving three key words or phrases that describe the symptoms of mania in the listed areas of functioning.

Area of functioning	Key words or phrases
Emotional	*elation, euphoric joy, irritability*
Motivational	
Behavioral	
Cognitive	
Physical	

B: Diagnosing Bipolar Disorders

1. DSM-IV criteria for a manic episode includes experiencing an ________________, expansive, or ________________ mood, as well as at least ________________ other symptoms of mania, for a minimum of one week.

2. If symptoms of mania are less severe and of shorter duration, the diagnosis would be a ____________________ episode.

3. Complete the following statements regarding the prevalence of bipolar disorders.

a. Bipolar _____ disorders are slightly more common than bipolar _____ disorders.

b. The prevalence of bipolar disorders is the same for men and women, at all socioeconomic levels, and in all ______________ groups.

c. The age of onset is usually between _____ and _____ years.

4. A diagnosis of ________________ disorder would be assigned to a person who experienced alternating periods of hypomanic and mild depressive symptoms.

C: Explanations of Bipolar disorders

The most promising clues for an explanation of bipolar disorders come from three areas of the biological realm—neurotransmitter activity, sodium ion activity, and genetic factors. Each of these is covered separately in this part of the Workbook.

1. Neurotransmitters

1. Describe one of the two findings that led researchers to believe that mania is related to abnormally high levels of norepinephrine.

____

____

____

2. Contrary to the expectations of theorists, research has shown that mania, like depression, is associated with a low supply of _______________.

3. Complete the following diagram which depicts the "permissive theory" of mood disorders.

Low _______________ activity	Plus	Low to moderate levels of _______________	Depression
	Plus	High levels of _______________	Mania

2. Sodium Ion Activity

1. When a neuron is stimulated, a series of events takes place. Complete the following statements related to these events:

a. Sodium ions move from the __________ side of the neuronal membrane to the __________ side

b. Electrochemical activations that travel down the length of the __________ results in the "__________" of the neuron.

c. __________ ions move from the inside to the outside of the neuron, returning it to the original __________ state.

2. What do researchers believe might be happening in the above series of events that:

   leads to mania? ______________________________

   leads to depression? ______________________________

3. Genetic Factors

1. Family pedigree studies have indicated that close relatives of a person with bipolar disorder have a _____ to _____ percent likelihood of developing the disorder, compared to 1% prevalence rate in the general population.

2. Studies involving close relatives and twins of those with bipolar disorders indicate that the more similar the _______________ _______________ of two people, the more similar their tendency to develop a bipolar disorder.

3. Complete the following description of the method used by researchers in genetic linkage studies.

a. Researchers select extended families that have high rates of bipolar disorder over several _______________.

b. They observe the pattern of distribution of bipolar disorder in family members.

c. They determine whether the bipolar pattern follows the distribution patterns of other family (inherited) traits such as:

____

Practice multiple-choice questions for this chapter begin on page 281.

Chapter 9

Treatments for Mood Disorders

Chapter Organization

Coverage of the treatments for mood disorders are divided between treatments for unipolar depression and bipolar disorders. The section covering unipolar treatments is broken down into examinations of different kinds of therapy. The two largest subsections are those looking at electroconvulsive therapy (ECT) and antidepressant drug therapy. Coverage of the treatment of bipolar disorders centers on the use of lithium. As with other chapters that focus on treatment of psychological abnormalities, an important aspect of the studies is how combinations of various specific therapies are sometimes used as treatments.

Be sure to read through each section before completing the exercises for that section.

Exercises

I: Treatments for Unipolar Depression

A variety of treatment approaches are available for persons suffering from unipolar depression. In the following section, exercises will cover three general categories of treatments: psychological approaches (psychodynamic, behavioral, and cognitive therapies), sociocultural approaches (interpersonal and couple therapies), and biological approaches (electroconvulsive therapy and antidepressant drugs). Additionally, exercises addressing trends in treatment are included at the end of this section.

A: Psychodynamic Therapy

1. Complete the following flow chart of information regarding psychodynamic therapy for unipolar depression.

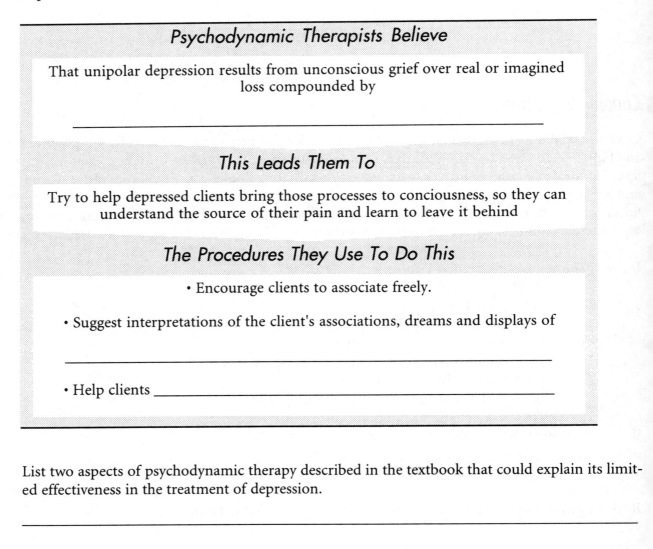

Psychodynamic Therapists Believe

That unipolar depression results from unconscious grief over real or imagined loss compounded by

____

This Leads Them To

Try to help depressed clients bring those processes to conciousness, so they can understand the source of their pain and learn to leave it behind

The Procedures They Use To Do This

- Encourage clients to associate freely.
- Suggest interpretations of the client's associations, dreams and displays of

  ____
- Help clients ____________________________________

2. List two aspects of psychodynamic therapy described in the textbook that could explain its limited effectiveness in the treatment of depression.

a. ____

____

b. ____

____

B: Behavioral Therapy

1. Complete the following table by listing and describing each of the components of Peter Lewisohn's influential behavioral treatment of depression.

Component	Description
1. *Reintroducing Pleasurable Events*	
2.	*Contingency managment approach that ignores depression behaviors and rewards positive behaviors*
3.	

2. Therapies that ______________ several of Lewisohn's strategies seem to reduce symptoms of ______________ to ______________ levels of depression.

C: Cognitive Therapy

1. Complete the following table summarizing the four phases of Beck's cognitive therapy of depression.

Phase	Description
1. *Increasing activities and Elevating Mood*	*preparation of a detailed weekly schedule that includes behavioral "assignments" designed to gradually involve the client in more activities*
2.	
3.	
4.	

2. Hundreds of studies have concluded that ______________ to ______________ depressed people improve markedly with cognitive therapy, and approximately 50 to 60 percent show a total elimination of depressive symptoms.

D: Interpersonal Psychotherapy

1. Complete the following table by first describing the key problem areas addressed in interpersonal therapy and then by giving examples of the therapist's tasks in each of these areas.

Problem areas	Description	Therapist's tasks
greif reactions	*feelings of grief and sadness after the loss of a loved one (e. g. through death or divorce)*	*explore relationship with lost person; help client express feelings toward lost person; encourage development of new relationships*
interpersonal role dispute		
interpersonal role transition		
interpersonal deficits		

2. Depressive symptoms were relieved in approximately _____ to _____ percent of clients treated with IPT, according to research findings.

3. Interpersonal Psychotherapy appears to be the most effective treatment for what kinds of clients?

____

E: Sociocultural Approaches: Couple Therapy

1. Research has indicated that as many as _____ of all depressed clients are in a dysfunctional relationship, and recovery from depression is likely to be _____ for these persons.

2. Describe the central goals of the behavioral marital therapist.

____

____

F: Electroconvulsive Therapy

1. In ________________ ECT, electrodes carrying 65 to 140 volts of an electrical current are placed on both sides of the patient's head, whereas in ________________ ECT, electrodes are placed on only one side of the head.

2. Complete the following list of characteristics of ECT.

a. The electrical current causes a ________________ that lasts from 25 seconds to a few minutes; after about _______ minutes the patient wakes up.

b. Typically, barbiturates and ________________ ________________ are used as part of the treatment.

c. ECT programs consist of _______ to _______ treatments over the course of two to four ________________.

3. Inducing convulsions as a treatment for depression has historical origins in an accident that occurred over 200 years ago. Provide the missing information in the following statement regarding the path that led from this accident to ECT.

a. Dr. W. Oliver induced convulsions in a patient when he overadministered the stimulant camphor in 1785. When the patient awoke he was apparently cured of his psychological problems.

b. Believing that epileptic convulsions prevented psychosis, Joseph von Menduna revived this treatment in the early 1930s by using the camphor derivative ________________ to induce convulsions.

c. ________________ ________________ therapy, a related technique which is also a dangerous procedure was developed at about the same time by Manfred Sakel.

d. A few years later, ECT was developed by ________________________ and his colleague Lucio Bini.

4. Describe the purpose of (a) barbiturates, and (b) muscle relaxants in ECT.

a. ____

b. ____

5. Approximately 60 to 70 percent of patients improve with ECT. What are some of the symptoms of the patients with the best improvement rates?

____

G: Biological Treatments: Antidepressant Drugs

The primary classes of drugs that are used to treat depression are the MAO inhibitors, the tricyclics, and the second-generation antidepressant drugs. Each of these kinds of drugs will be examined separately in the exercises below.

1. The MAO Inhibitors

1. The drug _______________ is the predecessor of the current MAO inhibitors such as Nardil and Parnate that are used to treat depression.

2. Complete the following exercises related to how researchers believe MAO inhibitors alleviate depression.

a. Recall (from Chapter 8) that in some people, depression seems to be associated with decreased activity of the neurotransmitter norepinephrine.

b. The enzyme MAO, which stands for _______________ interacts with norepinephrine and breaks it down so that it is no longer effective.

c. When the antidepressant drug MAO inhibitor is introduced into the system, what is prevented?

____

d. Summarize why MAO inhibitors act to alleviate depressive symptoms.

____

____

3. In this exercise explain (a) what tyramine is, and (b) how it can present a danger to people using MAO inhibitors.

a. _______________

____

b. _______________

____

2. Tricyclics

1. Before it was found to be effective in treating depression, the tricyclic drug _______________ was used unsuccessfully in the treatment of schizophrenia.

2. About _____ to _____ percent of mildly to severely depressed patients who take tricyclic antidepressant drugs improve, and experience decreases in psychological symptoms such as excessive _____ and physical symptoms such as poor _________.

3. Complete the following statements related to relapse among depressed patients who take tricyclic drugs.

a. About _____ percent of people will relapse within one year if they stop taking the drugs immediately after they experience relief.

b. the risk of relapse decreases significantly if patients continue t take the drugs for a period of approximately __________ after depressive symptoms disappear.

c. Some studies have indicated that patients who take full dosages of the drugs for _____ to _____ years after initial improvement — a strategy called "__________ therapy" — reduce their risk for relapse even more.

4. When neurons release neurotransmitters into the synapse, they simultaneously "recapture" some of the neurotransmitter by way of a pumplike mechanism in the nerve ending. Answer the following questions about this process.

a. What is the purpose of this reuptake process?

____

____

b. What might be "going wrong" in the reuptake process of depressed people?

____

____

c. How are tricyclics thought to alleviate depressive symptoms?

____

____

5. What observation did researchers make about the action of tricyclics on the reuptake mechanism that led them to question how these drugs alleviate depression?

____

____

3. *Second-Generation Antidepressants*

1. Some second-generation antidepressants such as Prozac (fluoxetine) are classified as selective ______________ ______________ ______________ (SSRIs) because they alter serotonin activity specifically, but do not affect other neurotransmitters in the brain.

2. List some of the (a) strengths, and (b) weaknesses of the second-generation antidepressants compared to older tricyclics. Read Box 9-4 on pages 294-95.

____

____

H: Trends in Treatment

1. In comparative outcome studies, ______________________, interpersonal (IPT), and ______________________ therapies appear to be equally and highly effective at alleviating depressive symptoms.

Below is a diagram relating to the ambitious National Institute of Mental Health outcome study of treatments for depression.

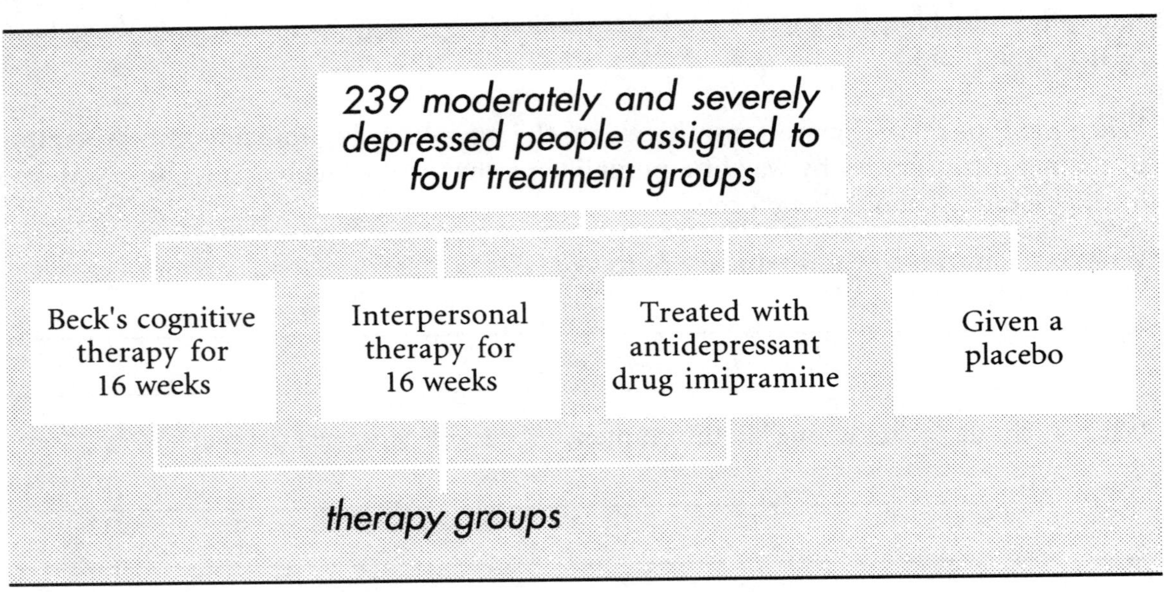

2. Answer the questions below relating to the findings of the National Institute of Mental Health outcome study of antidepressant therapy.

a. Describe improvements in the three therapy groups.

____

b. Describe the improvement in the placebo group.

____

c. What were the differences in how quickly the treatments worked in relieving depression?

____

____

3. ______________ therapy may be more effective than ______________ therapy at preventing relapses in depression, except when the latter therapy is continued for an extended period.

4. ______________ therapy is less effective in treating depression (particularly severe depression) than cognitive, interpersonal, or biological therapies.

5. A much disputed finding is that ______________ therapy does not appear to be effective in treating depression.

6. A combination of ______________ and ______________ therapy may be more helpful to depressed people than any single treatment, although the evidence for this is not consistent.

7. Complete the following statements that relate to biological treatments of unipolar depression.

a. ECT and antidepressant drugs seem to be more effective in treating depression, but ECT seems to act more __________.

b. Clinicians usually treat depressed people with ______________ first, and only if that treatment is unsuccessful will they consider ______________.

c. Research findings have indicated that _____ to _____ percent of people who do not respond to drug therapy are helped by ECT.

II: Treatments for Bipolar Disorders

1. Lithium therapy requires that patients undergo regular analyses of _____ and _____ in order for doctors to determine the correct dosage.

2. If lithium dosage is too low, the drug will be ineffective; however, if the dosage is too high, what are the potential results?

____

____

3. Improvement rates for people with manic symptoms are _____ percent and higher.

4. Improvement rates for people with manic symptoms are _____ percent and higher.

A: Lithium Therapy

1. Lithium therapy requires that patients undergo regular analyses of _____ and _____ in order for doctors to determine the correct dosage.

2. If lithium dosage is too low, the drug will be ineffective; however, if the dosage is too high, what are the potential results?

____

____

3. Improvement rates for people with manic symptoms are _____ percent and higher.

4. One study found that the risk of relapse is _____ times greater if patients stop taking lithium, suggesting that lithium may be a __________ drug (one that actually *prevents* symptoms from developing).

B: Adjunctive Psychotherapy

1. Most all clinicians agree that neither ____________ alone nor ____________ therapy alone is effective in treating bipolar disorders. In light of these beliefs, some clinicians utilize ____________ ____________ as an adjunct to lithium treatment.

2. Complete the following exercises relating to the concerns addressed by clinicians when psychotherapy is combined with lithium treatment.

a. What are some of the reasons patients give for disliking or rejecting lithium?

____

____

b. Recovering bipolar patients often experience social difficulties resulting from the loss of those close to them who were repelled by bipolar episodes. Returning to a certain kind of family environment may also cause problems. Specifically, what kind of family?

____

c. Psychotherapists provide information about the causes, common patterns, and practical implications of bipolar disorder. In therapy groups clinicians use an additional method to educate patients. Describe that method.

____

d. Bipolar disorders can lead to a host of problems in all aspects of a patient's life.

Therapists may help clients develop solutions for these difficulties.

3. Clinical reports suggest that combining psychotherapy with lithium treatment for patients with bipolar disorder leads to reduced ____________, better social functioning, and higher ____________ rates.

Practice multiple-choice questions for this chapter begin on page 283.

Chapter 10

Suicide

Chapter Organization

Chapter 10 is a thorough examination of the problem of suicide. The first section defines suicide and looks at the scientific methods involved in its study. Section two examines various factors that seem to precipitate suicide. The third section addresses how three major theoretical perspectives attempt to answer the central question, "Why do people commit suicide?" Patterns of suicide differ among age groups, and section four should help you to identify and explore these differences. The final section examines how clinicians treat people who attempt suicide, and identifies strategies for suicide prevention.

Be sure to read through each section before completing the exercises for that section.

Exercises

The following exercises cover chapter introductory material on page 304.

1. Statistics show that there are more than ______________ suicides each year in the U.S. and ______________ more unsuccessful attempts, called ______________________.

2. The textbook states that the actual number of suicides could be twice the official total. Give two reasons for the difficulty in obtaining accurate suicide statistics.

   a. ____

   b. ____

3. DSM-IV does not classify suicide as a ______________ ______________, although it is characterized by clinical features such as emotional turmoil, a breakdown in ______________ skills, and distorted perspective.

I: What Is Suicide?

1. Edwin Shneidman defines suicide as a self-inflicted death in which the person makes an ______________, direct, and ______________ effort to end his or her life.

2. Complete the following table by describing the characteristics of Shneidman's four categories of people who attempt or commit suicide. Then, read through the case examples provided and match each with the most appropriate category.

Category	Description of Characteristics	Example
Death seekers		
Death initiators		
Death ignorers		
Death darers		

Cases:

a. Sheldon repeatedly engages in high-risk activities such as drinking and driving, and mixing alcohol and drugs. When his girlfriend pleads with him to stop the dangerous behavior, Sheldon usually retorts with statements like: "You wouldn't care if I died, anyway" and "It would serve you right if I did kill myself one of these days."

b. After her suicide attempt by drug overdose, Jackie stated the following to a hospital psychiatric nurse: "I had thought about killing myself on and off for weeks. I would have a really bad day and almost do it, but then I'd feel a little better the next day and decide not to. Today was a really, really bad day—the worst."

c. Six-year old Marrianne is devastated after seeing the family dog, Jo-Jo, killed by a car in front of her house. Her parents try to comfort her by telling her that Jo-Jo is happy in heaven, but later she runs into the busy street and is nearly hit by an oncoming truck. When Marrianne's parents ask why she did what she did, she replies, "I wanted to go to heaven to make sure Jo-Jo is okay."

d. Antonio is a 72-year-old man who is suffering from advanced bone cancer. Certain that his last days will be filled with intolerable pain, Antonio asphyxiates himself in his car.

3. A person who plays an indirect, partial, or unconscious role in his/her own death might be classified in a category called ___________ death.

4. Define **chronic suicide** and list three behaviors that illustrate this form of suicide.

Definition:____

Behaviors:____

A: The Study of Suicide

1. Researchers utilize two primary methods in their studies of suicide. In this exercise, describe each type of research strategy, and then describe a limitation of that strategy.

Strategy I:

____

____

Limitation:

____

____

Strategy II:

____

____

Limitation:

____

____

B: Patterns and Statistics

1. ________________ affiliation, and in particular the extent to which people are devout in their beliefs, could account for national differences in suicide rates.

2. The male:female ratio for suicide attempts is roughly ___:___, while the male:female ratio for suicide completions is roughly ___:___.

3. Complete the following exercises in response to the question "Why do completed suicide rates differ between men and women?"

a. One factor is that men tend to use more violent methods such as shooting, ________________, and ________________________, while women often use less violent methods such as ________________ .

b. What do some researchers think sex role stereotypes have to do with the above?

____

____

4. According to research on marital status and suicide, which groups of people are...

a. at highest risk for suicide? ________________________

b. at moderate risk for suicide? ________________________

c. at lowest risk for suicide? ________________________

5. The suicide rate of white Americans is ____________ as high as the suicide rate for ______________ Americans and members of most other non-white racial groups.

6. The suicide rates of some Native Americans is an exception to the usual rule that white Americans have a higher suicide rate than non-white Americans. What are some of the factors that might account for the high rate among Native Americans?

____

II: Factors that Precipitate Suicide

A: Stressful Events and Situations

1. Give examples of recent and episodic stressors that might precipitate suicide.

____

____

2. Complete the following table by describing research evidence of the association between suicide and the delineated long-term stressors.

Long-term stressor linked to suicide	Description of Characteristics
Serious illness	
Abusive environment (See Figure 10-3 on textbook page 355)	*inmates in U.S. jails have 8 times the national suicide rate—over half occur on the 1st day in jail; high rates also seen for prisoners of war, Holocaust victims, and abused spouses and children*
Occupational stress	
Role conflict	

: Mood and Thought Changes

Sadness is one mood change that is associated with suicide. List some others.

____

Describe the most salient cognitive changes that seem to precipitate suicide.

____

____

____

C: Alcohol and Other Drug Use

1. Evidence gained from autopsies of suicide victims indicate that about _______ percent of them drank alcohol just before the act, and that one-fourth of these people were legally intoxicated at the time of death.

2. Alcohol may allow suicidal people to overcome their _____________ of committing suicide, lower inhibitions against _________________, and/or __________________ their ability to make rational decisions for themselves.

D: Mental Disorders

1. Which mental disorders are most often linked with suicide?

____

____

2. Why might psychiatric staff continue to monitor a patient for suicide risk even after his/her depression seems to be lifting?

____

____

3. People with terminal illnesses who attempt suicide are also likely to be suffering from an episode of __________________ ______________________.

4. One explanation of the link between substance abuse and suicide is that the lifestyle resulting from the abuse or a feeling of being hopelessly hooked on the substance or other drugs may lead to suicidal thinking. What is another explanation that is offered for the relationship between the two factors?

____

____

5. Among people with schizophrenia, suicide is most often associated with feelings of ____________________________, rather than being a response to hallucinations or delusions.

E: Modeling: The Contagion of Suicide

1. List the three kinds of models that most often seem to trigger suicide attempts.

____

2. Can you think of people that you know or have heard about that have modeled suicides or attempts on others? Write a paragraph describing the effects of that model on others' behavior.

____

____

____

____

Do people have a right to commit suicide? Read through Box 10-3 and consider your own views on this controversial question.

II: Explanations of Suicide

A: The Psychodynamic View

1. Many psychodynamic theorists believe that suicide results from ____________ and self-____________ anger.

2. Freud and others felt that through introjection, extreme ____________ toward a lost loved one could lead to unrelenting ____________ toward oneself. Suicide could be yet a further expression of this self-____________.

3. Freud suggested that human beings have a basic "death instinct," called ____________, that most people direct toward ____________ and suicidal people direct toward ____________.

4. Describe research findings supporting the psychodynamic theory of suicide in relation to (a) childhood losses, and (b) the "death instinct."

____

____

____

____

B: The Sociocultural View

1. Emile Durkheim proposed that a person's likelihood of committing suicide is strongly influencec by his or her involvement in social institutions and structures. Complete the following flow char by providing the missing information on social structures and Durkheim's three categories of sui cide.

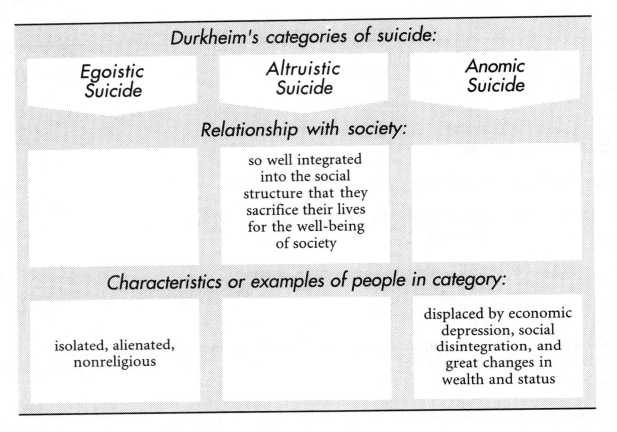

Durkheim's categories of suicide:		
Egoistic Suicide	Altruistic Suicide	Anomic Suicide
Relationship with society:		
	so well integrated into the social structure that they sacrifice their lives for the well-being of society	
Characteristics or examples of people in category:		
isolated, alienated, nonreligious		displaced by economic depression, social disintegration, and great changes in wealth and status

C: The Biological View

The exercises in this subsection together represent an interesting "story" of how the biological view of suici has evolved with continual research.

Over the past two decades, researchers using the family pedigree and twin study methods have found eviden (such as higher than expected rates of suicidal behavior among the close relatives of people who have attemp ed suicide) in support of the position that genetic and biological factors contribute to suicidal behavior. Oth theorists and researchers have argued that the same findings could just as easily be explained by non-biolog cal factors, such as modeling. More recently, researchers have provided stronger and more direct evidence f the biological view of suicide; this evidence is addressed in the following exercises.

1. Complete the following statements relating to the Asberg, et al., (1976) study of depressed patients and suicidal behavior.

a. The Asberg study measured 68 depressed patients' levels of 5-HIAA, a ________________, or by-product of brain serotonin.

b. In the study, of 20 patients with low levels of 5-HIAA, ____ made suicide attempts, compared to ____ from the group of 48 with higher 5-HIAA levels.

c. Researchers concluded that low serotonin levels may be a ________________ of suicide.

2. Another piece of evidence giving more direct support for the biological view of suicide is that autopsies have indicated that the brains of individuals who commit suicide have only __________ as many ________________ receptor sites as the brains of those who die by other means.

3. Since we have already learned that low serotonin activity is associated with depression, and that many depressed people attempt suicide, the findings covered in Exercises #2 and #3 might not seem important. However, two other investigations show evidence of a possible independent link between low serotonin and suicide. Complete the following statements relating to them.

a. Several studies have found that low serotonin levels among suicidal subjects who have no history of __________.

b. Another set of findings suggests that low serotonin levels are associated with __________ behavior, and with the commission of suicide by __________ means.

c. In sum, it appears that low serotonin activity may contribute to aggressive and __________ tendencies — in depressed and nondepressed people — that could lead to suicidal thinking and action.

V: Suicide in Different Age Groups

A: Children

1. Suicide attempts by children are often preceded by temper tantrums, morbid fantasies, and abuse by parents. List some other events and behavior patterns that have been found to precede childhood suicidal behavior.

____

____

2. What does recent research say about how common suicidal thinking is among "normal" children?

____

____

B: Adolescents and Young Adults

1. Suicide ranks __________ among causes of death in people between the ages of 15 and 24 in the U.S., after __________ and homicide.

2. What are some of the major warning signs of suicide in teenagers?

____

____

3. Suicidal behavior in teenagers has been linked to depression, as well as to experiences of both long-term and immediate stress. List some of the (a) long-term, and (b) immediate stressors that have been identified.

a. __________

b. __________

4. The ratio of suicide attempts to fatalities among teenagers is between 50 and 200 to one, suggesting that teenagers may be more __________ about killing themselves than people from other age groups.

5. Some studies suggest that 20 percent of college students have suicidal thoughts. Describe some of the factors that might play a role in suicide attempts among college students.

____

____

____

6. Complete the following list of the four perceived societal changes discussed in the textbook that could explain the recent dramatic rise in suicides among adolescents and young adults.

a. Competition for jobs, college positions, and academic and athletic honors is steadily increasing—leading to high levels of frustration and desperation in some.

b. Recently weakened ties in the family structure have resulted in alienation and rejection among the young, fitting Durkheim's notion of __________ suicide.

c. A propensity toward suicide may be increased by the availability of drugs and:

____

d. __________

____

C: The Elderly

1. Suicide rates among the elderly are higher than in any other age group, and may rank as high as ______________ among causes of death in this age group.

2. Briefly describe explanations for the lower rates (relative to elderly white Americans) of (a) elderly Native Americans, and (b) elderly African Americans.

a. ______________________________

b. ______________________________

V: Treatment and Suicide

A: Treatment after a Suicide Attempt

1. ___________ care is the primary need of victims immediately after they have attempted suicide.

2. Studies indicate that most suicidal people do not receive ______________ after a suicide attempt.

3. The first goal of therapy for people who have attempted suicide is to keep the client alive. What are two other primary goals?

a. ______________________________

b. ______________________________

B: Suicide Prevention

1. List some of the characteristics of a person who is "in crisis."

____

____

2. Complete the following table by putting yourself in the place of a crisis-line counselor at the Los Angeles County Suicide Prevention Center. List your primary tasks to accomplish when taking a crisis call. Then match the task with the statement that is most indicative of that particular task. The first is given.

Task	*Statement*
1. *Establishing a Positive Relationship*	*d.*
2.	
3.	
4.	
5.	

Statements:

a. "Do you have a suicide plan at this point? Do you have access to a gun or pills?"

b. "What is going on in your life right now that feels difficult to handle? Did something happen that made you think about killing yourself?"

c. "Instead of hurting yourself, I want you to come to the crisis center tomorrow morning. Will you agree to do that?"

d. "I can hear how overwhelmed you feel. I want you to know that I am here to listen to you and help you."

e. "Do you have a friend or family member who you feel you can talk to and trust? Who is that person?"

C: The Effectiveness of Suicide Prevention

Assessing the effectiveness of suicide prevention is difficult. The findings of such studies have not been consistent. While some studies indicate that in some communities, centers have had no effect on suicide rates—or even that rates have gone up after centers were established—these findings are not conclusive.

1. One investigator found that while suicide rates increased in some cities with suicide prevention centers, the rates increased __________ in cities without them.

2. A study of the Los Angeles Suicide Prevention Center indicated that among ____________________ people who did call the center, a much higher than average number were averted from committing suicide.

3. One certain implication of effectiveness studies of suicide prevention centers seems to be that they need to be more ________________ to and ________________ for people who are harboring thoughts of suicide.

Practice multiple-choice questions for this chapter begin on page 284.

Chapter 11

Psychological Factors and Physical Disorders

Chapter Organization

In this chapter you will become familiar with psychosocial factors that contribute to the development and maintenance of physical illnesses. Not all of the physical disorders are "real," as you will discover in the first two sections. Factitious disorders, for example, are "faked" ailments for which the patient hopes to receive some sort of gain. Section II looks at the somatoform disorders which are characterized by physical symptoms in the absence of an organically based medical condition, or preoccupation with a perceived physical defect. The bulk of Chapter 11 addresses the psychophysiological disorders. These are true physical illnesses that are significantly influenced by psychological factors such as personality and coping style.

Be sure to read through each section before completing the exercises for that section.

Exercises

I: Factitious Disorders

1. A person is said to be _______________________ when he or she "fakes" an illness in order to achieve an external gain such as financial compensation.

2. People with factitious disorders _______________________ produce symptoms as well, but they are motivated by internal rewards of maintaining a sick role.

3. Complete the following statement regarding characteristics of people diagnosed with factitious disorder with predominantly physical signs and symptoms.

a. Physical symptoms could be a total _______________________, self-inflicted, or an exaggeration of a pre-existing physical condition.

b. Many of these patients undergo painful testing and even _____________________, sometimes resulting in real medical problems.

c. If these patients are "found out," they generally deny the evidence, discharge themselves, and move on to a new, unsuspecting treatment center.

4. Munchausen syndrome is the most chronic form of factitious disorder. Describe a related factitious disorder, Munchausen by proxy.

____

____

II: Somatoform Disorders

In contrast to people with factitious disorders, people with somatoform disorders do not intentionally produce symptoms. Make sure you have read through the introductory material about somatoform disorders on page 339 of the textbook.

A: Hysterical Somatoform Disorders

1. Complete the following table summarizing three types of somatoform disorders.

Type	Description	Symptoms
Conversion disorders	*expression of psychological problems in the form of on or more physical symptoms*	*called "pseudoneurological" include paralysis, blindness, anesthesia, aphonia*
Somatization disorders		
Pain disorders		

2. The textbook discusses several key distinctions used by diagnosticians to distinguish hysterical somatoform disorders from "true" medical problems. Complete the following summary relating to those distinctions.

a. *Neurological and Anatomical Inconsistencies:* Symptoms that are inconsistent or impossible when compared to the manner in which the nervous system works.

Example: ______________________________

b. *Unexpected Course of Development and Consequences:* ______________________________

____

B: Preoccupation Somatoform Disorders

1. People diagnosed with ______________________ interpret normal physical symptoms as a sign of __________.

2. People suffering from body dysmorphic disorder, or ______________________, become preoccupied with imagined or exaggerated __________________ in their appearance.

3. List some of the aspects of appearance that are of most concern to people diagnosed with body dysmorphic disorder.

____

____

C: Views on Somatoform Disorders

1. Explanations for the preoccupation somatoform disorders are most similar to the cognitive and behavioral theories of ____________________ disorders.

2. The ancient Greeks believed that hysterical disorders were experienced when the ______________ of a sexually ____________________ woman would wander throughout her body in search of fulfillment, producing a physical symptom wherever it lodged.

3. The current belief that hysterical ailments are caused by psychological factors dates from the work of Liébault and Bernheim in late nineteenth century France. What was the key to Liébault and Bernheim's discovery?

____

____

____

The textbook discusses three main views of somatoform disorders separately. The Workbook covers each part separately as well.

1. The Psychodynamic View

1. Complete the statements about Freud's view of hysterical somatoform disorders.

a. Freud believed that because hysterical disorders could be treated with hypnosis, these disorders represented a ____________________ of underlying ____________________ conflicts into physical symptoms.

b. According to Freud, if parents overreact to a girl's "sexual" feeling toward her father during the __________________ stage, she will not adequately resolve the emotional conflict (or complex) and could experience sexual ____________ throughout her adult life.

d. Specifically, what did Freud propose would happen when the adult woman's sexual feelings are triggered which could lead to a hysterical disorder?

____

____

2. Although today's psychodynamic theorists agree with Freud that hysterical disorders reflect an unconscious, anxiety-arousing conflict that is converted into more tolerable physical symptoms that symbolize the conflict, they now focus on two mechanisms that seem to be part of the hysterical somatoform disorders. Define the mechanisms (a) primary gain, and (b) secondary gain.

a. ____

____

b. ____

____

2. The Behavioral View

1. The behavioral view of the hysterical somatoform disorders emphasizes the ______________ gained by the patient by manifesting the disorder.

2. Research has supported the behaviorists view that people with hysterical disorders are __________ with an illness, and are therefore able to adopts its __________.

3. What is the primary difference between the behavioral view and the modern psychodynamic view of hysterical disorder?

____

____

3. The Cognitive View

1. Cognitive theorists suggest that the hysterical somatoform disorders serve to ____________________ distressing emotions such as anger, depression, guilt, and jealousy in a "__________ language" that is familiar and comfortable to the patient.

2. According to adherents of the cognitive view, people who have difficulty acknowledging their emotions or expressing them to others are candidates for a hysterical disorder. Who else do they believe is susceptible to this disorder?

____

____

D: Treatments for Somatoform Disorders

Hysterical somatoform disorder sufferers tend to resist psychotherapy because they believe they have physical rather than psychological ailments. The exercises relate to treatments used when these individuals give up on the medical alternatives.

1. People with preoccupation somatoform disorders are usually treated with __________ and __________ interventions that are also utilized for people suffering from anxiety disorder (specifically, __________ disorders).

Read the following sample case.

Sample Case

Rita has sought treatment for her mysterious physical symptoms from six medical professionals at four hospitals. Her symptoms include a sensation of numbness that "travels" across her scalp and face, frequent abdominal pain, and paralysis of her legs. The last doctor she visited could find no organic (physical) basis for her condition even after an extensive series of tests, and finally advised Rita to seek psychotherapy. Although she initially resisted, Rita decided that she had better do what the doctor advised or she might not be able to receive further medical services from the hospital.

2. Complete the following table by writing in the names of the therapeutic techniques used against hysterical somatoform disorder described in the textbook, as well as sample statements you might use for each technique if your were the therapist assigned to treat Rita.

Technique	Sample therapeutic statement
Insight	*"Rita, I would like you to talk to me about your childhood as well as your life right now."*
Suggestion	
	"Rita, I noticed that you walked very quickly into my office today. It's just wonderful that you've been able to suppress the paralysis."

3. Which of the techniques in Exercise #2 seems to be the most effective?

____

III: Psychophysiological Disorders

Physicians and psychologists have long recognized that some physical conditions, such as certain skin problems, ulcers, and heart conditions result from an interaction of physical and psychological/behavioral factors. These disorders, unlike the somatoform disorders, are characterized by actual medical conditions.

In the textbook and Workbook, the shorthand term "psychophysiological disorders" is used to indicate those medical conditions that are significantly affected by psychological factors, rather than the current "psychological factors affecting medical condition" diagnostic term delineated by DSM-IV. Before moving to the exercises in this section, let's take a closer look at the DSM-IV classification scheme for these "psychophysiological" disorders.

DSM-IV Classification of Psychological Disorders

DSM-IV recognizes that psychological and behavioral factors probably play a role in nearly all medical conditions. However, according to DSM-IV:

"This category should be reserved for those situations in which the psychological factors have a clinically significant effect on the course or outcome of the general medical condition or place the individual at a significantly higher risk for an adverse outcome."

(p. 676, APA, 1994)

According to DSM-IV, the psychological factors (including personality traits and coping styles) are coded on Axis I. The accompanying medical condition is coded on Axis III. For example, a patient might be diagnosed with the following:

Axis I: Type A Style (pressured, hostile behavior) Affecting Cardiovascular Disease

Axis III: Cardiovascular Disease; recent Myocardial Infarction

A: "Traditional" Psychophysiological Disorders

1. This exercise focuses on the "traditional" psychophysiological disorders: ulcers, asthma, chronic headaches, hypertension, and coronary heart disease. Complete the table. It was designed to assist in organizing the information in this section.

Ulcer	
Description	*lesions that form in the wall of the stomach (gastric ulcers) or in the duodenum (peptic ulcers) causes pain, vometing, and stomach bleeding*
Psychological factors	*environmental stress, intense anger and/or anxiety, dependent personality traits*
Physiological factors	*bacterial infections, excessive secretions of gastric juices; weak lining of stomach or duodenum*

Asthma	
Description	
Psychological factors	*generalized anxiety, dependency traits, environmental stress, dysfunctional family relationships*
Physiological factors	

Chronic Headaches	
Description	*muscle contraction (tension): pain to back or front of head or back of neck; migraine: severe or immobilizing aches on one side of the head*
Psychological factors	
Physiological factors	

Hypertension	
Description	
Psychological factors	
Physiological factors	*diet high in salt; dysfunctional baroreceptors (nerves in the arteries that signal the brain that blood pressure is too high)*

Coronary Heart Disease (CHD)	
Description	*blockage of coronary arteries—angina pectoris: extreme chest pain; coronary occlusion: destruction of heart tissue; myocardial infarction: heart attack*
Psychological factors	
Physiological factors	

The rest of subsection A. is broken down into two parts, which the Workbook will also cover separately.

1. The Disregulation Model of Traditional Psychophysiological Disorders

1. The disregulation model proposes that our brain and body usually establish ________________ ________________ loops that maintain steadily-operating physical processes.

Study Figure 11-3 on page 350of the textbook—Schwartz's disregulation model. Then compare it to the following figure which shows an application of this negative feedback system to the regulation of blood pressure.

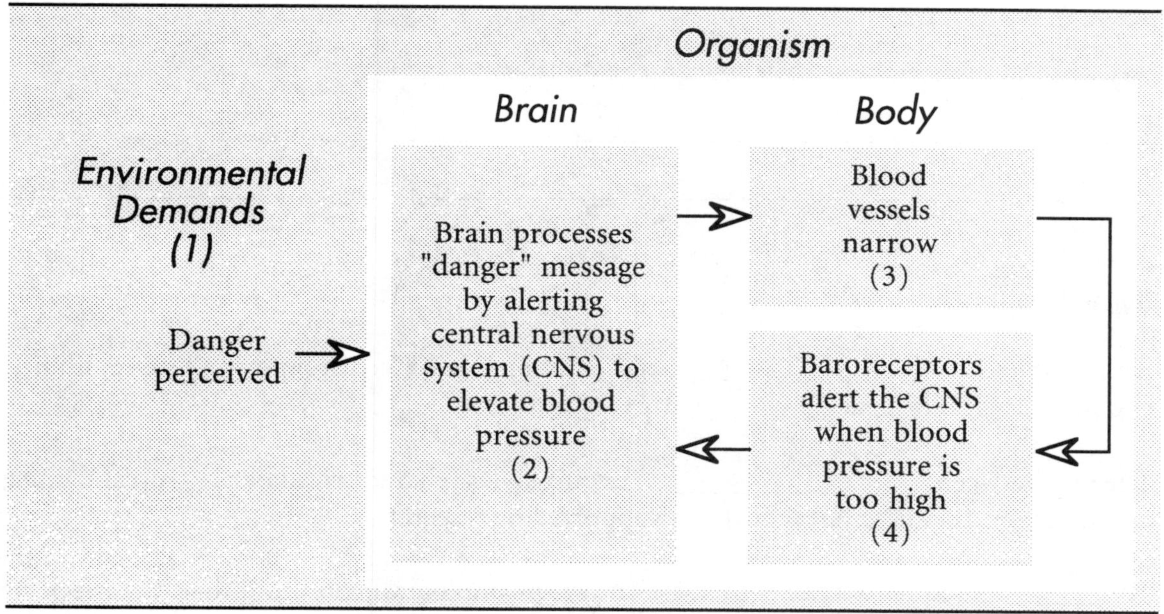

2. If any part of the feedback loop fails to operate properly, the body enters a state of ________________ which might result in a ____________________ disorder.

3. List one of the problems that could occur in each of the numbered "phases" of the blood pressure feedback system that could result in hypertension.

a. (1) The person faces many environmental stressors, such as a divorce or the loss of a job. These stressors could result in an excessive increase in blood pressure.

b. (2) ____________________

____

c. (3) ____________________

____

d. (4) Baroreceptor malfunctioning—failure to alert CNS of rising blood pressure.

2. Sociocultural Factors

The following exercises examine three areas of difficulty that could contribute to problems in the body's feedback system (i.e., disregulation) and result in a psychophysiological disorder.

• Extraordinary Environmental Pressures

1. Give examples of the three kinds of sociocultural factors that could lead to feedback system disregulation: (a) wide-ranging stressors, (b) chronic social circumstances, and (c) transient stressors.

a. war, natural disaster, large scale man-made disaster

b. ____________________

c. ____________________

• Psychological Factors

2. Certain needs, ____________________, and emotions may increase a person's susceptibility to psychophysiological disorders.

4. The link between "____________________" coping styles (characterized by pent-up and unexpressed emotions) and poor physical health is supported by research.

5. Type _____ personality style is the best known psychological condition that can affect the development of ____________________ ____________________ disease.

• Biological Factors

Review the exercise in Chapter ??? on page ???of the Workbook regarding how the autonomic nervous system (including the sympathetic and parasympathetic systems) works. Then study the diagram below. It depicts Hans Selye's model describing the relationship between stress and the autonomic nervous system (ANS). Selye held that people respond to stress with what he called the general adaptation syndrome, composed of three sequential stages.

	Alarm Stage	Resistance Stage		Exhaustion Stage
Threat perceived	Physical arousal stimulated by the sympathetic nervous system	Parasympathetic nervous system attempts to calm or counteract arousal	Continued threat perceived	Resistance fails. Organs become overworked and break down
				Physical illness results

B: "New" Psychophysiological Disorders

Like the textbook, the Workbook will study five areas of "new" psychophysiological disorders separately.

1. Stress and Susceptibility to Illness

1. In the late 1960s, researchers ________________ and ________________ developed the ________________ ________________ Rating Scale, which assigned a numerical value to life stressors that people commonly experience.

2. In the scale the stressor is assigned a certain number of ________________ ________________ ________________ (LCUs) that corresponds to the degree that both positive and negative life events impact on people.

3. Complete the following exercise relating to research methods used to study the relationship between LCUs and the onset of illnesses.

a. In retrospective studies, subjects were asked to remember their life events and illnesses.

b. What was the main problem with retrospective studies?

____

c. To rule this problem out, researchers began to conduct prospective studies—studies that predict ________________ health changes on the basis of ________________ life events.

2. Psychoneuroimmunology

1. Psychoneuroimmunology examines the links between ______________________________.

2. ____________________ (viruses and bacteria) as well as cancer cells "invade" the body and trigger the immune system to go into action.

3. In this exercise, describe the functions of the three groups of lymphocytes in the body's immune system that are described in the textbook.

a. Helper T-cells identify antigens and then ____________________ and trigger the production of other immune cells.

b. What is the function of killer T-cells?

____

c. B-cells produce ____________________, or immunoglobulins, which are protein molecules that recognize and bind to a specific antigen and mark it for ____________________.

4. The Role of Personality Style

1. Complete this table by describing the basis of research by David McClelland et al., on a personality style they believe is linked to immune system dysfunction.

Aspect of research	Description
Personality style	*inhibited power motive style (a strong desire for prestige and influence over others that has been inhibited or suppressed)*
Characteristics of style	
Illness linked to style	*upper respiratory infections*
Psychological link of style to illness	

2. Now complete this exercise on a study of the relationship of academic stress, power motive style, and immune system functioning (ISF) in 64 dental students.

a. *Means of "test" of ISF:* Measuring levels of secretory immunoglobulin (S-IgA), an antibody in human saliva which helps fight off upper respiratory problems.

b. *Method:* Researchers measured students' S-IgA during periods of low and high __________ stress. They also measured their power motive styles to see if those styles affected the relationship between __________ and ISF.

c. *Findings:* __________

____

3. Describe Type C personality style, which has been linked to poorer cancer prognosis.

____

____

5. The Role of Social Support

1. Research findings indicate that the immune system functioning of people who have few social supports and feel __________ is more poor in times of stress compared to people who do not share these characteristics.

2. Describe the findings of a study that supports the link between social support and immune system functioning.

____

____

C: Psychological Treatments for Physical Disorders

1. __________ medicine is the field that combines physical and psychological strategies to treat or __________ medical problems.

2. Complete this table which summarizes the most common psychological treatments for the psychophysiological disorders.

Intervention	Description	Illness treated
Relaxation training	Patients taught to relax muscles, which curbs anxiety by reducing sympathetic nervous system activity	essential hypertension, headaches, insomnia, asthma
Biofeedback training		
Meditation		
Hypnosis		
Cognitive interventions		
Insight therapy		
Combination of approaches		

Practice multiple-choice questions for this chapter begin on page 286.

Chapter 12

Eating Disorders

Chapter Organization

The first two sections of Chapter 12 provide coverage designed to help you understand the characteristics of both anorexia nervosa and bulimia nervosa, as well as descriptions of the similarities and differences between these two eating disorders. Section III, the biggest part of the chapter, focuses on various explanations for anorexia and bulimia that have been proposed by theorists and clinicians representing different perspectives. As with the coverage of other disorders presented in the textbook, it is likely that multiple factors and circumstances interact in the development of eating disorders, and there is probably no one "right" explanation. Finally, Section IV examines treatment approaches used by clinicians on those suffering from these distressing and physically dangerous disorders.

The Workbook also directly covers material in Box 12-2, "Obesity: To Lose or Not to Lose."

Be sure toread through each section before completing the exercises for that section.

Exercises

I: Anorexia Nervosa

Until recently, anorexia nervosa and bulimia nervosa were viewed as very distinct disorders with different characteristics and causes which required different kinds of treatment. Although it is true that the varieties of eating disorders do have important differences, clinicians now realize that the similarities are significant as well.

1. In ____________________ type anorexia, people move from cutting out sweets and fattening foods to cutting out other foods in their diet.

2. Complete the list of facts concerning anorexia nervosa.

a. ____________ to _____ percent of people with anorexia nervosa are female.

b. The average age of onset is between _____ and _____ years.

c. About __________ percent of the female population develops the disorder.

d. The disorder often develops following a particularly ____________________ event in the person's life.

e. Between ___________ and _____ percent of people with anorexia nervosa die, typically from medical problems associated with ______________________.

3. In the following table complete the summary of the central features of anorexia nervosa by providing an example of each feature.

Features	Examples illustrating features
Drive for thinness	*the patient fears she will not be able to control her eating and that she will become obese*
Preoccupied with food	
Cognitive dysfunction	
Personality and mood problems	
Medical problems	

II: Bulimia Nervosa

1. Bulimia nervosa is also known as ____________________ syndrome.

2. Complete this list of symptoms of bulimia nervosa according to DSM-IV.

a. Recurrent episodes of ________________ eating.

b. Recurrent inappropriate ____________________ behavior to prevent weight gain.

c. Body weight and shape strongly influence the person's ____________________.

d. The disturbance is not part of a pattern of anorexia nervosa.

3. List the types of compensatory behaviors engaged in by people with (a) purging-type bulimia nervosa, and (b) non-purging type bulimia nervosa.

a. ____

b. ____

A: Binges

1. Complete this table by giving a description of the typical aspects of a binge that are listed.

Features	Examples illustrating features
Setting of binge	*in secret*
Types of food chosen	
Binge triggers	
Feelings at start of binge	*unbearable tension, irritability, removed, powerless*
Feelings during binge	
Feelings after binge	

B: Compensatory Behaviors

1. Describe the results of the following kinds of compensatory behaviors: (a) self-induced vomiting, (b) laxative abuse.

a. ____

____

b. ____

____

2. Describe the results of the Telch and Agras study of binge eating behaviors of overweight people who followed a low calorie and behavioral weight loss program.

____

____

____

C: Bulimia Nervosa vs. Anorexia Nervosa

1. Bulimia nervosa and anorexia nervosa have key similarities as well as important differences. Each of the following 26 characteristics are found in patients suffering from eating disorders. Put the letter for each into the appropriate box following the list: "Bulimia nervosa" if it is more likely to be found in a sufferer of that disorder, "Anorexia nervosa" if it is more likely to be found in an anorexic person, or "Both" if the characteristic is a similarity of both disorders. (Be sure to study Table 12-2 on textbook page 383 in addition to coverage on pages 382-384.)

a. become easily frustrated and bored
b. consider their social life unsatisfactory
c. dental problems are more likely
d. driven to become thin
e. fearful of becoming obese
f. feel dominated by conflicts about eating
g. feel their family support is low
h. less familial disposition to obesity
i. frequently change friends
j. less concern over being sexually active
k. have disturbed attitudes toward eating
l. have gone through intense dieting
m. have difficulty controlling impulses
n. have trouble identifying internal states
o. history of dramatic mood swings
p. hypokalemia is more likely
q. likely to display more obsessive qualities
r. more likely to reject typical "femininity"
s. more likely to abuse alcohol and drugs
t. more likely to have internal bleeding
u. more likely to have amenorrhea
v. emotionally overcontrolled
w. preoccupied with weight and appearance
x. suffering depression and anxiety
y. recognize their behavior is pathological
z. tend to deny family conflict

Bulimia (11)	Anorexia (7)	Both (8)

Refer to Box 12-2 on textbook pages 380-1 for the following.

Box 12–2

1. About _____ percent of adults in the United States are obese by medical standards.

2. Complete the following table by listing one research finding that supports each of the causal factors involved in obesity that are listed.

Features	Examples illustrating features
Genetic factors	
Biological factors	*researchers have found a possible link between obesity and deficits in serotonin levels*
Environmental factors	

3. Researchers generally agree that people who attempt to lose weight should set _______________ and _______________ goals for themselves.

III: Explanations of Eating Disorders

A: Societal Pressures

1. The textbook describes several pieces of evidence that since the 1950s, Western culture's image of the "perfect" female form has steadily become thinner. Describe the findings related to "Miss America," "Playboy," or "diet articles."

____

____

2. Fashion modeling, acting, dancing, and athletics are professional areas where thinness is highly valued. Think of other professions where this might be true?

____

3. Complete the following exercise relating to eating disorders and socioeconomic level, race, and gender.

a. In past years, white American women in upper socioeconomic levels expressed more concern about thinness and dieting than what two other groups of women?

____

b. However, in recent years the emphasis on thinness and dieting has been embraced by women of all ____________ and ____________ groups, and the prevalence of eating disorders has increased as well.

c. Research also indicates that increased emphasis on male thinness and dieting in recent years has been accompanied by increases in eating disorders among men.

B: Family Environment

1. Research findings suggest that about half of the people with eating disorders come from families who seem to emphasize ____________________, physical appearance, and ____________.

Theorist Salvador Minuchin believes that "enmeshed family patterns" can lead to eating disorders. Study the chart on enmeshed family patterns below and then complete the exercises relating to it which follow.

Characteristics of enmeshed family "set the stage" for disorders

- family members are overinvolved with each other's affairs
- family members are overconcerned about each other's welfare
- little romm for family members' individuality and autonomy
- parents too involved in the lives of their children
- family members are discouraged from speaking about their own ideas and feelings
- families can be clinging and foster dependency
- children not seen as individuals by parents, but rather as appenages who can make the lives and experiences of the parents more complete

Conflict arises during adolescence

During adolescence, these characteristics come into conflict with the natural tendency toward independance among children

As a result, problems can develop

The family responds to the conflict by subtly forcing the child to take on a "sick" role (to develop an eating disorder or some other pattern)

2. The chart lists negative characteristics of the enmeshed family. List any aspects of the pattern that could be viewed as positive.

____

3. When a child in an enmeshed family assumes the "sick" role, the family is able to maintain the illusion of living in harmony. The sick child "needs" her family. What is the role that the other family members take on?

____

C: Ego Deficiencies and Cognitive Disturbances

1. Study the following completed (top) diagram which shows how Bruch proposed children of "effective" parents were raised. Then give the missing information in the diagram below it showing how eating disorders can develop in children of "ineffective" parents.

Effective parents attend to their children's expressions of biological and emotional needs	Children develop a sense of self-control and are able to differentiate between states of internal need	Children become autonomous, confident, and self-reliant individuals

Ineffective parents define their children's ______________ ______________ ______________ for them	Children fail to develop cohesive self-concept, and are unable to differentiate between internal need states— —children rely on other people (parents) to tell them what they need and when they need it	As adolescents, children feel ______________ because they are unable to establish ______________	To overcome these feelings, children try to achieve extreme ______________ over their body size and shape, and ______________

2. Children who are "successful" in the attempt for control described in the chart can be headed toward which eating disorder?

____

3. Children who are not "successful" in the attempt for control described in the chart can spiral toward which eating disorder?

____

D: Mood Disorders

1. In the following table, summarize the research findings that support the notion that people who suffer from mood disorders are predisposed to develop eating disorders.

Research topic	*Findings*
Major depression	
Close relatives	
Neurotransmitter activity	
Medications	*the dysfunctional eating patterns of those with eating disorders are often helped significantly by antidepressant drugs*

E: Biological Factors

1. The ________________ hypothalamus (LH) and the ________________ hypothalamus (VMH), the two parts of the hypothalamus that control eating, have become the focus of biological researchers studying eating disorders.

2. The functions of the LH and VMH have been studied in laboratory animals. Complete the exercises relating to the effects of the following actions upon these two parts of the hypothalamus.

a. What happens when the LH is stimulated?

The animal eats even if it has just been fed.

b. What happens if the LH is destroyed?

____

c. What happens if the VMH is stimulated?

____

d. What happens if the VMH is destroyed?

____

3. Researchers think that the LH and VMH set up a "weight ____________________" in the body that predisposes people to maintain a stable body weight, called the weight set point.

IV: Treatments for Eating Disorders

Current treatments for eating disorders vary depending on the symptoms, behaviors, and circumstances of each client. However, all treatments are comprised of two broad components, or dimensions: 1) correcting the eating pattern that is endangering the client's health, and 2) addressing the psychological and situational factors that led to and maintain the eating disorder.

A: Treatments for Anorexia Nervosa

Most clinicians devise treatment plans for their clients that include individualized therapeutic goals for each client, as well as specific strategies that the clinician might use to address those goals. Additionally, clinicians recognize that all strategies have strengths and limitations that might have an impact on whether any one strategy will "fit" for a particular client. Thus, clinicians sometimes identify "important clinical issues" in regard to the strategies they use to help clients.

Read the following sample case that will be used in an elaborate exercise relating to the treatment of anorexia nervosa that follows it.

Sample Case

Josie S. is a fifteen-year-old female who was referred to the City Hospital's Department of Psychiatry because she is believed to be suffering from anorexia nervosa. Josie is 5 feet 6 inches tall. In the last six months, her weight dropped 59 pounds, from 142 to 83 pounds. She appears emaciated and is physically weak. Josie reached menarche at age 11, but has not had a period in 16 weeks. Her parents state that although they really wanted Josie to lose some weight "because she was too big to wear all the nice clothes" they bought for her, they are now concerned because she is refusing to eat meals at home. Josie reports that she feels fine and "doesn't understand all the fuss because I am still a fat pig."

1. This exercise has been designed to give you a thorough understanding of some of the important concepts and issues involved in the treatment of eating disorders. In the exercise, you will put yourself in the place of the therapist assigned to treat Josie's anorexia nervosa. You are to complete the "treatment plan" on the following pages. It has been designed to look like a "real" treatment plan. The plan's two halves relate the two dimensions most common to treatments of all eating disorders.

City Hospital – Department of Psychiatry

Treatment plan for:	Josie S.—
Therapist:	
Diagnosis:	Anorexia Nervosa

Treatment dimension: Weight restoration and resumption of eating	
• Goal #1	provision of nourishment if Josie's disorder is life-threatening
Treatment strategy	tube and intravenous feedings
Clinical issues regarding strategy	clients are usually uncooperative; set up power struggle between patient and clinician
• Goal #2	reverse Josie's starvation habits
Treatment strategy	use antipsychotic and/or antidepressant medication
Clinical issues regarding strategy	
• Goal #3	restore Josie's weight
Treatment strategy	use operant conditioning approach
Clinical issues regarding strategy	approach has limited effectiveness; Josie might not maintain initial weight gain unless other interventions are employed
Goal	restore Josie's weight
Treatment strategy	utilize supportive nursing care for Josie
Clinical issues regarding strategy	

Treatment dimension: Address Josie's psychological problems	
• Goal #1	build autonomy and self-awareness
Treatment strategy	help Josie become aware of difficulty expressing autonomy and exercising control in appropriate ways; help Josie recognize and trust own feelings
Clinical issues regarding strategy	important not to tell client what she is experiencing internally because if she is very conforming, she will agree even if interpretation is not accurate
• Goal #2	correct Josie's distorted cognitions
Treatment strategy	
Clinical issues regarding strategy	
• Goal #3	change dysfunctional interactions within Josie's family
Treatment strategy #1	support each family member's personal space
Treatment strategy #2	
Clinical issues regarding strategy	

: Treatments for Bulimia Nervosa

reatment programs for bulimia nervosa emphasize education as well as therapy. Specific treatment strategies re addressed in the following exercise.

1. Complete this table summarizing treatment strategies for bulimia nervosa. Find two examples of strategies for each type of treatment approach, and then summarize the effectiveness of each approach.

Treatment approach	Examples	Effectiveness
Individual insight therapy		*psychodynamic, cognitive, and combined approaches effective*
Group therapy		
Behavioral therapy		*decrease in eating anxiety; decreased bingeing and purging*

Examples:

a. Group meals in which clients plan and eat a meal together, while discussing thoughts and feelings

b. free association and interpretation of clients underlying conflicts about lack of self-trust and need for control

c. exposure and response prevention

d. teaching that having an eating disorder is not "strange" or shameful

e. evaluation and alteration of maladaptive beliefs toward food, eating, and weight (e.g., "I must lose weight in order to be happy")

f. keeping diaries of eating behavior, body sensations, thoughts, and feelings

2. Complete the following statements regarding the aftermath of bulimia nervosa.

a. As with anorexia, relapses are usually precipitated by a new ________________ in the person's life.

b. Of clients treated for bulimia, ______ percent almost immediately stop their binge-purge behaviors and stabilize their eating habits, 40 percent show a moderate response to treatment, and the remaining ______ percent show no improvement in bulimic behaviors.

c. One study showed that almost one-third of recovered bulimic clients relapsed within ____________ years of treatment, usually within ____________ months after treatment ended.

d. Follow-up studies indicate that after treatment, most clients are less ________________ than when they were diagnosed with bulimia, and about one-____________ show improvements in work, home, and social interactions.

Practice multiple-choice questions for this chapter begin on page 287.

Chapter 13

Substance-Related Disorders

Chapter Organization

This chapter covers a great many topics relating to drugs and how their misuse can lead to changes in human behavior, emotions, and thought. Sections I through IV cover major categories of these substances: depressants (including alcohol), stimulants, and hallucinogens and cannabis. Section V discusses what happens when substances are mixed. Section VI looks at the major theoretical explanations for substance-related disorders. Finally, Section VII explores the most prominent treatments for the disorders, many of which arise from various theoretical perspectives.

Be sure to read through each section before completing the exercises for that section.

Exercises

Match numbers 1–6 below with the appropriate letter from the list a–f.

1. _____ Intoxication

2. _____ Hallucinosis

3. _____ Substance abuse

4. _____ Substance dependence

5. _____ Tolerance

6. _____ Withdrawal

a. Condition in which a person needs increasing doses of a substance in order to keep obtaining the desired effect.

b. A state of perceptual distortions and hallucinations.

c. Condition in which people experience unpleasant symptoms when they suddenly stop taking or reduce their dosage of a drug.

d. Addiction—physical dependence on a drug.

e. A temporary syndrome in which the person exhibits impaired judgment, mood changes, irritability, slurred speech, and loss of coordination.

f. An excessive and chronic reliance on drugs, in which the drugs occupy a central place in a person's life.

I: Depressants

A: Alcohol

1. More than five percent of all adults are heavy drinkers, which means that they consume at least __________ drinks on at least __________ occasions during the past month.

2. The ratio of male heavy drinkers to female heavy drinkers is more than __________ to one.

Ethyl alcohol consumption affects the physiological, cognitive, and emotional states of people who consume progressively more amounts of it. Study this diagram which illustrates these progressive effects.

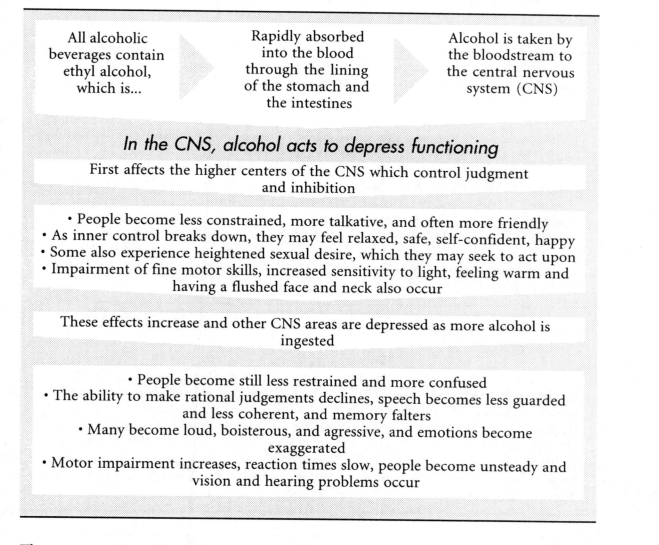

All alcoholic beverages contain ethyl alcohol, which is...

Rapidly absorbed into the blood through the lining of the stomach and the intestines

Alcohol is taken by the bloodstream to the central nervous system (CNS)

In the CNS, alcohol acts to depress functioning

First affects the higher centers of the CNS which control judgment and inhibition

- People become less constrained, more talkative, and often more friendly
- As inner control breaks down, they may feel relaxed, safe, self-confident, happy
- Some also experience heightened sexual desire, which they may seek to act upon
- Impairment of fine motor skills, increased sensitivity to light, feeling warm and having a flushed face and neck also occur

These effects increase and other CNS areas are depressed as more alcohol is ingested

- People become still less restrained and more confused
- The ability to make rational judgements declines, speech becomes less guarded and less coherent, and memory falters
- Many become loud, boisterous, and agressive, and emotions become exaggerated
- Motor impairment increases, reaction times slow, people become unsteady and vision and hearing problems occur

The concentration of ethyl alcohol in the __________________ determine its effect on body chemistry.

Women have significantly ______________________ of the stomach enzyme called alcohol ______________________, the enzyme that breaks down alcohol before it enters the blood.

• Alcohol Abuse and Dependence

5. Each of the following sample cases illustrate one of three broad patterns of alcohol abuse described in the textbook. Make up a name for each pattern that will help you remember it (if your instructor has given names, use those). Then underline the parts of each description that are typical for that pattern.

Sample Cases

Name of pattern:

Almost every day of Alan's life in the last six years has been built around alcohol. This is his fourth year in college, but he hasn't progressed much since he rarely makes it through the entire term of a class. Alan usually blames "rotten" professors. Most days Alan gets up at lunch time (he's learned not to attempt morning classes), and meets friends at a fast food restaurant. Invariably he orders just a jumbo soft drink, which he proceeds to spike with alcohol. If he hasn't drunken too much, and if he isn't too hung-over, he might then go to a class or two. Often however, Alan goes straight from "lunch" to a bar, where he nibbles on the buffalo wings they put out at happy hour and drinks copious amounts of beer until he stumbles home and passes out.

Name of pattern:

There are over twenty times as many people attending Rebecca's college as there are living in her home town. She is the first member of her family to go to college, and she wants to make every one proud of her. Rebecca gets excellent grades because she works very hard, never missing a class and spending a good part of the evenings in the library. After a long day of studying though, she usually goes to her room and drinks alone for at least a couple of hours. Rebecca gets up early on Saturdays to go to the library. However, her Saturday afternoons and Sundays are spent just like her weekday evenings—drinking alone in her room.

Name of pattern:

Ric is probably the most intelligent and hardest-working undergraduate in his college's math department. He loves his classes and he pushes himself tremendously to maintain a near-perfect academic record. Whenever a big test is approaching, he vanishes for several days so he can devote himself entirely to studying. The results are always the same—an A+. Once the test is over, Ric makes up for lost time by partying every bit as hard as he studies. If a test falls on a Thursday, he probably won't draw a sober breath from that night until Monday morning. Stories of these episodes and of his drunken exploits during school vacations have become legendary among his friends. Ric is glad for this, since he himself often remembers little of what he does while drunk.

• Personal and Social Impact of Alcoholism

6. List some of the social costs of alcoholism.

____

____

Take a few moments to consider some of the damaging physical effects of chronic and excessive alcohol consumption. Make sure you understand how alcohol consumption can lead to each of the following physical problems:

- *Fatty liver and cirrhosis of the liver*
- *Heart failure, irregularities of heart functioning, blood clots*
- *Immune system impairment, susceptibility to certain diseases*
- *Malnutrition, Wernicke's encephalopathy, Korsakoff's syndrome (see below)*

7. Chronic alcohol use can result in malnutrition, since alcohol contains no nutritional value, but lowers a person's desire for food. Furthermore, alcohol-related vitamin and mineral deficiencies can result in mental disorders, such as Wernicke's encephalopathy and Korsakoff's syndrome. Complete this diagram relating to these disorders.

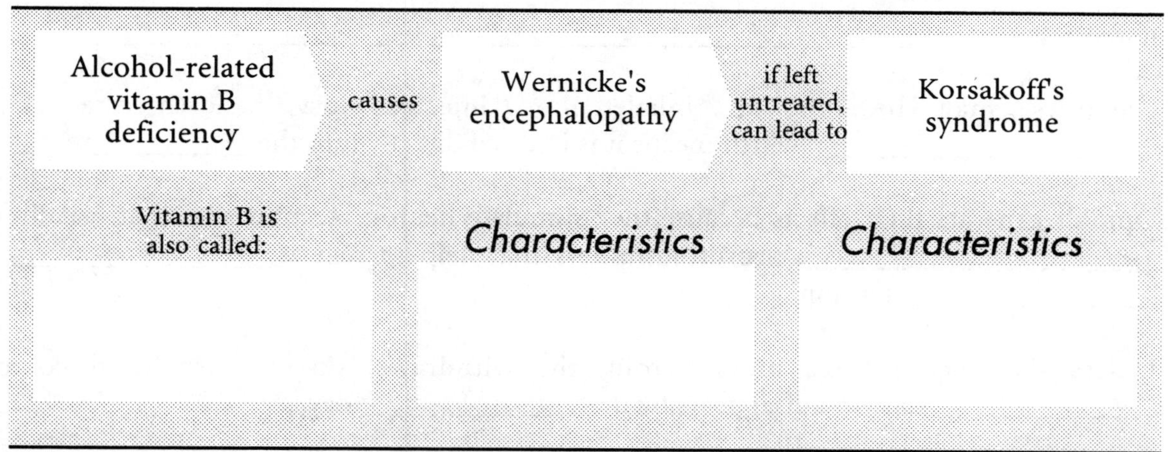

3: Sedative-Hypnotic Drugs

. Sedative-hypnotic drugs produce a sedative or ________________ effect, and at high doses are ________________ inducers.

. Like benzodiazepines, low doses of barbiturates reduce anxiety by ________________ activity of the neurotransmitter ________________.

3. Complete these questions relating to the results of higher doses of barbiturates on the reticular formation.

a. The reticular formation is the body's ____________ center and is responsible for keeping people awake and alert.

b. High doses of barbiturates depress ____________ reflexes and muscles.

c. Overdoses can result in ____________ failure and ____________ blood pressure, leading to a coma and even death.

C: Opioids

Be sure to read the material about the many uses and misuses of opioids from the use of opium in ancient times through the development of synthetic opioids in our day.

1. Describe the central characteristics of the following opioid drugs:

opium: ____________

heroin: ____________

methadone: ____________

narcotics: ____________

2. Narcotics may be smoked, inhaled, or injected just beneath the skin, or "____________," which means it is injected directly into the ____________.

3. Opioids generate their effects because they stimulate neuron receptor sites that usually receive ____________, neurotransmitters that help to relieve ____________ and ____________ tension.

4. Unless the person takes more heroin, the withdrawal distress usually peaks by the ____________ day, and disappears by the ____________ day.

II: Stimulants

Cocaine and amphetamine use stimulates activity of the central nervous system, resulting in effects such as increased blood pressure and heart rate, and intensified behavioral activity, thought processes, and alertness.

A: Cocaine

Make sure you read about the dramatic surge in the number of people in the U.S. who have tried cocaine over the course of the last few decades. Today, almost 3% of the U.S. population have been dependent on cocaine at some point in their lives.

1. Describe the high experienced by those who use cocaine.

____

2. Cocaine produces its effects because it overstimulates the central nervous system by releasing excessive amounts of which three neurotransmitters?

____

3. If a person with a physical dependence on cocaine decides to stop what are the withdrawal symptoms that may result from abstinence?

____

____

4. New forms of cocaine have produced an increase in abuse and dependence on the drug. Complete the statements regarding these recent forms.

a. In the technique called _______________, the pure cocaine basic alkaloid is chemically separated from processed cocaine, vaporized by heat from a flame, and inhaled with a pipe.

b. Crack is a cheaper form of cocaine with the ability to induce more persistent and intense drug _______________ than most other drugs.

c. About 1 percent of high school seniors say they have used crack in the past year.

Take some time to consider the many ways in which cocaine can be an extremely dangerous drug to your health. Make sure you understand how cocaine use can lead to each of the following physical problems:

- *Cocaine overdose (effects on the brain and body)*
- *Irregular heart functioning*
- *Fetal cocaine syndrome*

B: Amphetamines

1. Amphetamines are taken in the form of _______________, can be injected, or are ingested in such forms as "ice" and "_______________", counterparts of free-basing cocaine and crack, respectively.

2. Complete the list of physiological and psychological similarities between amphetamines and cocaine.

a. They both increase energy and alertness and reduce appetite in low doses.

b. Both cause an emotional _______________ as they leave the body.

c. Both stimulate the CNS by increasing the release of the neurotransmitters _______________, norepinephrine, and _______________.

Read the following sample case relating to amphetamine abuse.

Sample Case

Margaret is a full-time college student, holds a part-time job, and is also on the cross-country team. While competing in a track meet one week ago, Margaret started her race feeling good and full of energy. At the one-mile mark, however, she felt a wrenching pain in her hamstring muscle. She pushed herself to run, but had to drop out of the race as she approached the two mile mark. Margaret felt exhausted, and the pain in her leg was excruciating. After being examined by a physician, Margaret learned that in addition to tearing several ligaments, she had tested positive for amphetamines. She confessed to her coach that she had been using increasing amounts of Dexedrine in order to maintain the energy she needed to keep up with the demands of her life.

3. Using the concepts of tolerance and dependence, how would you explain Margaret's increased amphetamine use and subsequent injuries?

____

____

____

____

C: Caffeine

1. List the most common forms in which caffeine is consumed.

____

2. Caffeine affects the CNS by stimulating the release of which three neurotransmitters?

____

3. The possible physiological effects of caffeine include disruption of the performance of complex motor tasks and interference with both duration and quality of sleep. Listed below are several physiological processes. Put an "I" before those that caffeine increases, and a "D" before those it decreases.

____ Arousal

____ General motor activities

____ Heart rate

____ Respiration

____ Secretion of gastric acid by stomach

____ Vigilance

III: Hallucinogens

1. Psychedelics are chemical substances that affect sensory experiences, producing sensations that are sometimes called ________________.

2. LSD was derived by the Swiss chemist Albert Hoffman in 1938 from a group of naturally occurring drugs called ________________ ________________.

3. If a person using LSD has sensations that "cross," for example, he or she can "see" musical vibrations in the air, that person is experiencing ________________.

4. The immediate effects of LSD wear off in about ____________ hours.

Study this diagram that shows how LSD produces the characteristics of a "trip."

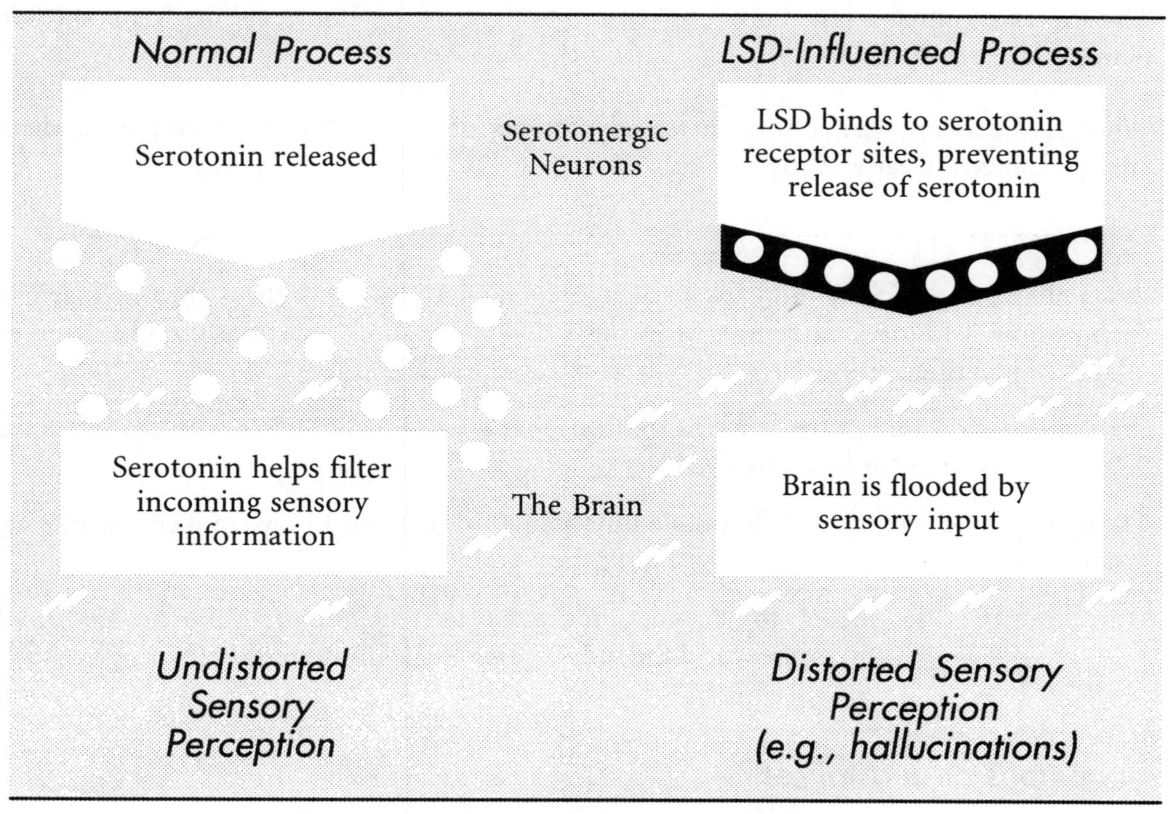

5. Even though LSD use does not result in significant tolerance or withdrawal, it poses serious risks—even to first-time users. Complete the following questions relating to the three primary risks related to LSD.

a. LSD is so remarkably ________________ that a dose of any size is likely to elicit powerful perceptual, emotional, and behavioral reactions—which are sometimes extremely unpleasant (i.e., a "bad trip").

b. List the three types of hallucinogen-induced disorders.

____

____

c. A hallucinogen ____________ ____________ disorder, or the flashback—sensory and emotional changes that recur long after the LSD has left body—is experienced b about a quarter of LSD users.

IV: Cannabis

1. Cannabis is harvested from the leaves and flowers of the ____________ plant, and its mair active ingredient is tetrahydrocannabinol, or ____________.

2. The effects of cannabis last about ________ to ________ hours, although mood changes car persist.

3. What is the main reason why increased patterns of marijuana abuse and dependence hav emerged since the early 1970s?

____

4. Researchers have become more aware of the potential negative effects of chronic marijuana use such as how it induces panic attacks in some. Complete these questions summarizing evidenc related to identified risks.

a. Marijuana's increased potency seems to mean that it can now interfere with performance of th complex sensorimotor tasks involved in ____________.

b. Marijuana's interference with cognitive functioning means that heavy smokers operate at a grea disadvantage at ____________ and in the ____________.

c. Other health risks linked to chronic marijuana use include irregularities in the humar ____________ system and the functioning of the immune system.

V: Combinations of Substances

All three subsections of Section IV are treated in the following exercises.

1. Sometimes when two or more drugs that have similar effects on the body (such as alcohol an antianxiety drugs) are ingested simultaneously, users will develop ____________ for them.

2. Often, drugs are mixed in ignorance of the dangerous consequences. However, increasingly thi kind of multiple drug use, or ____________ use seems to be done knowingly becaus the user enjoys the synergistic effects.

VI: Explanations of Substance-Related Disorders

A: The Sociocultural View

The sociocultural theory of drug abuse and dependence proposes that the people most likely to develop problems are those whose societies create an atmosphere of stress and those whose families value, or at lease tolerate, drug taking.

1. Complete the following statements regarding research that has tended to support the sociocultural theory regarding drug abuse and societal stress.

a. Higher rates of ____________________ have been found in regions of the U.S. where ________________ is more common or where more people are laid off.

b. People in lower ______________________ classes have higher drinking and substance abuse rates than other classes.

c. Very high rates of heroin addiction were documented among American soldiers in ________________.

d. Lower rates of alcohol abuse were found among ethnic and religious groups in which the ____________________ of drinking are clearly defined.

B: The Psychodynamic View

1. Psychodynamic theorists suggest that people who abuse substances were not __________________ enough during childhood, and that they subsequently try to meet their need for comfort and support by relying on others, or on drugs.

2. The psychodynamic hypothesis that some people develop a "substance abuse personality" is supported by research findings indicating that, compared to others, people who abuse substances are more likely to have what kinds of personality characteristics?

____

3. What is the major problem with studies that have purported to identify personality traits of people with or prone to substance abuse problems?

____

C: The Behavioral View

There are three primary behavioral theories that attempt to explain substance-related disorders: the reinforcement (operant conditioning) theory, the opponent-process theory, and the classical conditioning theory. Read the following sample case. The exercise after the case will ask you to apply it to each of these three theories.

Sample Case

Glenn started using alcohol at age fifteen. Always rather shy and socially awkward, he found that drinking helped him "loosen up" enough to interact with his peers, who he had avoided in the past. By age eighteen, Glenn was known as a real "partyer." He drank nearly every day, and often experienced blackouts. Glenn managed to get into college, but dropped out at the end of his first semester because his grades were so poor. He got a job at a convenience store, and was fired for coming to work intoxicated. Depressed and broke, Glenn asked an acquaintance if he could "crash" at his place until he found another job. It turned out that the acquaintance sold heroin. Glenn continued his heavy drinking, and within three months of moving in, he was also hooked on heroin. He tried to quit, but whenever his roommate brought out his drug paraphernalia, Glenn would succumb to an overpowering urge to shoot up. The fact that he would become depressed, anxious, and physically ill after going without heroin for even a day or two, made it even more difficult to quit.

1. How would each of the following behavioral theories explain Glenn's increasing heroin and alcohol use?

a. *Reinforcement (operant conditioning) theory:* In a sense, Glenn is medicating himself against his general uneasiness and depression with the drugs. By ingesting the drugs he is able to achieve a (temporary) sense of well-being.

b. *Opponent-process theory:* ______________________________

____

____

c. *Classical conditioning theory:* ______________________________

____

____

D: The Genetic and Biological View

1. There are several lines of research that have implicated genetic factors in the development of substance abuse and dependence. Complete this table by summarizing the findings from each area of research.

Research area	*Study or studies*	*Summary of findings*
Twin studies	Goldstein, 1994; Kaij, 1960	*in 54% of cases where one identical twin abused alcohol, so did the other; compared to a 28% concordance rate among fraternal twins*
Adoption studies	Goldstein, 1994; Goodwin et al., 1973	
Gene mapping	Blum & Noble, 1993; Blum et al., 1991	

Recent advances in technology have enabled researchers to explore the biological underpinnings of drug dependence. The diagram below relates to a line of study that has pinpointed some of the biological processes that produce drug tolerance and withdrawal symptoms.

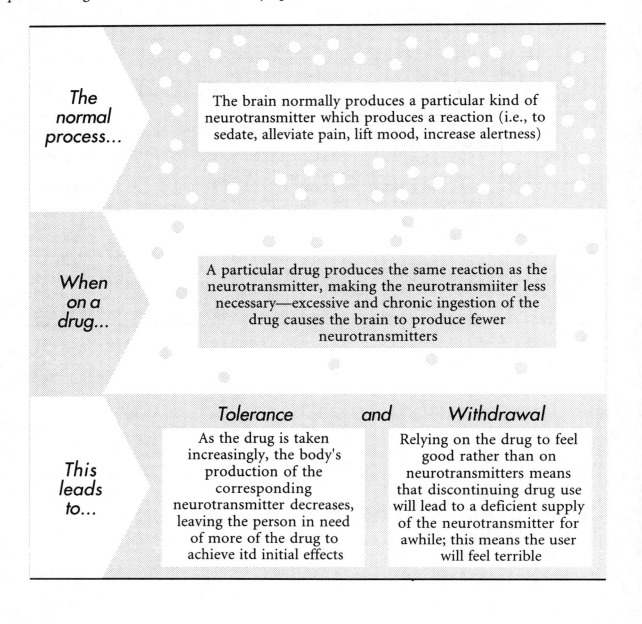

The normal process...	The brain normally produces a particular kind of neurotransmitter which produces a reaction (i.e., to sedate, alleviate pain, lift mood, increase alertness)	
When on a drug...	A particular drug produces the same reaction as the neurotransmitter, making the neurotransmiiter less necessary—excessive and chronic ingestion of the drug causes the brain to produce fewer neurotransmitters	
This leads to...	*Tolerance* As the drug is taken increasingly, the body's production of the corresponding neurotransmitter decreases, leaving the person in need of more of the drug to achieve itd initial effects	*and* *Withdrawal* Relying on the drug to feel good rather than on neurotransmitters means that discontinuing drug use will lead to a deficient supply of the neurotransmitter for awhile; this means the user will feel terrible

2. The previous diagram lists neither specific drugs nor specific neurotransmitters. Complete the table below by providing the names of the neurotransmitters that become deficient when a person abuses the identified substance.

Drug(s)	Neurotransmitter(s)
alcohol & benzodiazephines	
opioids	
cocaine or amphetamines	
marijuana	*unknown natural equivalent of THC*

3. An important question for researcher and clinicians is, "why are drugs so rewarding?" Complete the statements below that relate to one answer from the biological perspective.

a. Drugs seem to activate a __________ center or "pathway" in the brain the extends from the ventral tegmental area to the nucleus accumbens to the __________ __________.

b. It appears that when activity of the neurotransmitter __________ is stimulated in this pathway, pleasure is experienced.

VII: Treatments for Substance-Related Disorders

1. One problem facing researchers trying to determine if treatment is effective for substance abuse disorders is that it is difficult to determine if treatment is the crucial component in any one person's success, relapse, or failure. List two other difficulties facing these researchers.

____

____

2. Substance abuse treatment interventions are usually combined either with each other or with other formats, such as __________________ therapy or __________________ therapy.

A: Psychodynamic Therapies

1. Psychodynamic therapists help clients with substance-related disorders to __________ and resolve underlying conflicts and then move toward __________ their styles of living.

2. Psychodynamic therapies do not appear to be very effective on their own in treating substance-related disorders, but have been combined successfully with ____________________ and ____________________ treatments.

B: Behavioral and Cognitive-Behavioral Therapies

Match the numbers 1–6 below with the appropriate option from the list a–f below the numbers. Numbers 1–6 are widely used behavioral treatments for substance-related disorders. Options a–f represent examples of these treatments.

1. ____ Aversion conditioning

2. ____ Covert sensitization

3. ____ Teaching alternatives

4. ____ Contingency training

5. ____ Behavioral self-control training (BSCT)

6. ____ Relapse-prevention training

a. A client is taught to identify high risk situations and to identify and practices strategies that will help him interrupt the pattern of abuse before it gets out of hand.

b. A man who is alcohol dependent is given a nausea-producing chemical injection at the same time he drinks alcohol.

c. For six weeks running, a woman with a history of cocaine abuse has been submitting "clean" urine specimens in return for incentives.

d. Whenever she takes a drink, a woman who is alcohol dependent imagines gruesome scenes of the carnage after a terrorist bombing.

e. A man with a drinking problem signs up for a night school class that meets on his normal "night on the town;" he practices telling his "drinking buddies" that he cannot join them.

f. A client chronicles his drinking habits and then applies strategies to control her alcohol intake in the future.

C: Biological Treatments

1. Briefly describe the two primary methods or strategies of detoxification.

a. ____

b. ____

2. The relapse rates of people who fail to pursue ____________________ after withdrawal tend to be high.

3. Antagonist drugs are used to avoid a ____________________ of drug abuse and dependence after a successful withdrawal from the drug.

4. Complete the following statements regarding various antagonist drugs.

a. Disulfiram, or ____________________, is given to people being treated for alcohol problems, and produces a terrible physical reaction when taken with alcohol.

b. While narcotic antagonists are sometimes used for people who are dependent on ________________, they are more often considered too dangerous for this treatment.

c. The narcotic antagonist ____________________ is thought to hold great promise in the treatment of alcoholism.

d. Newly developed antibodies are being studied as a possible cocaine antagonist.

D: Sociocultural Therapies

1. Alcoholics Anonymous (AA) was founded in 1935 and today has over two million members worldwide. Describe two or three of the features and emphases of AA.

____

____

2. What is the purpose of the residential treatment program?

____

____

3. A growing number of therapist believe that ____________________ to each patient's unique life challenges can be the best defense against the environmental and social stresses that can lead to abuse problems.

4. What are two of the numerous problems, not adequately considered in the past , that face women who are substance abusers?

____

____

E: Prevention

1. Prevention programs can differ greatly in their emphases and approaches. In particular, they may target different levels of a society's structure. Complete this exercise by filling in the missing strategies that might be employed in a program attempting to prevent the abuse of alcohol.

a. *Individual:* Educate people about the long-term health hazards of excessive and chronic alcohol use.

b. *Family:* ______________________________

____

c. *Peer group:* ______________________________

____

d. *School:* Encourage schools to require counseling for students involved in rule infractions relating to alcohol and drug abuse

e. *Community:* ______________________________

____

Practice multiple-choice questions for this chapter begin on page 289.

Chapter 14

Sexual Disorders and Gender Identity Disorder

Chapter Organization

Each of the two main sections of this large chapter deal with one of two kinds of sexual disorders. The subsections of Section I each contain a great deal of important information about sexual dysfunctions. Most of the subsections of Section II deal with the paraphilias. The final section covers gender identity disorder, which is sexually-related, but not well understood.

The Workbook also directly covers material in Box Box 14-4, "Homosexuality and Society."

Be sure to read through each section before completing the exercises for that section.

Exercises

I: Sexual Dysfunctions

1. What is the definition for sexual dysfunction given in your textbook?

____

____

2. DSM-IV categorizes sexual dysfunctions according to the phase of the sexual response cycle that is most affected by the specific dysfunction. The following tables organize sexual dysfunctions by those phases. Provide the missing information on the characteristics of each phase and on the symptoms of dysfunctions. Ignore the "Dysfunction prevalence" columns for now.

Phase: Desire	
Phase characteristics	

Dysfunction name	Dysfunction symptoms	Dysfunction prevalence
Hypoactive sexual desire		m f
Sexual aversion	*revulsion, disgust, and fear regarding sex*	m *unknown* f *unknown*

Phase: Arousal	
Phase characteristics	*increased heart rate, muscle tension, blood pressure and respiration; pelvic vasocongestion leads to male erections and female vaginal lubrication and genital swelling*

Dysfunction name	Dysfunction symptoms	Dysfunction prevalence
Male erectile disorder	*(formerly called frigidity) failure of lubrication and swelling*	m
Female arousal disorder		f

Phase: Orgasm	
Phase characteristics	

Dysfunction name	*Dysfunction symptoms*	*Dysfunction prevalence*
Premature ejaculation		m
Male orgasmic disorder	*inability to reach orgasm despite adequate stimulation*	m
Inhibited female orgasmic disorder		f *10–30%*

Phase: Resolution	
Phase characteristics	

A: Disorders of the Desire Phase

1. In defining hypoactive sexual desire, DSM-IV refers to a "deficient" level of sexual desire without specifying what a "deficient" level is. The statements given in boxes in this exercise illustrate some of the problems that can arise from this lack of specificity. Below each boxed statement, formulate a counter-statement that shows its limitations. The first is already completed.

The average frequency of sex for married couples is two to three times per week, so anything less is "deficient."

a. This is an average of the general population. Averages within large groups, such as age levels or races, may be much higher or lower than 2–3 times per week.

Frequency of intercourse is a good estimator of sexual desire, because people who do not have sex frequently probably do not desire it, and people who do have sex frequently probably do desire it.

b. ______________________________

____

When partner A complains that partner B does not want to have sex enough, it is a good indication that partner A has hypoactive sexual desire.

c. ______________________________

____

2. Clinicians usually do not diagnose hypoactive sexual desire unless the client desires sex less than once every __________ __________.

3. Elevated __________ levels can produce diminished sex drive in men, and high levels of __________ can interfere with the sex drives of both men and women.

4. Complete the following table by giving two examples of each psychological factor that could interfere with sex drive or cause sexual aversion.

Psychological factors	*Examples*
Situational factors	*increased life stress of having a baby when both parents are employed*
Personal beliefs	*being raised in an antisexual culture or religion*
Personality characteristics	
Relationship issues	*feeling pwerless and very dominated by the other in a relationship*
Sexual trauma	

B. Disorders of the Excitement Phase

Traditionally the causes of erectile failure were assumed to be either psychological or organic. Currently, clinicians believe that this problem is a result of interacting biological and psychological factors.

1. ________________ abnormalities—which are abnormalities in the structure of the penis and blood flow through the penis—are more commonly the cause of erectile failure than are hormonal problems.

2. List four factors that could lead to erectile failure related to abnormality in the structure of and blood flow through the penis.

____

____

Examine this diagram which depicts a primary psychological mechanism that can result in erectile failure: performance anxiety and the spectator role.

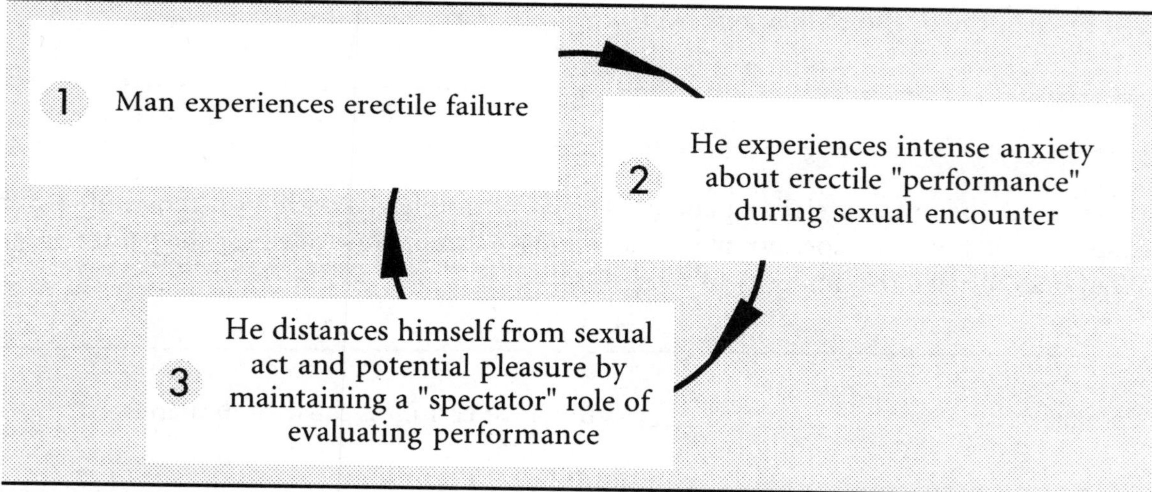
1 Man experiences erectile failure
2 He experiences intense anxiety about erectile "performance" during sexual encounter
3 He distances himself from sexual act and potential pleasure by maintaining a "spectator" role of evaluating performance

According to the performance anxiety theory of erectile failure, whatever the initial reason for the erectile failure, the resulting anxious, self-evaluative spectator role becomes the reason for the ongoing problem.

3. Barlow further suggests that performance demands cause fear and anxiety in dysfunctional men, and lead nondysfunctional men to focus on the sexually stimulating aspects of a sexual encounter, which acts to ________________ arousal.

C. Disorders of the Orgasm Phase

. Complete the statements regarding the men most prone to premature ejaculation.

. Young men who are ________________ ________________.

b. Men who have sex infrequently; the sensory ________________ in the penis is influenced by the frequency and the ________________ of sexual activity.

2. Theorists have formulated several hypotheses about why some men experience premature ejaculation. Complete the following list of these hypotheses.

a. Men learned as adolescents that they needed to ejaculate quickly when masturbating in order to minimize the risk of being discovered by their parents.

b. Men who ejaculate prematurely do not accurately perceive their own ________________ ________________, and thus cannot control their ejaculations.

3. Physiological conditions that can affect arousal and orgasm among women include diabetes, neurological diseases, ________________ changes in skin sensitivity, and the structure of the ________________ and vaginal walls.

D. Sexual Pain Disorder

1. List three of the possible situations from which vaginismus can result.

____

____

2. When a sex therapist receives a patient who has been referred with a diagnosis of "psychogenic dyspareunia," it usually does not mean that there isn't an organic cause for the painful intercourse. What does it mean in a majority of instances?

____

3. Damage caused by ________________ is the most common cause of dyspareunia.

4. Psychogenic dyspareunia usually reflects a simple lack of ________________.

Be sure to read Box 14-3, "Sex Role Myths," on textbook pages 460500–1. The myths about sexuality that are discussed pervade our culture in the form of media messages, themes in books and movies, and generational legacies of unchallenged stereotypes of men and women. Try to pick out the myths that you may have heard—or even that you may have believed in the past to the detriment of an intimate relationship. You might also want to consider how society can move beyond these stereotypes and their destructive power on our culture.

E: Treatments of Sexual Dysfunctions

In 1970, Masters and Johnson published the book "Human Sexual Inadequacy." It described a revolutionary approach to the treatment of sexual dysfunction which came to be called "sex therapy." While the approach has been modified, the original components remain intact. In some ways you can think of this approach as a generic program, and not necessarily focused on any one dysfunction.

1. This exercise calls for a summary of each component of Masters and Johnson's sex therapy. For each component, be sure to include a brief statement regarding the specific issues being addressed and the therapist tasks and/or techniques. The first (and lengthiest) is done for you.

Component 1
Assessment and Conceptualization of the Problem

a. Understanding past and current factors that might have caused or maintain the patient's problem is the emphasis. Along with a thorough medical examination, the therapist gathers information on the patient's life history, as well as current emotions, attitudes, and behaviors. Sex therapists expect to treat both partners since they stress that a sexual dysfunction is the responsibility of both. The technique of "dual sex co-therapy" is not currently in wide practice.

Component 2
Natural Responsibility

b. ____

____

____

____

Component 3
Education about Sexuality

c. ____

____

____

____

Component 4
Attitude Change

d. ____

Component 5
Elimination of Performance Anxiety and the Spectator Role

e. ____

Component 6
Increase Communication and the Effectiveness of Sexual Techniques

f. ____

Component 7
Change Destructive Lifestyles and Marital Interactions

g. ____

The rest of this subsection relates to treatments for the major sexual dysfunctions covered in this chapter. Each dysfunction is covered separately.

As you read the following sample case, put yourself in the place of a therapist treating the couple for hypoactive sexual desire.

Sample Case

Chad and his partner Don have contacted you, a sex therapist, for counseling related to Chad's hypoactive sexual desire. Chad and Don have been together for five years, and have enjoyed a healthy, mutually-satisfying relationship until about six months ago when Chad became extremely reluctant to engage in sexual activity with Don. In fact, Chad tells you that he "can't stand to be touched in any way, and having sex is out of the question." When you question Chad about his life experiences, you discover that he had been involved in a highly abusive relationship just prior to meeting Don. Chad's ex-partner, Marc, was an alcoholic who could be physically and sexually abusive when intoxicated. Chad described the sexual aspect of that relationship as having been "highly coercive and manipulative."

You ask Don when he thinks the problem with Chad's low sex drive started, and he says it was about the time he lost his job. After pausing to remember, Don states, "I was really depressed and stressed out, and I know I took some of that out on Chad. I started drinking more than I usually do, and several times I came home pretty drunk. Now that I think of it, some of those times I wanted to have sex with Chad and he really freaked out. I guess I haven't been very sensitive to Chad's feelings. What should we do, Doctor?"

2. For each phase of Friedman and LoPiccolo's (1988) sequential model for treating hypoactive sexual desire and sexual aversion, give specific examples and strategies that are applicable to Chad and Don's treatment.

Phase	Examples of strategy
Affectual awareness	
Insight	If Chad's feelings of anxiety, fear, and vulnerability concerning sex were triggered by a belief that Don was "turning into another Marco," it is important that he sees this as the probable cause of his aversion
Cognitive and enotional change	
Behavioral interventions	

II: Paraphilias

On the following pages, the Workbook covers eight of the nine subsections of Section II together. The final subsection, "SocietalCultural Norms and Sexual Labels," is covered together with Box 14-4.

1. Complete the following chart that summarizes the descriptions, causes, and treatments for the paraphilias.

Fetishism	
Description	recurrent, intense sexual urges that involve the use of nonliving objects (e.g., women's undergarments, shoes) which may be smelled or touched
Causes	psychodynamic: these are defense mechanisms against anxiety of normal sexual contact; behavioral: they are acquired through classical conditioning
Treatment	behavioral: aversion therapy, covert sensitization, and masturbatory satiation which is designed to produce boredom in clients who are told to masturbate for long durations to fetishistic fantasies

Transvestic fetishism (transvestism, cross-dressing)	
Description	*those with disorder (almost exclusively heterosexual males) have a recurrent need to dress in clothes of the opposite sex in order to become sexually aroused*
Causes	*behavioral: as children, those with the disorder were operantly conditioned, or reinforced, for cross-dressing*
Treatment	*no specific treatments described in textbook*

Exhibitionism	
Description	
Causes	
Treatment	

Voyeurism	
Description	*recurrent and intense sexual urges to spy on people as they undress or have sex; usually begins before age 15 and is chronic*
Causes	
Treatment	*no specific strategies described in textbook; however, typical strategies used for treatment of paraphilias could be applied (e.g., covert sensitization, masturbatory satiation, relapse-prevention training)*

Frotteurism	
Description	
Causes	
Treatment	*no specific treatments described in textbook; usually disappears after the age of 25*

Pedophilia	
Description	
Causes	
Treatment	*behavioral: orgasmic reorientation, in which clients are conditioned to become sexually aroused by other stimuli; aversion therapy; and masturbatory satiation; cognitive-behavioral: relapse prevention training focuses on identifying triggering situations and the development of healthier coping strategies*

Sexual masochism	
Description	*recurrent sexual urges and fantasies that involve being made to suffer (e.g., through pain, humiliation)*
Causes	
Treatment	*no specific treatments described in textbook*

Sexual sadism	
Description	
Causes	*behavioral: as children, the sexually sadistic might have been classically conditioned to become aroused when inflicting pain, or may have seen models engaging in sexual sadism; cognitive, psychodynamic: may feel sexually inadequate and insecure; biological: evidence of abnormal endocrine functioning*
Treatment	*no specific treatments described in textbook*

Similar to sexual dysfunctions, the paraphilias are defined partly through comparisons to "normal" sexual behavior as dictated by the society in which these conditions or behaviors occur. Some behaviors, such as certain paraphilias that involve harming people, more clearly warrant a diagnostic "label." Generally however, clinicians are very careful about assigning the "sexual disorder" label to people because of the stigma and self-revulsion that can result.

Homosexuality is a good example of a "behavior" that clinicians once diagnosed as a paraphilia, but now consider a normal variation in human sexuality. This gradual shift and the public debates over issues involving homosexuality are discussed in Box 14-4 on pages 472-3 of the textbook.

Box 14-4

Complete the following statements regarding the landmark studies by Alfred Kinsey et al. (1948, 1953) and the occurrence of homosexuality.

Kinsey's studies suggested that four percent of the male population were ________________ homosexual.

The studies further found that 37 percent of the male population had had a homosexual experience that led to ________________.

The studies suggested that the occurrence of homosexuality among women was one-half to one-third that of men.

These findings shocked and astonished people. Why do you think people had this reaction?

____

One of the myths about homosexual individuals is that they suffer from gender confusion. List another myth.

____

3. One of the primary goals of the homosexual community is to be treated exactly as male-femal couples are treated in the eyes of the law. Give two examples of rights that heterosexual couple are afforded that are not consistently given to homosexual couples.

____

____

III: Gender Identity Disorder

1. In gender identity disorder, or _______________, people feel that they have been assigne the wrong sex.

2. List some of the characteristics of people who have gender identity disorder.

____

____

____

3. People with gender identity disorder are not _______________. In other words, they do nc cross-dress in order to achieve sexual arousal.

4. The ratio of transsexual males to transsexual females is _______ to 1.

5. There does not appear to be strong empirical support for the psychological o _______________ theories of the causes of gender identity disorder.

Although hormone therapy and psychotherapy are effective in helping many transsexuals lead satisfying liv that reflect their "true" gender role, some transsexual individuals undergo sex-reassignment surger Approximately 1000 such surgeries are performed in the United States each year. Sex-reassignment surgery a highly controversial procedure, and research has not been able to settle the debate regarding its long-ter effectiveness.

6. Complete the following statements regarding sex-reassignment procedures.

a. Surgery is preceded by one or two years of _______________ treatments.

b. For men, the surgery consists of _______________ of the penis, creation of an artifici _______________, and plastic surgery.

c. For women, the surgery consists of bilateral _______________, hysterectomy, and sometim _______________ (the surgical creation of a functioning penis) or the implantation of a sil cone prosthesis.

7. The long-term psychological outcome of sex-reassignment surgery is not well established, bu untreated gender identity disorder among adults is usually _______________.

Practice multiple-choice questions for this chapter begin on page 290.

Chapter 15

Schizophrenia

hapter Organization

hapter 15 is the first of two chapters examining various aspects of schizophrenia. The chapter is divid-d into two sections. The first deals with the disorder from a clinical perspective. The first subsection of ection I is particularly important because it describes and categorizes the symptoms of schizophrenia. he categories of the disorder are a subject that will come up again and again in this chapter and the next. he second section examines the various theoretical perspectives on the disorder. Pay particularly close tention to the biological views of schizophrenia, as it is the foundation for most of the material in hapter 16, which specifically deals with the treatments of schizophrenia.

e sure to read through each section before completing the exercises for that section.

Exercises

The following exercises cover chapter introductory material on pages 479-481.

1. In 1911, a Swiss psychiatrist named Eugen ________________ first used the term schizophreni (meaning ________________ ________________) to describe this group of disorders.

2. Although the term schizophrenia is often misused for multiple personality disorder, it actuall denotes these three points:

a. a ____________________ of thought processes;

b. a split between ________________ and ________________, and

c. a withdrawal from ________________.

3. Approximately ____________ percent of the world populations meets DSM-IV criteria for schiz ophrenia.

4. Figure 15-1 on page 481 illustrates the fact that people in lower socioeconomic groups are mor likely to suffer from schizophrenia than wealthier groups. Complete this list of possible reasons fo this fact.

a. The stress of __________ could lead to schizophrenia.

b. Schizophrenia could cause people to:

____

5. For this exercise, complete the paragraph describing the prevalence of schizophrenia by drawing line through the incorrect option within each set of parentheses.

Schizophrenia prevalence rates are higher among people in (~~higher~~/lower) socioeconomic group Neither gender appears to be at higher risk, but the age of onset is earlier among (men/women While divorced people have (higher/lower) rates than either married or single people, the exac reasons for this are not clear. The rate among African Americans compared to the rate amon white Americans is (equal/higher). When socioeconomic class and marital status are factored ou the rates are (equal for the two races/slightly higher among African Americans).

I: The Clinical Picture of Schizophrenia

1. DSM-IV classifies schizophrenia as a single disorder with different "faces." A number of clinician hold a contrary view. Describe that view.

____

A: Symptoms of Schizophrenia

Symptoms of schizophrenia can be grouped into three categories: positive symptoms, so named because they represent bizarre "additions" to or "excesses" of normal behavior; negative symptoms that represent "deficits" of normal behavior; and psychomotor symptoms that reflect unusual or bizarre motor behaviors.

Exercises in this subsection are broken down into one part for each of the three categories of symptoms. Within these category parts, exercises are broken down further into specific symptoms.

1. Positive Symptoms

Delusions

1. Delusions are ideas that schizophrenic people believe fervently, but that have no basis in _______________ and are often _______________.

2. Complete this exercise by describing the type of delusion and then by matching the example that best illustrates each type.

Type of delusion	Description	Example
Persecution	*irrational belief that one is being threatened, plotted against, spied upon, etc.*	
Reference		
Grandeur		
Control		

Examples:

a. Lowell eats at a Chinese restaurant every day. At the end of each meal, he reverently reads the message in the fortune cookie and carefully writes it down in a notebook. He believes that the messages are written specifically for him.

b. [Excerpt from a letter to a newspaper] Beware of the plot of destruction orchestrated by so-called 'door-to-door salesmen.' They come to my home 20 or 100 times a day, always snooping around and wanting to kill me. They say they are selling things, but they lie! They carry guns and knives and explosives. Beware! You could be the next victim!

c. Over the past two years, Lea has become convinced that thoughts are being put in her brain by alien life forms conducting mind-control experiments. Lately she has become certain that the aliens want her to disguise herself as Madonna and appear on television.

d. While watching the national college basketball championship on television, Margaret becomes convinced that she is determining the outcome of the game by manipulating the players with her mind

• Disorganized Thinking and Speech

3. Many people with schizophrenia display positive formal ________________ disorders that are manifested in the form of peculiar __________ and __________ patterns of thinking.

Match the numbers 4–6 below with the appropriate option from the list a–d below the numbers.

4. ____ loose associations

5. ____ neologisms

6. ____ perseveration

7. ____ clang

a. Made-up words that have meaning only to the person using them

b. Using rhyme as a guide to formulating thoughts and statements

c. Repeating words and statements over and over again

d. Rapidly shifting from one topic to another, making inconsequential and incoherent statements and apparently believing them to make sense (also called derailments)

• Heightened Perceptions and Hallucinations

8. People with schizophrenia often report a heightened sensitivity to ______________ and ______________, making it difficult for these individuals to attend to relevant stimuli.

9. One study demonstrated that compared to non-schizophrenic subjects, subjects with schizophrenia were less able to pick out a target __________ when they listened to a recording that also contained distracting __________ speech, showing attention problem these subjects.

10. Attention problems in people with schizophrenia may be related to smooth __________ movement (the ability to keep one's head still and track a moving object back and forth with one's eye

11. Define the term hallucination.

____

12. __________ hallucinations are the most common form of hallucination and are most likely to occur during the times of __________ or inattention.

13. Research has suggested that people with schizophrenia actually "hear" sounds that they attribute to __________ sources; the area of the brain that is most active during an auditory hallucination is __________ area (the area associated with speech production).

Match the numbers 11–16, representing the types of hallucinations, with the example from letters a–e that best illustrates each type of hallucination.

14. ____ auditory

15. ____ tactile

16. ____ somatic

17. ____ visual

18. ____ gustatory

19. ____ olfactory

a. While on a cross-country flight, Norman starts to see his fellow passengers as grotesque, green-colored monsters.

b. Lil, an office worker, quits her job when she can no longer bear smelling the "stench of death" that she can smell coming from her vent. No one else can smell the odor.

c. While at the mental health clinic, Phil tells the counselor taking information from him that she will have to get rid of her wristwatch if she wants him to be able to answer the questions. "It's ticking so loud that I can't hear your voice," he shouts.

d. Much to the consternation of her family and doctor, Bernadine insists against all medical evidence to the contrary that she has "grapefruit-sized" tumors throughout her body.

e. Roger, a guest at a nice hotel, calls the front desk to say that his room is "crawling with spiders." When the hotel investigates and finds no spiders, Roger contends that he could feel the spiders running over his body all night long.

f. At her nephew's wedding, Fay stands by the punchbowl and warns the other guests not to drink the punch because she tasted poison in it.

• Inappropriate Affect

20. In some cases, inappropriate affect may come about as a result of another positive symptom of schizophrenia. Give one such explanation for this example:

    Jerry, a man with schizophrenia, shows extreme anger at the same time he wins $500 playing the state lottery.

    ____

    ____

2. Negative Symptoms

• Poverty of Speech

1. Complete these exercises relating to the forms of poverty of speech.

a. Alogia is a decreased ____________ and ____________ of speech characterized by brief and empty replies.

b. Poverty of content is when a schizophrenic person actually says quite a bit but:

    ____

• Blunted and Flat Affect

2. What is the difference between blunted affect and flat affect?

    ____

3. Blunted or flat affect may reflect ________ ,a lack of pleasure and enjoyment.

• Disturbances in Volition

4. Schizophrenic people who display avolition, or ____________, feel drained of energy and ____________ in normal goals, are unable to initiate or complete a normal course of action, and commonly also display ____________.

• Social Withdrawal

5. Schizophrenic people withdraw from the "real" external world and become preoccupied with their own ____________ and ____________., leading to deterioration in social skills.

3. Psychomotor Symptoms

1. The psychomotor symptoms of schizophrenia are collectively known as "catatonia." Complete this box by providing the names of the types of catatonia being described.

Type of catatonia	*Description*
	assuming awkward, bizarre positions for long periods of time
	indefinitely maintaining postures into which they have been placed by someone else
	being totally unaware of and unresponsive to the external world, remaining motionless and silent for long stretches of time
	moving excitedly, sometimes with wild waving of arms and legs
	remaining in an unmoving, upright posture for hours and resisting efforts to be moved

B: The Course of Schizophrenia

1. While approximately _______ percent of schizophrenic patients recover completely, the majority show signs of residual ___________________.

2. The several characteristics that are predictive of recovery in schizophrenic patients include good premorbid functioning. List two other characteristics.

____

C: Diagnosing Schizophrenia

1. Complete this list of DSM-IV diagnostic criteria for schizophrenia.

a. Signs of schizophrenia present for at least ___________ months.

b. For at least one of these months, an active phase of the disorder that includes at least ___________ major symptoms.

c. Deterioration from previous levels of ___________________.

2. Kraepelin delineated the hebephrenic, ______________, and ______________ patterns of schizophrenia.

3. Like Kraepelin, the DSM-IV categorizes types of schizophrenia based on descriptions of patients' behaviors. In this table, write key words that will help you remember the central features of each type of disorder. Then, match each type with the example that best illustrates it.

Category	Key words for central factors	Example
Disorganized		
Catatonic		
Paranoid		
Undifferentiated		
Residual		

Examples:

a. Daniel lost his job as a corporate attorney about a year ago, which seemed to trigger an intense phase of schizophrenic symptoms. Most of them have passed, but Daniel no longer seems to show much emotion about anything.

b. Jenny excitedly waves her arms about wildly in an attempt to fight off the "evil spirits" who tell her they are going to hurt her.

c. Albert lives in a large city where he is homeless. He spends most days sitting in a small park, speaking to no one and quietly laughing and grimacing as thousands of people walk past him.

d. Bob is convinced that government agents trying to kill him because President Kennedy has "spoken" to him, telling Bob the truth about his assassination.

e. Ellen is a 45-year old ex-teacher, who had to quit her job when her schizophrenic symptoms took over her life. She can usually be found sitting in her kitchen, where she often will barely move a muscle for hours at a time.

4. Researchers and clinicians are increasingly labeling schizophrenia cases either "Type I" or "Type II." The distinctions have proven useful in predicting the course and the prognosis of the disorder. For each letter a–g, assign either a "I" or a "II" according to which type of schizophrenia the information best applies.

a. _____ dominated by positive symptoms such as delusions and hallucinations

b. _____ dominated by negative symptoms such as flat affect and poverty of speech

c. _____ worse premorbid adjustment

d. ____ better response to antidepressant drugs

e. ____ is linked to structural abnormalities in the brain

f. ____ is linked to biochemical abnormalities in the brain

g. ____ has a better prognosis

II: Views on Schizophrenia

A: Biological Views

Coverage of this subsection is broken down into its three parts—genetic factors, biochemical abnormalities, abnormal brain structure.

1. Genetic Factors

1. Although it seems clear that the risk of developing schizophrenia is significantly greater in people who are closely related to schizophrenic probands, the trend does not (in itself) establish a genetic basis for the disorder. Why?

____

2. If genetic factors were at work in schizophrenia, ________________ twins would have a higher concordance rate for the disorder than ________________ twins.

3. What have studies shown with regard to the fact stated above in Exercise 2?

____

4. Using a technique called ___________ researchers have examined families with high rates of schizophrenia and compared gene segments taken from family members with and without schizophrenia.

5. Research which seemed to indicate that abnormalities on chromosone S could indicate a predisosition to develop schizophrenia was greeted as a possible breakthrough. However, follow-up studies have dampened this enthusiasm. What are the possible explanations for the different findings?

____

____

2. Biochemical Abnormalities

The first of the two distinct biological views of the development of schizophrenia centers on the dopamine hypothesis. It states that in schizophrenia, neurons that use the neurotransmitter dopamine fire too often and thus transmit too many messages, leading to symptoms of the disorder. Researchers formulated this hypothesis after observing some interesting effects of antipsychotic medications known as phenothiazines.

1. Complete the statements below by writing in the effects of the given situations, all of which support the link between dopamine and schizophrenia.

a. Parkinson's patients who take too much L-Dopa:

____

b. Schizophrenic patients who take L-Dopa:

____

c. People with amphetamine psychosis who are given antipsychotic drugs:

____

2. Amphetamines induce or exacerbate psychotic symptoms because they ____________ dopamine ____________ activity in the brain.

3. Research has indicated that antipsychotic drugs and dopamine bind to many of the same sites. What conclusion was drawn from this finding?

____

____

4. A number of studies have led researchers to tentatively conclude that dopamine synapses in the brain are overactive—especially ________ receptors.

5. Researchers now believe that the dopamine synapses of schizophrenic people are overactive because of a ____________ than usual number of dopamine receptors—again, especially ________ receptors.

While there is significant evidence that D-2 receptors are heavily implicated in schizophrenia, recent research suggests that these receptor sites are not THE answer to the causal question of schizophrenia. These findings that challenge the dopamine hypothesis have largely been the result of the introduction of "atypical antipsychotic" drugs such as clozapine. These drugs act on some receptor sites other than D-2 receptors and are often more effective treatment than traditional antipsychotic drugs.

6. Complete these questions on the role of atypical antipsychotic drugs in leading to alternative "challenging" hypotheses about biological causes of schizophrenia.

a. Traditional antipsychotic drugs bind to and block primarily _______ receptors, but few if any _______ receptors, while atypical drugs bind to both of these receptors, and might be more effective than the traditional antipsychotics.

b. Clozapine also binds to ________________ receptors, suggesting that this neurotransmitter may also be important with regard to schizophrenia.

c. Researchers have observed that Type ____ cases of schizophrenia are more responsive than Type _____ cases to the traditional antipsychotic drugs, and that Type _____ cases are often responsive to atypical antipsychotic drugs.

d. Researchers increasingly suspect that the dopamine hypothesis may be relevant only for Type I schizophrenia and that Type II may have a totally different biological cause.

3. Abnormal Brain Structure

The second distinct biological view of the cause of schizophrenia relates to abnormal brain structure. It has been strengthened by research in the last decade that has linked Type II schizophrenia with specific structural abnormalities in the brain.

1. Researchers have found that many schizophrenic people have enlarged ________________ on the ____________ side of their brains.

2. List characteristics of schizophrenic people with this brain abnormality.

____

____

3. It may be that enlarged ventricles indicate that nearby brain regions have atrophied. What are the three findings that support this view.

a. ____

b. ____

c. ____

4. According to the viral theory of schizophrenia, symptoms come about as a result of a virus entering the brain during the ________________ period and remain latent until puberty or young adulthood when it is reactivated by ________________ changes or another viral infection.

5. Summarize the evidence for the viral theory of schizophrenia related to:

a. season of birth

____

____

b. fingerprints

____

____

c. viral reactions

____

____

B: Psychological Views

In this subsection, each of the leading psychological theories of schizophrenia is addressed in its own part.

1. The Psychodynamic View

1. Complete these statements regarding Freud's theory of the development of schizophrenia.

a. Regression, the first part of the two-part process, is when a person regresses to a pre-ego state o primary ____________________ resulting in "self-indulgent" symptoms such as neologisms, loos associations, and delusions of grandeur.

b. During the second part, the person attempts to regain ___________ control and establish contac with the external world, resulting in "reality substitution" symptoms such as hallucinations.

2. List some of the characteristics found in mothers of schizophrenic people which seem to disagre with the so-called schizophrenogenic mother notion that such women are cold, domineering, an impervious to their children's needs.

____

2. The Behavioral View

1. "Since symptoms of schizophrenia can be altered by conditioning techniques, it must mean tha the disorder is caused by conditioning." Counter this statement.

____

3. The Cognitive View

1. The cognitive explanation might explain the fairly high prevalence of ____________________ delu sions among the elderly.

C. Sociocultural-Existential Views

1. Sociocultural theorists believe that the ___________ itself causes many of the features of schizo phrenia.

2. What did the Rosehan study demonstrate with regard to the power of social labeling?

____

Bateson's double-bind hypothesis suggests that children respond to their parents' mutually contradictory messages by developing schizophrenic symptoms. Read this sample case relating to this hypothesis, and then complete the exercise following it.

Sample Case

Pamela is the ten-year-old daughter of divorced parents who are constantly in conflict with each other, particularly concerning visitation issues. Here is an example of a typical interaction between Pamela and her parents:

Mother: (sarcastically) Pamela, you know it is very important that you go to your father's this weekend,. because it was part of our agreement.

Pamela: Do you want me to stay with you this weekend? I could call him...

Mother: No, I want you to go. I'll be fine here by myself. (crosses arms, facial expression of anger)

Pamela: Well...okay. Are you sure?

Mother: Yes, of course I'm sure. (Mother hugs Pamela and begins to cry)

Pamela then goes to her room and sits on her bed. She feels confused and paralyzed. Should she go to her father's house and risk hurting her mother? However, her mother said she wanted her to go. Pamela knows that if she doesn't go, her father will be angry with her.

3. Restate (a) the mother's primary communication, and (b) her metacommunciation.

a. _______________

b. _______________

4. What does research indicate about the validity of the double-bind hypothesis?

____

5. While no single family systems view has yielded much research support, the study of families of schizophrenic people have yielded three trends that support some aspects of the family systems view. One is that parents of schizophrenic people display more conflict. List the other two.

a. _______________

b. _______________

6. Sociocultural theorists believe that the ____________________ itself causes many of the features of schizophrenia.

7. R. D. Laing's theory asserts that we find meaning in our lives by finding our true selves, which is difficult because society requires us to develop "false selves" to meet the demands and expectations of others. Complete the following question's regarding Laing's conceptualization of schizophrenia.

a. Because they cannot meet the needs of their families and society, some people withdraw into an inner search for strength and purpose.

b. According to Laing, what would happen if these people were left to themselves?

____

c. However, society responds by telling these people they are ____________________.

d. Yielding to society's ____________________, these individuals assume the role of patient and submit to treatments that actually produce more symptoms.

Practice multiple-choice questions for this chapter begin on page 291.

Chapter 16

Treatments for Schizophrenia

Chapter Organization

This chapter examines a variety of treatments for people with schizophrenia. The first section takes a look at past and present trends in institutional care, and focuses on the use of milieu therapy and token economy programs in hospitals and residential care facilities. The discovery of antipsychotic drugs has revolutionized the treatment of schizophrenia. This crucial component of the treatment process is explored in the second section. The next section looks at psychotherapy. Psychotherapy can provide schizophrenic people and their families with the knowledge and skills to function effectively in the community—especially when patients are helped by medication. The final section covering the community approach shows how this treatment can provide necessary services to schizophrenic people who require support in the community. As you study, you will learn that there are still substantial inadequacies in the community mental health system which psychologists are attempting to address on a continuing basis.

Be sure to read through each section before completing the exercises for that section.

Exercises

I: Institutional Care

A: Past Institutional Care

1. Phillipe Pinel's practice of ________________ treatment spread to the U.S. resulting in the creation of large __________________ __________________ rather than asylums to care for mentally disturbed individuals.

2. Required by U.S. law, ________________ hospitals were established so that institutional care would be available to both poor and rich people.

3. Complete these questions about the 100-year decline in mental health care that began in the mid-nineteenth century.

a. Priorities of public mental health institutions changed dramatically from ____________________ to custodial, or order-keeping.

b. During this time, hospitals increasingly relied upon ____________________ restraints, isolation, and ____________________ to treat disruptive patients.

c. "Advanced" forms of intervention included medically debilitating approaches such as ____________________.

d. The social breakdown syndrome was a result of institutionalization itself. Its symptoms included:

____

B: Improved Institutional Care

During the 1950s, milieu therapy (based on humanistic principles) and token economy programs (based on behavioral principles) gained prominence as methods of treatment in institutions for mentally ill people. Exercises in this subsection cover the two approaches separately.

1. Milieu Therapy

1. Humanistic theorists proposed the basic premise of milieu therapy. Complete the list of the two basic components of this premise.

a. Institutionalized patients deteriorate mainly because they are deprived of opportunities to develop self-respect, independence, and to engage in meaningful activity—all experiences basic to healthy human functioning.

b. ____

____

2. The psychiatrist Maxwell Jones converted a psychiatric hospital ward into a therapeutic community. Give two more examples of how this community differed from traditional institutional care.

a. *Patients were called residents, who were assumed to be able to make decisions about their own lives.*

b. ____

c. ____

3. Researchers have had difficulty assessing the effectiveness of milieu therapy because milieu approaches vary so much between ____________________, and the approach has been applied to patients with different ____________________.

4. Research indicates that chronic schizophrenic patients in milieu programs improve at higher rates than do patients in ____________________ programs, and the approach has proven to be an effective adjunct to other hospital treatments.

2. The Token Economy

1. Token economy programs apply the systematic application of ________________ conditioning techniques.

2. Clinicians set up ____________________ programs in order to facilitate patients' gradual development of more difficult or demanding behaviors.

3. Summarize the effectiveness of the structured token economy implemented by Paul and Lentz (1977) by describing the results at the time periods listed.

a. Seven months into the program, many patients were regularly demonstrating appropriate behavior in each area that was targeted.

b. By the end of the program (after four and a half years):

____

c. At a follow-up eighteen months after the end of the program:

____

4. Paul and Lentz also compared the effects of the token economy program with two other kinds of treatment. Generally how did the results (a) compare to those of the milieu program, and (b) compare to those of the custodial program?

a. ____

b. ____

5. The primary problem in studies that examine the effectiveness of token economy programs is the failure to use ________________ groups.

The following two questions ask you to play the role of a psychologist who is working in a hospital that employs a token economy program.

6. Suppose that one of your colleagues proposes a token economy that requires patients to earn tokens to buy pillows, meals, and any "outdoor" time in the fresh air. Write a statement on the ethical and legal problems this program would give the hospital.

____

____

____

7. Suppose that another colleague has been treating a woman who insisted on talking to her "evil twin" every day in the mirror. After six months in your colleague's token economy program, the woman stops this behavior.

a. Critique your colleague's subsequent claim that the program had "worked."

____

____

b. How might your colleague rebut your critique?

____

____

II: Antipsychotic Drugs

1. Complete these statements that delineate the history of the antipsychotic drugs.

a. The group of antihistamine drugs called the ____________________ were administered by the surgeon Henri Laborit to try to prevent a sudden drop in blood pressure in anesthetized patients undergoing surgery.

b. Laborit found that the drug ________________ in particular calmed and relaxed his patients, even when they were awake.

c. Because of their calming effects, researchers speculated that this group of drugs could be used to treat ____________________ disorders.

d. After being tested in laboratory and clinical settings, chlorpromazine was marketed as the first antipsychotic drug under the trade name __________________.

e. Since the discovery of this drug, other antipsychotics have been developed and are known collectively as the __________________ drugs.

A: The Effectiveness of Antipsychotic Drugs

1. Antipsychotic drugs are the single most effective intervention for schizophrenia. Complete the following statements regarding the effectiveness of these drugs.

a. Patients improve most within the first _____ months of antipsychotic drug treatment.

b. Research strongly indicates that people with Type I schizophrenia, dominated by __________ symptoms, are helped more by antipsychotic medications and show higher __________ rates compared to those with Type II schizophrenia.

c. Compared to women, men with schizophrenia require ________ doses and respond __________ readily to antipsychotic drugs.

2. Research strongly indicates that people with Type I schizophrenia, dominated by __________________ symptoms, are helped more by antipsychotic medications and show higher ____________________ rates compared to those with Type II.

B: Unwanted Effects of Antipsychotic Drugs

1. ____________________ effects are movement abnormalities that are produced by antipsychotic medications, and are classified as medication-induced ____________________ disorders by DSM-IV.

2. Approximately 20-40% of patients taking antipsychotic drugs experience Parkinsonian symptoms, as well as related symptoms of dystonia and akathisia. Describe the characteristics of each of these unwanted side effects of antipsychotic drugs.`

Parkinsonian symptoms: ________________________________

dystonia: ________________________________

akathisia: ________________________________

3. Parkinsonian, dystonia, and akathisia symptoms are related to reductions in __________ activity in the area of the brain called the __________ __________ that are caused by the drugs.

4. In about 1-2% of patients (especially _______ patients) antipsychotic drug use results in __________ __________ syndrome, a potentially fatal reaction characterized by fever, rigidity, and autonomic dysfunction.

5. Complete the following statements about **tardive dyskinesia**.

a. It is called the late appearing movement disorder because symptoms do not appear until the patient has been on antipsychotic medication for at least ____________.

b. What are the symptoms of tardive dyskinesia?

____

c. Approximately _____ percent of people who take antipsychotic drugs for an extended period develop tardive dyskinesia.

d. Patients at greater risk for developing tardive dyskinesia include patients over _____ years of age and people with Type _____ schizophrenia.

6. Imagine that you are training a group of psychiatric residents on appropriate antipsychotic prescription procedures. What three points will you emphasize?

a. If the patient does not respond to neuroleptic drugs, you should:

____

b. When you begin a neuroleptic drug regimen for a patient, you should prescribe the ________________ dosage possible.

c. After the patient re-establishes nonpsychotic functioning you should:

____

7. Because so many chronic schizophrenic patients rely on neuroleptic drugs in order to control their symptoms, researchers have attempted to find ways to predict relapse so they can better determine the appropriate (and most conservative) medication dosages. Describe two ways relapse can be predicted.

a. ____

b. ____

C: New Antipsychotic Drugs

Because some schizophrenic patients do not respond to, or cannot tolerate the effects of traditional neuroleptic drugs, new antipsychotic drugs have been developed to treat them. By far the most effective and widely used of these drugs are clozapine (Clozaril) and resperidone (Resperdole), which have been found to be 80–85 percent effective, as compared to rates of 65–75 percent for traditional antipsychotic drugs.

1. In addition to being more effective drugs, the atypical antipsychotics have has several other advantages over traditional neuroleptic drugs. Complete this list of advantages.

a. Atypical antipsychotic drugs cause few ________________ symptoms because it does not block ________________ receptors.

b. Even after prolonged treatment, it doesn't cause ____________ ____________.

2. A major concern with clozapine is that it can lead to ______________________, a potentially fatal drop in white blood cells in 1–2 percent of its users.

3. Because of the potential risks associated with clozapine use, the U.S. Food and Drug Administration has regulated it. How?

____

____

II: Psychotherapy

Although some clinicians have treated schizophrenic people with psychotherapy alone (emphasizing a trusting and understanding relationship), the majority of practitioners today recognize that medication is a crucial component of the treatment process. Insight therapy, social therapy, and family therapy can be very helpful to patients especially after medication has relieved symptoms such as delusional thoughts and incoherence that are barriers to therapeutic interventions.

A: Insight Therapy

1. Regardless of their theoretical orientation, the insight therapists who are more ______________ in working with schizophrenic patients are the most effective.

2. Along with gaining a patient's trust and being active in therapy, what are some of the other methods that successful insight therapists use when treating schizophrenic patients?

____

____

B: Family Therapy

1. About 25–40 percent of recovering schizophrenic patients live in the community with ________________, siblings, ________________, or________________.

2. People with schizophrenia whose relatives have high levels of ____________________ ________________ (i.e., high levels of criticism, emotional over-involvement, and hostility) have higher relapse rates compared to those whose relatives are less emotional.

3. Psychoeducation also helps family members become more ________________ in their expectations, more ________________ of deviant behavior, less guilt-ridden and confused, and more willing to try new patterns of interaction and communication.

4. Psychoeducation also helps the schizophrenic person in what ways?

____

____

C: Social Therapy

1. Clinicians who use social therapy in the treatment of schizophrenia focus on the development of problem-solving, decision-making, and social skills in their patients. List two other "practical" interventions in this form of therapy.

____

2. In their study of the effectiveness of social therapy, Hogarty et al. found that chronic patients needed ______________ to avoid rehospitalization, and that patients who also received social therapy adjusted to the __________________ and avoided rehospitalization most successfully.

IV: The Community Approach

Match numbers 1–4 below with the appropriate letter from the list a–d.

1. ____ "Revolving door" syndrome

2. ____ John F. Kennedy

3. ____ Deinstitutionalization

4. ____ Community Mental Health Act

a. The movement of thousands of chronic mental patients from hospitals to communities hospitals to community mental health centers

b. Called for a "bold new approach" to the treatment of mental disorders in 1963

c. Required communities to provide a full range of mental health services to psychiatric patients

d. Patients are released from hospitals, rehospitalized shortly thereafter, then released again, readmitted again, etc.

A: Effective Community Care

In order to address the needs of people with schizophrenia, the community care approach provides a range of services that are designed to maximize the potential of these individuals to live and function in the community.

1. Complete this summary table by describing the central characteristics of each component of the community care approach.

Category	Key words for central factors
Coordinated services	*community mental health centers provide medication, therapy, and emergency care; they also coordinate services of other agencies in a designated "catchment area"*
Short-term hospitalization	
Partial hospitaliztion	
Halfway houses	
Occupational training	

B: Inadequacies in Community Treatment

1. In any given year, approximately _____ percent of people with schizophrenia do not receive any form of treatment services.

2. One inadequacy in community treatment for people with schizophrenia is poor coordination of services, including minimal ______________________ between agencies and no overall strategy for the provision of services.

3. Poor coordination between state hospitals and community mental health centers often results in mental health centers being unaware when a state hospital releases a patient into their community. Give a reason why this situation exists.

____

____

In addition to the shortage of needed community programs, there is an increasing trend in community mental health services away from their stated goals. Those goals are to: (1) assist patients suffering from acute mental illness, (2) circumvent hospitalization before it becomes absolutely necessary, and (3) provide services to patients who have just been released from the hospital.

4. In fact, only about ten percent of patients treated by community mental health centers are schizophrenic. To what services are these centers devoting increasing resources?

____

____

5. There are three factors that seem to contribute to the shift in community mental health priorities from serving more disabled populations (such as schizophrenic people) to less disabled people. Describe and explain these factors in this table.

Factor	Description/explanation
Characterisitics of professionals and patients	
"NIMBY" syndrome	
Allocation of funds/resources	

6. Where do people with schizophrenia go after they have been discharged from the hospital? Answer this question by giving the destination of each of the percentages listed

a. 25 to 40 percent: *return to their families*

b. 5 to 15 percent: ______________________

c. Up to 35 percent: ______________________

7. As many as one out of every __________ homeless people have a severe mental disorder such as schizophrenia.

C: The Promise of Community Treatment

1. A number of innovative community programs have been developed to address the problems that have been described. In this table, describe the purpose and services of these programs.

Program	Purpose	Services
Task Force on Homelessness and Severe Mental Illness		
National Alliance for the Mentally Ill (NAMI)	*a national interest group that promotes community treatment for schizophrenic and other chronic patients*	

Practice multiple-choice questions for this chapter begin on page 293.

Chapter 17

Disorders of Memory and Other Cognitive Functions

Chapter Organization

Chapter 17 covers some fascinating topics and some intriguing studies that have been done in the area of memory disorders. It is divided into two sections. The first explores dissociative, or inorganic, disorders of memory and identity, and the second looks at disorders of memory with an organic cause. The three main types of dissociative disorders—dissociative amnesia, dissociative fugue, and multiple personality disorder—are each examined in their own subsections. The largest subsection in the first half examines four explanations of dissociative disorders. Along with discussions of the psychodynamic and behavioral views (the foundations of which should be very familiar to you by now) are discussions of two explanations which are unique to these disorders: state-dependent learning and self-hypnosis. The second section starts out with a series of brief discussions that describe the current state of scientific understanding of memory. Following that are sections that describe the two main types of organic disorders of memory—amnestic disorders and dementias—as well as one that covers current treatments for these types of disorders.

Be sure to read through each section before completing the exercises for that section.

Exercises

I: Dissociative Disorders

A: Dissociative Amnesia

1. According to DSM-IV, people with dissociative amnesia manifest an inability to remember important information, usually of a stressful or ________________ event in their lives, which cannot be attributed to an ________________ cause.

Read this sample case that is the basis for an exercise relating to the different kinds of amnesia.

Sample Case

Clara, the proprietor of a popular inn on the beach, was quite busy one fateful June day. The inn was at full capacity with 60 guests—all of whom seemed to be making requests at the same time for more towels and pillows, extra room keys, and use of the fax machine. Clara managed to get through dealing with an angry guest, a Mr. Barnes, who demanded to have a "bigger room facing the ocean," and then decided it would be an ideal time to escape the chaos and obnoxious guests by running to the bank to make a deposit.

Standing in line, Clara became lost in her thoughts about the big dinner that evening at the inn. She heard a scream behind her, and turned to see four men wearing Richard Nixon masks and carrying guns. The gunmen shot out the cameras on the walls and ordered everyone to drop to the floor. One of them threatened to shoot all of the bank tellers if any of them activated the alarm. Face down on the floor, Clara shut her eyes and silently prayed. She was so frightened that she had trouble breathing. Suddenly, more shots were fired and Clara felt a man falling on top of her. She opened her eyes to see the man all bloody and writhing on the floor next to her. Clara screamed, for which she received a sharp kick to the shoulder and a threat that if she didn't "shut the hell up" she would "be next." The next few minutes were a blur. Clara heard the gunmen running shortly before the police swarmed into the bank.

> After waiting what seemed like hours, Clara was checked out by a doctor and then interviewed by the police. She was finally allowed to return to the inn—six hours after she left for what she thought would be a brief errand. For the next few weeks, Clara felt as if she were in a fog and had difficulty remembering details about the traumatic event she had experienced.

2. Using this case, apply a description of the pattern of forgetting that would illustrate the kinds of amnesia listed.

a. *Localized amnesia:* Clara is able to recall her hectic day at the inn, including her run in with Mr. Barnes, but can't remember a thing about being in the bank. She can recall everything after waking up at the inn the day after the robbery.

b. *Selective amnesia:* ____

____

____

c. *Generalized amnesia:* ____

____

____

d. *Continuous amnesia:* ____

____

____

3. People with dissociative amnesia show deficits in episodic memory, but not semantic memory. Complete the definitions of these two types of memory.

a. Episodic memory is a person's ______________________ memory of personal ______________ and other highly personal material.

b. Semantic memory is memory of ______________________, encyclopedic, or ______________ information.

. Give an example of an event more ordinary than military experiences that might precipitate dissociative amnesia.

____

Dissociative amnesia has been linked to child sexual abuse as well. This link has stirred considerable controversy over the reality of "repressed" memories, which is examined in Box 18-2, "Repressed Childhood Memories vs. False Memory Syndrome." Read the box and think about your reaction to the controversy.

B: Dissociative Fugue

1. According to DSM-IV, people with dissociative fugue forget their personal ____________, flee to a different ____________, and might even establish an entirely new identity.

2. For some people with dissociative fugue, the disorder is relatively brief—lasting only a few hours or days. In others, the fugue is more extensive. Complete this list of four characteristics of those who have the more extensive fugue state.

a. They establish a well-integrated new identity.

b. They may have personal ____________ that they never displayed before.

c. Usually they are more ____________ and less ____________ during the fugue state.

3. List two ways in which dissociative fugue and dissociative amnesia are similar.

a. ____________

b. ____________

4. Usually fugues end ____________ and recovery of memories is ____________.

C: Multiple Personality Disorder (Dissociative Identity Disorder)

1. A person with multiple personality disorder (MPD), manifests ____________ or more distinct subpersonalities, one of which—the primary or ____________ personality—dominates the others and appears more frequently.

2. The transition from one subpersonality to another can be ____________ and dramatic, and is typically precipitated by a ____________ event.

3. Complete these statements relating to the onset and prevalence of MPD.

a. Most cases of MPD are first diagnosed in late ____________ or young ____________.

b. However, symptoms of MPD usually appear in childhood before the age of ______, after the child experiences some form of ____________.

c. It is estimated that as many as 97 percent of MPD patients have histories of having been physically and/or ____________ abused.

d. For every man diagnosed with MPD, there are between ____________ and ____________ women diagnosed with the disorder.

4. Complete the brief descriptions of the characteristics of the three kinds of relationships between subpersonalities in this table.

Type	*How the subpersonalities relate to each other*
Mutually amnesic	*they have no awareness of each other*
Mutually cognizant	
One-way amnesic	

. Complete this table by giving examples of the differences between and among the subperonalities in people who suffer from MPD

Types of differences	*Examples of differences*
Personality characteristic	*one subpersonality might be fun-loving, spontaneous, and optimistic; another might be hostile and aggressive; a third might be shy, withdrawn, and passive*
Vital statistics	
Abilities and preferences	
Physiological activity	

Some researchers suggest that cases of so-called MPD are actually iatrogenic, or unintentionally caused by practitioners. Complete the list of ways in which they say therapists create this disorder during therapy.

Therapists subtly ________________ the existence of alternate personalities.

While the patient is ________________ ________________, therapists elicit the personalities.

c. Therapists may ________________ multiple personality patterns by becoming more interest-ed in a patient when he or she displays symptoms of dissociation.

D: Explanations of Dissociative Disorders

Explanations for dissociative disorders have been offered by psychodynamic and behavioral theorists. Newe theories that explain these disorders in terms of state-dependent learning and self hypnosis combine aspects the cognitive, behavioral, and biological perspectives. Each of these views will be covered separately.

1. The Psychodynamic View

1. The psychodynamic view posits that people with dissociative disorders use th ________________ ________________ of repression excessively in order to prevent painfu memories from reaching conscious awareness.

2. According to psychodynamic theorists, people with dissociative amnesia and fugue unconscious-ly use a single ________________ episode of repression to avoid confronting a very traumati event.

3. While amnesia and fugue usually represent one-time occurrences resulting from a single represse event, multiple personality disorder is an ________________ style of coping triggered b extremely ________________ childhood experiences, according to the psychodynamic the-ory.

4. In order to escape an abusive and dangerous world, children take to flight symbolically by regu-larly ________________ to be another person who is ________________ looking on fro afar.

5. The bulk of support for the psychodynamic view of the dissociative disorders is provided b ________________ ________________.

2. The Behavioral View

1. Complete these questions about the behavioral view of dissociative disorders.

a. The view holds that dissociation is a response acquired through ________________ ________________.

b. Those affected have learned that momentarily forgetting a horrific event leads to a reduction ________________.

c. The relief resulting from this reduction ________________ the act of forgetting and increas the likelihood of more forgetting in the future.

2. Complete the list of the similarities between the behavioral and the psychodynamic views of dissociative disorders.

a. The disorder is precipitated by a traumatic event.

b. The disorder represents a way of ________________ extreme ________________.

c. ____

3. Here are two statements representing beliefs of psychodynamic theorists about dissociative disorders. Explain the differences between each statement and the behavioral view of these disorders.

a. *From the start, disorders represent unconscious but purposeful attempts to forget.*

____

b. *A hardworking unconscious is keeping the individual unaware that he or she is using dissociation as a means of escape.*

____

. State-Dependent Learning

. What is the central idea underlying state-dependent learning?

____

____

. One explanation for state-dependent learning phenomena is that a certain ________________ level has a set of remembered thoughts, events, and skills "attached" to it.

. Some research has pointed to a structure in the brain's limbic system—the ________________—as the regulator of the arousal state to memory link.

. People with dissociative disorders may have extremely narrow and ________________ state-to-memory links, which could mean that certain memories would be exclusively tied to a particular ________________ level.

While state-dependent learning proponents point to consistencies between their explanation and the personality shifts seen in people with MPD, efforts to tie the theory to dissociative disorders keeps running into what major problem?

____

____

4. Self-Hypnosis

1. Hypnosis is defined as the deliberate induction of a sleeplike state in which the person shows a very high degree of ________________.

2. Complete the list of three examples of how hypnosis may be used.

a. Hypnosis can suspend a person's ________________ functioning so that they become temporarily blind, deaf, or insensitive to pain.

b. It can help people remember events that occurred in the past, but were long forgotten.

c. It can make people forget facts and events, as well as their personal identity—a phenomenon that is called ________________ ________________.

3. Complete this description of the three-step process that many researchers use to examine the effects of hypnosis on memory and recall.

a. Subjects are asked to memorize certain material (such as a list of words).

b. ________________

c. ________________

4. Hypnotic suggestion seems to influence ________________ memories more than ________________ memories.

5. Complete this list of the three parallel features of hypnotic amnesia and dissociative disorders that provide support for the hypothesis that dissociative disorders represent a form of self-hypnosis.

a. ________________

b. ________________

c. Events are more readily forgotten than basic knowledge.

E: Treatments for Dissociative Amnesia and Fugue

1. The primary goal of psychodynamic therapy in treating dissociative disorders is to guide patients to ________________ and search their unconscious in the hope of bringing the forgotten experiences back to the level of consciousness.

2. In hypnotic therapy or ________________ for dissociative disorders, therapists hypnotize patients and then guide them to recall the forgotten events.

3. The idea behind therapy involving injections of sodium amobarbital or sodium pentobarbital is that these drugs lower inhibitions, and thus might help patients regain lost memories. What are the main drawbacks to this rarely-used treatment?

____

____

F: Treatments for Multiple Personality Disorder

1. As you have done before, this exercise calls upon you to imagine that you are a clinician. This time you have been called upon to create a treatment plan for a patient named Maggie N., who suffers from multiple personality disorder. Note that the phases of the treatment plan correspond to the parts of subsection F. in the textbook.

City Hospital - Department of Psychiatry

Treatment plan for: Maggie N.—

Therapist:

Diagnosis: Multiple Personality Disorder

Tratment Phase I: Recognizing the Disorder	
• Goal	*form an alliance with primary and subpersonalities*
Strategy	1. *establish a safe therapeutic atmosphere* 2. *establish contacts with each subpersonality*
• Goal	*help Maggie recognize her disorder*
Strategy	1. *introduce subpersonalities to each other under hypnosis* 2.
• Goal	*provide adjunctive therapies*
Strategy	1. *(group)* 2. *(family)*

Tratment Phase II: Recovery of Memories	
• Goal	*use therapeutic strategies to help Maggie remember "missing" life events*
Strategy	1. 2. 3.
Potential Obstacles	*1. certain subpersonalities may serve as "protector" against... [complete:]* *2. Maggie could be at risk for engaging in self-destructive behaviors in this stage, so if necessary consider restraints or hospitalization*

Tratment Phase II: Recovery of Memories	
• Goal	*use therapeutic strategies to help Maggie remember "missing" life events*
Strategy	1. 2. 3.
Potential Obstacles	*1. certain subpersonalities may serve as "protector" against... [complete:]* *2. Maggie could be at risk for engaging in self-destructive behaviors in this stage, so if necessary consider restraints or hospitalization*

Tratment Phase III: Integration	
• Goal	
Strategy	1. 2. 3.
Potential Obstacles	1.

Tratment Phase IV: Post-Integration	
• Goal	*help Maggie develop the social and coping skills she needs so that she won't have to dissociate in order to function in the world*

I: Organic Disorders Affecting Memory and Identity

The first three brief subsections of Section II—"Memory Systems," "The Anatomy of Memory," and "The Biochemistry of Memory."—will be covered together.

1. Researchers have been unable to identify a well-defined region of the cerebral cortex that corresponds with the function of memory, leading to the view that memory is a ________________ rather than a place in the brain.

2. Even though the brain has no storehouse for memories, researchers have identified areas that seem to play a role in short- and long-term memory processes. Complete the table below by listing the structures that are important to memory, and then describing the results of lesions to each area.

Brain area	Key structures	Result of lesions
Temporal lobes	*hippocampus and amygdala*	
Diencephalon		*problems encoding new information*
Connection between temporal lobes and diencephalon		*memory loss*

3. While it has been suggested that newly learned information in the brain follows a circuit, and that memory disorders may result from any disruption in this circuit, it is also thought that memory is ________________—meaning that if one pathway on the circuit is disrupted, alternative routes may be available.

4. Explain the effect known as long-term potentiation.

____

____

D: Amnestic Disorders

1. People with amnestic disorders (which are organic disorders), may or may not suffer from ________________ amnesia—a lack of memory of events that occurred before the event that caused the amnesia, but always exhibit ________________ amnesia, which is characterized by inability to learn and recall new information.

2. In anterograde amnesia, it is as though information can no longer cross from short- to long-term memory, which are linked to the brain's ______________________ lobes and ______________.

3. Korsakoff's syndrome, also called Alcohol-Induced Persisting ______________ Disorder, affects about 5 percent of people with chronic alcoholism and occurs when the ______________ is damaged as a result of a deficiency of the vitamin ______________ caused by excessive drinking and poor diet.

4. Wernicke's encephalopathy, which is the name for the first stages of Korsakoff's syndrome, is treated with large doses of ______________.

5. Describe what happens when a Korsakoff's patient confabulates?

____

____

6. Vascular diseases can cause lesions in the brain that are associated with memory impairment. List three other traumas that may result in amnestic disorders.

____

E: Dementias

1. Both amnestic disorders and dementias are associated with severe memory loss; but with dementias, at least one other ______________ function is also impaired.

The effects of Alzheimer's disease will be explored in more depth in Chapter 20. For now, you should know that it eventually disrupts nearly all cognitive abilities, including memory and sense of identity.

2. Other cortical dementias include Creutzfeldt-Jakob disease, a pattern of dementia caused by a ______________, and ______________ disease, which affects the frontal and temporal lobes of the brain.

3. Complete the following list of facts concerning Huntington's disease.

a. *Description:* ____

b. *Onset:* late 30s, early 40s, or younger

c. *Effects:* causes ______________, instability, and anxiety, and severe ______________ amnesia early in its course

4. Parkinson's disease is a slowly progressive neurological condition marked by:

____

____

. Parkinson's disease is closely tied to low levels of the neurotransmitter ____________________ in the brain.

: Treatments of Amnestic Disorders and Dementias

. Clinicians who treat people with amnestic disorders and dementias must identify the type and cause of each patient's disorder. Complete the list of ways in which they accomplish this goal.

. Clinicians take a complete life history, checking for individual and family histories of alcohol use and dementia.

. ____

____

. ____

____

ractice multiple-choice questions for this chapter begin on page 294.

Chapter 18

Personality Disorders

Chapter Organization

Chapter 18 looks at personality disorders—an active and sometimes controversial area of abnormal psychology. The DSM-IV distinguishes ten personality disorders, and the three main sections of the chapter cover the three different groups, or clusters into which the DSM-IV puts them. Each disorder is covered from three standpoints, with a description of the symptoms and behaviors associated with it first. Then come the explanations of each disorder offered by theorists of the various theoretical perspectives. Finally the treatments of each perspective practiced by clinicians of the differing perspectives is discussed. As you read the descriptions of the disorders you will notice many similarities between them, as well as to disorders of other types which you have already studied. These similarities are part of the reason why the classification and diagnosis of personality disorders is sometimes controversial. This subject is summed in the fourth and final section of the chapter.

Be sure to read through each section before completing the exercises for that section.

Exercises

The following exercises cover chapter introductory material on pages 567-69.

1. Complete these exercises about the concepts that form the basis of this chapter.

a. The term personality refers to the ________________ and enduring patterns of inner experience and outward ________________ displayed by each individual.

b. The enduring ________________ with which we interact with our surroundings are called personality traits, that can be the result of intrinsic characteristics, ______ ______, or a combination of the two.

c. Those with a personality disorder are frequently unable to do this. List some of the characteristics of a personality disorder described in the textbook.

____

____

2. Personality disorders are classified in DSM-IV as Axis ____ disorders because they usually do not have periods of significant ________________ and do not vary greatly in intensity or improve over time.

3. Personality disorders often coexist with Axis ____ disorders, a relationship called __________.

I: "Odd" Personality Disorders [Cluster A]

1. Because some of the behaviors seen in the "odd" personality disorders are similar to those seen in schizophrenia, some clinicians suggest they are among the **schizophrenia-spectrum disorders**. Complete the questions about this notion.

a. Findings have shown that compared to others, those with "odd" personality Cluster A disorders are more likely to qualify for an ________________ diagnosis of schizophrenia.

b. They are also more likely to have close ________________ with schizophrenia.

c. However, it may just be that clinicians have difficulty doing what?

____

A: Paranoid Personality Disorder

1. List key word and phrases that describe the central features of the paranoid personality disorder.

____

____

2. Unlike schizophrenia, the ____________________ of people with a paranoid personality disorder are not usually so far out of the bounds of reality to be considered ____________________.

3. Between 0.5 and 2.5 percent of adults, and apparently more ____________ than the other gender, have paranoid personality disorder.

Psychodynamic theorists propose several ways a paranoid personality disorder can emerge from parental mistreatment, hostility, and absence of consistent nurturing. Study this diagram showing potential "outcomes" for people who experience this sort of parental environment, and who later develop a paranoid personality disorder.

Parental mistreatment, hostility, and absence of consistent nurturance leads to three potential outcomes

Children come to view all environments as hostile and dangerous, resulting in a basic distrust of others	Children project feelings of hostility and rage onto others, leading to feelings of persecution	Children see self as inadequate and different from others; they rationalize rejection with a belief that others must be jealous of their "specialness"

All three outcomes result in

Paranoid Personality Disorder

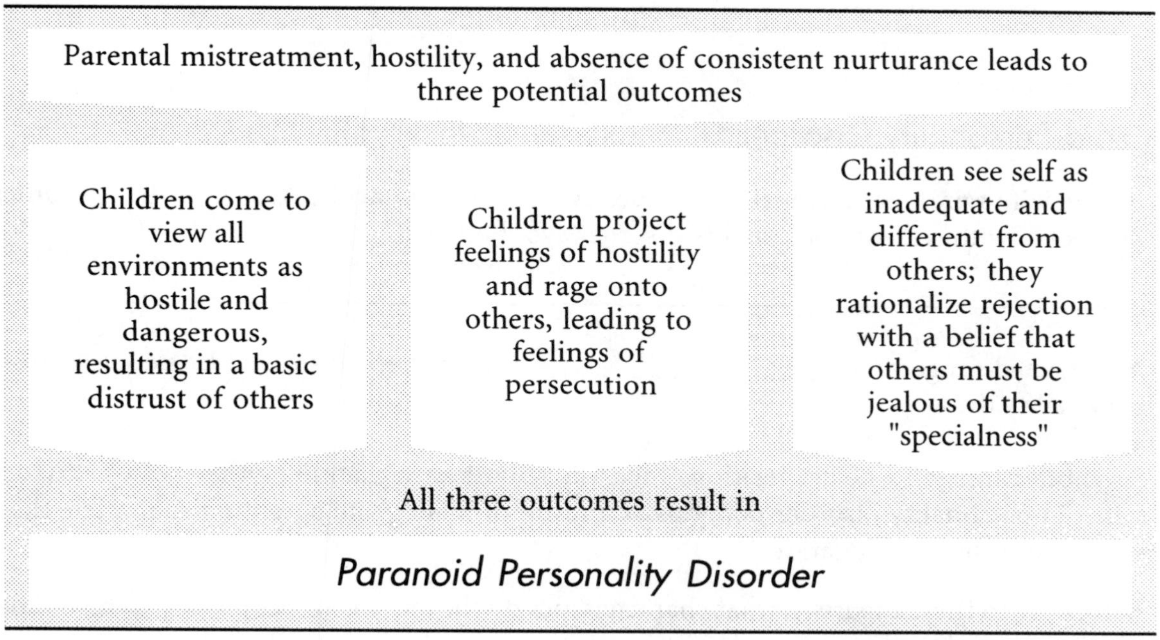

4. A possible ________________ factor in paranoid personality disorder was shown by one study of Australian twin pairs that found a high concordance of excessive suspiciousness.

5. One reason that clinicians find it difficult to treat people with paranoid personality disorder is that unless they are in crisis, few of these individuals think they need therapy. What is another reason?

____

____

6. Complete this table by describing the central foci of the approaches listed in treating people with paranoid personality disorder.

Approach	Central focus
Object relations	
Cognitive	

B: Schizoid Personality Disorder

1. People with paranoid personality disorder avoid social contact because they distrust others. Why do people with schizoid personality disorder avoid others?

____

2. A restricted range of _______________ expression is displayed by people with schizoid personality disorder.

3. Psychodynamic and object relations theorists hypothesize that, like other personality disorders, schizoid personality disorder develops as a result of inadequate parenting. Complete these questions about these explanations.

a. According to these theorists, what characteristics do the parents of people with schizoid personality disorder tend to have?

____

b. Unlike those with paranoid personality disorder, who react with distrust and hostility, those with schizoid personality disorder suffer an inability to _______________ or _______________ love.

c. Vulnerability to rejection leads them to develop a defensive strategy of shunning all relationships.

C: Schizotypal Personality Disorder

1. People with schizotypal personality disorder experience extreme discomfort in close _______________, cognitive or perceptual _______________, and behavioral eccentricities.

2. _______________ _______________ is a distinctive characteristic of people with schizotypal personality disorder that causes them to converse in a vague manner, making statements that are inappropriately elaborate and difficult to follow.

3. Some studies have suggested that the "positive" symptoms such as magical thinking are more common in ________________, while the negative symptoms such as constricted emotions are more typical in the other gender.

4. People among the estimated three percent of adults with a schizotypal disorder are more likely to have ________________ ________________ and to have been hospitalized with another mental disorder than the general population.

5. It is tempting to conclude that schizotypal personality disorder is tied solely to schizophrenia, but it has also been linked to ________________ disorders.

I: *"Dramatic" Personality Disorders*

A: Antisocial Personality Disorder

1. What are two other terms used for people with antisocial personality disorder?

____

2. DSM-IV stipulates that although a diagnosis of antisocial personality disorder cannot be given until the person is at least _____ years of age, evidence of antisocial behaviors are typically seen before the age of 15.

3. What are some of the antisocial behaviors typically seen before age 15 in people who will later be diagnosed with antisocial personality disorder?

____

____

4. Typical characteristics of people with antisocial personality disorder include deceitfulness, an inability to work ________________ at a job, financial ________________, impulsiveness, irritability, and aggressiveness.

5. Up to 3.5 percent of adults are diagnosed with antisocial personality disorder; men are ____________ times more likely to be diagnosed than women, and ____________ Americans are more likely to receive the diagnosis than ____________ Americans.

6. Complete the following diagram that explores the possible relationships between antisocial personality disorder and substance-related disorders.

Early substance abuse loosens inhibitions and contributes to...	Antisocial personality disorder causes increased vulnerability and contributes to...	A common cause, such as the need to take risks, contributes to...
•	•	• •

Box 17-2

Researchers such as David Lykken have studied antisocial personality disorder for more than 40 years in an attempt to answer the question "Why do people with the disorder seem unable to learn from negative experiences or weigh the potential consequences of their behavior before they act?" Read through Box 18-2, A Lesson Not Learned, for a glimpse into research that attempts to answer this important question.

B: Borderline Personality Disorder

Read the following case study related to borderline personality disorder which will be followed by an exercise

Case Study

Belinda T. is a 27-year-old woman who decided to seek therapy from Dr. Platt, an established and highly-regarded clinician. During the initial interview, Belinda told Dr. Platt the following: "Things have been getting worse and worse for me. Even when it seems like I'm having a good day, suddenly something goes wrong and I get depressed, or so mad that I see red. [1] A few nights ago I smashed every glass plate in my house, and kicked my dog so hard that I had to take him to the vet. [2] The next day I felt so horrible that I drank until I passed out. I get to feeling really awful and alone, like I'm a big nothing inside. Sometimes I cut my arms and stomach with a razor. [3] When I feel the pain and see the blood, I get a rush...almost like I feel more "real." [4] This therapy is my last chance; if it doesn't work I may as well just give up and die."

Dr. Platt agreed to work with Belinda in therapy, and made a provisional diagnosis of borderline personality disorder. After her first therapy session, Belinda told her friends that Dr. Platt was "the most wonderful person in the world," and that she had never met anyone with such understanding and compassion. She said that she was certain Dr. Platt could help her. But just five sessions later, Belinda confronted Dr. Platt by saying,, "You are an unfeeling, incompetent bitch! You are the one who needs a shrink." [5] Dr. Platt responded by asking,, "I wonder if some of your anger is about my being on vacation last week?" Belinda confirmed Dr. Platt's hypothesis by angrily claiming that Dr. Platt had deserted her and no longer cared about her. [6] Sobbing, Belinda rolled up her sleeve and revealed several new cuts on her arm. "Look at what you made me do! Please don't leave me alone again, I can't stand it. The next time you cancel a session I might kill myself." [7]

1. Each of the numbered statements in this sample case relate to a particular characteristic of people who suffer from borderline personality disorder. Match each statement with the characteristics (a–g) that follow.

   [1] ____ [2] ____ [3] ____ [4] ____ [5] ____ [6] ____ [7] ____

   Characteristics:

a. Anger is expressed in aggressive, violent behavior directed outward

b. Fearing desertion, manipulative behavior, such as suicidal threats are used to maintain relationships.

c. Anger is expressed and directed inward through self-destructive and self-mutilating behaviors.

d. Vacillation between overidealizing and devaluing others in relationships.

e. Dramatic, often sudden shifts in mood.

f. Rage and extreme disappointment are felt when expectations, particularly about others "being there" at all times in a relationship, are not met.

g. Self-destructive and self-mutilating behavior can serve to relieve chronic feelings of boredom and emptiness, and to validate "personhood."

2. Complete the following statements regarding the prevalence and course of borderline personality disorder.

a. About 75 percent of the estimated two percent of the general population with borderline personality disorder are __________________.

b. Women are more likely to engage in ______________________ behavior, and to have co-existing ________________ disorders.

c. Men are more likely to have co-existing ______________________ personality disorders, attention-deficit, and conduct disorders.

d. The symptoms of the disorder seem to peak during ________________ adulthood, and decrease with age.

3. Psychodynamic research has focused on the excessive fear of ________________ in people with borderline personality disorder, which has led to a hypothesis that parents' lack of acceptance causes a loss in self-esteem, dependency, and difficulty in coping with ________________.

4. Describe a research finding that supports the psychodynamic explanation of borderline personality disorder.

____

____

5. Early trauma such as childhood ________________ and ________________ abuse are prevalent in people diagnosed with borderline personality disorder.

6. Biological factors that have been implicated in borderline personality disorder include low ________________ activity (linked to aggression against self and others), abnormalities in ____________ sleep (associated with depression), and abnormal ________________ activity (linked to transient psychotic symptoms).

C: Histrionic Personality Disorder

1. List key words and phrases that describe the characteristics of people with histrionic personality disorder.

____

____

____

2. Psychodynamic theorists believe that histrionic people defend against deep fears of ________________ by being overly emotional and inventing crises so that other people will act ________________ toward them.

3. Many cognitive explanations focus on the lack of substance and extreme __________ of those with the disorder, and on their underlying assumptions that they are __________ to care for themselves.

4. Sociocultural theorists point to society's ______________ and expectations that encouraged childishness in women, resulting in histrionic behaviors that may be viewed as a caricature of ________________ as our culture once defined it.

5. What is a central goal in the treatment of histrionic personality disorder?

____

6. Histrionic individuals bring their unreasonable tantrums, seductiveness, and demands into the therapy. What is difficulty clinicians face with these patients?

____

D: Narcissistic Personality Disorder

1. Narcissistic personality disorder is characterized by excessive grandiosity, need for admiration, and lack of empathy. Read the lettered statements below made by a man with a this disorder and then describe the characteristic of the disorder that is being displayed in the spaces for letters a–f following the statements.

   Statements:

a. I think it's quite obvious that I saved the company's ass with my work on that project. I set a standard for the industry. The work could be described as nothing less than brilliant.

b. I am convinced that within two years, I will be a multi-millionaire, I'll have a luxury apartment on Park Avenue, as well as one in Paris. About fifteen-hundred people will be working for me.

c. Almost nobody is savvy enough to understand how my mind works. Maybe Bill Gates or Ted Turner...no, I doubt if even they could understand me.

d. All that time you spent lying around the hospital really added to the amount of work they gave to me.

e. So they're giving Patterson the company humanitarian award—what a joke. They should have given it to me. I find it hard to believe that they'd give it to a man who can't stand the fact that my office is bigger than his. Some humanitarian he is!

f. They're blaming me that we lost the account I was working on. I don't know why I even bother sometimes. My work isn't accomplishing a thing. I might as well not even get out of bed in the morning.

a. grandiose sense of self-importance, exaggeration of achievements, arrogance

b. ____

c. ____

d. ____

e. ____

f. ____

2. Of the less than one percent of the adult population who have narcissistic personality disorder, up to 75 percent are ____________________.

3. Psychodynamic theorists propose that cold and rejecting parents cause children to feel rejected and unworthy, and that some of these children grow up to defend against these feelings by telling themselves they are perfect. Complete the statements regarding two psychodynamic theories that go further in their explanation of narcissistic personality disorder.

a. Object relations theorists believe that early negative treatment disrupts a critical process of ____________________ between children and their parents and leads to a grandiose self-image that helps them maintain illusions of self-sufficiency.

b. Self theorists feel these children are deprived of mirroring. What does this mean?

____

____

4. Behavioral and cognitive theorists give a very different explanation of narcissistic personality disorder, suggesting that these people were treated too ____________________ early in life.

5. Cognitive therapists try to change the ways narcissistic people think by improving how they react to ____________________, increasing their ability to empathize, and changing all-or-nothing thinking.

III: "Anxious" Personality Disorders

A: Avoidant Personality Disorder

1. List key words and phrases that describe the central characteristics of the avoidant personality disorder.

____

____

____

2. Complete the following questions relating to the relationship between avoidant personality disorder and social phobias.

a. Some symptoms are common to the two disorders such as low ____________________ and fear of ____________________.

b. However, there are important differences such as the fact that people with social phobias primarily fear social ____________________, whereas people with avoidant personality disorder mostly fear social ____________________.

c. Also, avoidant personality disorder is common among those with chronic depressive disorder.

3. Psychodynamic theorists suggest that after being repeatedly ____________________ by parents, children experience self-deprecation, distrust of others, and a belief that "I am unlovable"—all of which contribute to avoidant personality disorder.

4. The __________________ view of avoidant personality disorder suggests that because of past criticisms, those affected expect and fear __________________, misinterpret people's reactions, and discount positive feedback.

5. Describe one challenge therapists face in the treatment of patients with avoidant personality disorder.

____

____

6. Treatment for avoidant personality disorder is very similar to treatment for people with __________________ disorders such as social phobias.

B: Dependent Personality Disorder

1. Complete this table by giving an example of a behavior that illustrates each characteristic of dependent disorder listed.

Characteristic	*Example of behavior*
Submissive behavior	
Lack of self-confidence	*allow others to make important decisions for them*
Fear of separation	
Excessive need to be taken care of	
Extreme distress	

2. Key concerns for clinicians in the treatment of dependent patients include how to get them to accept __________________ for themselves, and what to do about the patient's ______________ or parents - who may be playing a role in the maintenance of dependent behaviors.

3. Psychodynamic therapists must inevitably work through the dependent patient's __________________ of dependency needs onto the therapist.

C: Obsessive-Compulsive Personality Disorder

1. People with obsessive compulsive personality disorder are preoccupied with orderliness, __________________, and mental and interpersonal ______________.

2. Complete this table by providing the usual result or outcome of each characteristic of obsessive-compulsive personality disorder listed.

Characteristic	Example of behavior
Fixation on organization and details	
High standards for self and others	*inability to delegate responsibility or to work in a team*
Fear of making mistakes	
Inflexible morals, ethics, and values	*judgmental attitude towards others; restricted expression of affection; stilted, superficial relationships*
Miserly behavior	

3. Describe the demographic characteristics of a typical person among the 1.0 to 1.7 percent of the population with an obsessive-compulsive personality disorder.

____

4. While about 20 percent of people diagnosed with obsessive-compulsive (anxiety) disorder also have an obsessive-compulsive personality disorder, no specific link has found empirical support. Complete these questions about this relationship.

a. The symptoms of the anxiety disorder are ego-______________, meaning they are unwanted, while the symptoms of the personality disorder are ego-______________, meaning the person rarely wishes to resist them.

b. The functioning of people with the __________________ disorder is more likely to be impaired.

5. Freudian theorists use the term _____ __________ to describe the person with obsessive-compulsive personality disorder; this term relates to the view that due to parent's harsh toilet training methods, these individuals try to contain anger and instincts to mess — leading to behavioral characteristics of orderliness and inhibition.

6. Cognitive theorists believe that illogical thinking processes, such as black-or-white ____________________ thinking , maintain the symptoms of people with obsessive-compulsive personality disorder.

IV: Personality Disorders: Dilemmas and Confusion

1. The personality disorders are misdiagnosed more often than any other category of disorders in the DSM-IV. List three reasons for these diagnostic difficulties.

a. Diagnostic criteria for the personality disorders consist of __________ traits rather than observable behaviors

b. There are __________________ in personality disorders within the same cluster.

c. A wide range of people are often diagnosed with the __________ personality disorder.

2. Describe and example of how diagnostic criteria for the personality disorders continue to change.

____

____

____

Practice multiple-choice questions for this chapter begin on page 296.

Chapter 19

Disorders of Childhood and Old Age

Chapter Organization

Chapter 19 focuses on the various disorders affecting children and the elderly. The mental dysfunction of both children and the elderly can be caused by a variety of factors, including stress, trauma, and biological abnormalities. Section I describes the disorders of childhood and adolescence. Section II covers the long-term disorders of autism and mental retardation that begin in childhood. Section III discusses the various disorders that can appear in later life, much as mood disorders and dementia.

Be sure to read through each section before completing the exercises for that section.

Exercises

I: Disorders of Childhood and Adolescence

1. About ______ of children and adolescents in the U.S. experience a diagnosable mental disorder.

2. ________________ with mental disorders outnumber ________________, which is interesting since the prevalence of disorders by gender is generally the opposite in adulthood.

3. What are two possible reasons for the gender shift described in Exercise #2?

a. ____

b. There are special and increased pressures placed on ________________ in Western society.

A: Childhood Anxiety Disorders

1. (Study Figure 19-1 on textbook page 601.) It has been suggested that the higher anxiety levels of children of racial minorities results from living in ________________, more deprived, or ________________ environments.

2. Like adults, children can suffer from specific phobias or ________________ phobias, or ________________ anxiety disorders.

3. Children who suffer from separation anxiety disorder experience ________________ anxiety whenever they are separated from ______________ or a parent.

4. Anxiety disorders in children can also develop as a result of some unique features of childhood. For each unique feature listed, give an example of something that might contribute to the development of an anxiety disorder.

a. *Compared to adults, children have few experiences with the world.*

____

b. *Children are highly dependent on and influenced by their parents.*

____

c. *Today's society exposes children to many frightening images and messages.*

____

5. In the treatment technique known as play therapy, children express their conflicts and feelings indirectly by playing with toys, drawing, and making up stories. What does the therapist do in play therapy?

____

____

B: Childhood Depression

1. Depression rates do not differ by gender before the age of 11, but by age 16, ________________ are twice as likely to suffer from it than the other gender.

2. Among the factors implicated in childhood depression that are similar to those implicated in adult depression are learned ____________________, loss, low norepinephrine activity, major life change, rejection, or ongoing ______________.

3. Successful treatments for childhood depression include combinations of ________________ therapy, social skills ____________________, and family therapy; however, the use of antidepressant drugs has not been clearly

C: Disruptive Behavior Disorders

1. In this table, summarize the characteristics and prevalence rates of the two types of disruptive behavior disorders listed.

Disorder	Characteristics	Prevalence
Oppositional defiant disorder		2–16% in children
Conduct disorder		

2. Children between the ages of 8 and 18 who break the law are often labeled ____________________ ____________________ by the legal system.

3. Give one example of a parental behavior that has been associated with the emergence of conduct disorders.

____

4. Treatment for conduct disorders is more effective with children under the age of ________, because disruptive behavior patterns stabilize as a child grows older.

5. Complete these statements regarding the various treatments for children with conduct disorders.

a. Even though the approaches involving family ______________________ appear to be the most effective in treating this disorder, its seems to succeed far better in changing a child's behavior in the home, than outside of it.

b. Out-of-home approaches such as school-based interventions and skill training (teaching the child to cope with ________________) have had only limited success.

c. Drug therapy has also been used to help control ____________________ outbursts in children with conduct disorders.

D: Attention-Deficit Hyperactivity Disorder

1. The different diagnoses of attention-deficit hyperactivity disorder (ADHD) involve behaving overactively and impulsively, and attending very poorly to tasks. If both of these areas of functioning are impaired in a child, the diagnosis is "ADHD, combined type." List the other two potential diagnoses.

____

2. Give one piece of evidence for a genetic factor in ADHD.

____

3. A popular biological theory of ADHD suggests that it is a form of minimal ________________ ________________, but this view has not been consistently supported by research.

4. Complete the questions relating to the drug treatment for children with ADHD.

a. The stimulant drug methylphenidate (Ritalin) is prescribed for 1–2 percent of school-age children and has a ____________________ effect.

b. Methylphenidate increases the ability of children to perform ________________ and to solve complex problems, and also controls ____________________ behavior.

5. Behaviorists use operant conditioning treatments that involve teaching parents to systematically ________________ appropriate behavior—a method that seems most effective when it is combined with ________________ therapy.

E: Elimination Disorders

1. Complete these questions regarding enuresis, the usually involuntary bed-wetting or wetting of one's clothes.

a. The child must be functioning at the age of at least ______ years before a diagnosis of enuresis is warranted.

b. Prevalence of enuresis ____________________ with age for both sexes.

c. A ____________________ event such as hospitalization, the birth of a sibling, or entrance into ____________________ can percipitate the resumption of bed-wetting even after the child has been dry prior to these events.

2. Describe the explanations for enuresis by theorists of the (a) psychodynamic, (b) family systems. (c) behavioral, and (d) biological perspectives.

a. *it is a symbol of other conflicts and thus a symptom of a more general disorder*

b. ______________________________

c. ______________________________

d. ______________________________

3. Study the top part of this diagram describing a classical conditioning approach to the treatment of enuresis, and then provide the appropriate components that are missing from the bottom part of the diagram.

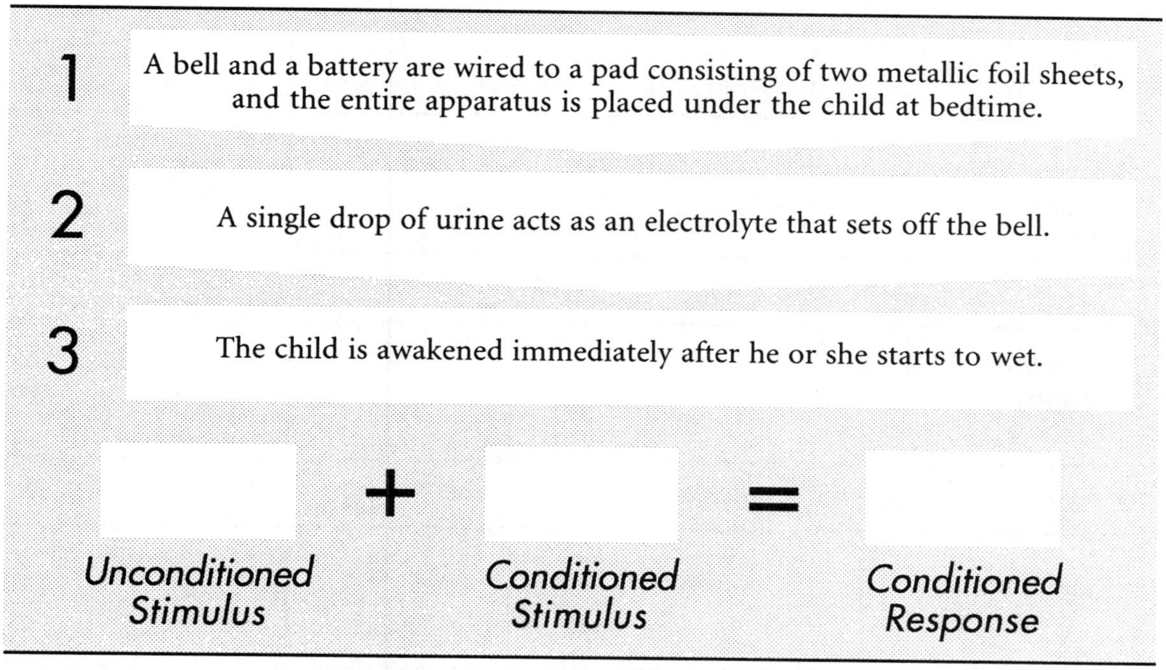

1 A bell and a battery are wired to a pad consisting of two metallic foil sheets, and the entire apparatus is placed under the child at bedtime.

2 A single drop of urine acts as an electrolyte that sets off the bell.

3 The child is awakened immediately after he or she starts to wet.

______	+	______	=	______
Unconditioned Stimulus		Conditioned Stimulus		Conditioned Response

F: Disorders of Learning, Communication, and Coordination

1. Complete this table that summarizes the disorders of learning, coordination, and communication delineated by DSM-IV.

Disorder	Characteristics	Prevalence
• *Learning Disorders*		
Mathematics disorder	*math skills are markedly below the child's intellectual capacity*	*1% of children*
Disorder of written expression		
Reading disorder, or dyslexia		
• *Developmental Coordination Disorder*		
Developmental coordination disorder		
• *Communication Disorders*		
Phonological disorder		
Expressive language disorder		
Mixed receptive/ expressive language disorder		
Stutter		

II: Long-Term Disorders that Begin in Childhood

A: Autistic Disorder

1. The symptoms of autistic disorder appear before the age of ______, and include extreme unresponsiveness to others, poor communication skills, and behave in a highly restricted and ____________________ manner.

2. Complete these statements that relate to the prevalence and course of autism.

a. Between 4 and 5 children out of ______________ are autistic.

b. Approximately ______ percent of autistic children are boys.

c. ______________ out of three autistic children remain severely impaired into adulthood.

3. Autistic children can display many behaviors that indicate a profound unresponsiveness to, and lack of interest in, other people (e.g., failure to make eye contact with parents). List three other examples of these behaviors.

____

____

4. About half of autistic children fail to speak or develop language skills. Those who do develop some level of verbal skills show many peculiarities in their communication patterns. Complete this description of these patterns.

a. In ____________________, the child repeats exact words and phrases spoken by others without comprehension.

b. An example of ____________________ ____________________ would be an autistic child saying "You want to watch TV now" when he or she wants to watch television.

c. Autistic children who are unable to name objects have ______________________________ ____________________, and might use odd or incorrect speech inflections.

Read this sample case, ignoring the numbers in brackets for now.

Sample Case
Jodie is a 10-year-old autistic girl. Her parents are constructing a deck on the back of their house, and Jodie is having great difficulty dealing with this change, even though her parents are careful to keep everything in the house the same.[1] Further, they are puzzled by the fact that Jodie does not seem to hear the extremely noisy electric saw but will turn her head if one of the workers drops a nail.[2] Most distressing is the fact that when Jodie is agitated, she will bang her head on the wall repeatedly[3], a behavior that prompted her parents to keep a protective helmet in the closet. Jodie's parents have noticed other unusual, but less frightening behaviors in their child. For example, Jodie insists on picking up "dust bunnies" from underneath furniture and keeping them in her pocket at all times.[4] She will take plates out of the kitchen cupboard, sit on the floor, and spin them around for hours on end.[5] Jodie also seems fascinated by twirling her fingers near her face, an activity that seems to have a calming affect when she is upset.[6]

5. As illustrated by this case, autistic children display very unusual responses to their environments. Describe each feature of autism listed in the table, and then match the feature with the appropriate example in sample case about Jodie.

Feature	Description of behavior	Example
Preservation of sameness	*autistic children are upset by changes in their environment or routine, and may respond to even minor changes by screaming or having tantrums*	*1.*
Attachment to objects		
Fascination with movement		
Self-stimulatory behaviors		
Self-injurious behaviors		
Disturbed and paradoxical perceptual reactions		

6. In conjunction with other treatments, ________________ drugs, and B^6 vitamins in combination with ________________ can increase attention and reduce self-stimulatory behaviors in autistic children.

7. ________________ therapies that try to encourage the development of a bond between the autistic child and his or her parents by providing a warm, and accepting environment, are less popular than in the past

8. What are the goals of behavioral interventions for autistic children?

____

____

9. ________________ techniques attempt to get autistic children to imitate appropriate behaviors of others, and ________________ conditioning strategies reinforce adaptive behaviors in the autistic child.

10. Many therapists use nonverbal means, such as sign language, to communicate with autistic individuals. Complete this table by describing the other types of communication training strategies therapists use.

Strategy	*Description of behavior*
Simultaneous communication	
Augmentative communication systems (general)	

3: Mental Retardation

1. About _____ percent of the population receives a diagnosis of mental retardation, and about three-fifths of those diagnosed are ________________.

2. A DSM-IV diagnosis of mental retardation is warranted if a person develops the following symptoms before the age of 18.

a. A person manifests subaverage general ________________ functioning (an IQ of ________ or below), and

b. displays concurrent deficits or impairments in present adaptive behavior—that is to say, they cannot meet set standards in at least two of these skill areas:

____

3. Complete this list of statements which relate to concerns about the validity of intelligence tests.

a. Correlations between IQ scores and ________________ performance range from 40 to .75, which is a less-than-perfect relationship.

b. Nor are scores highly correlated with job ________________ or social ________________, areas that would seem to rely on intellectual ability.

c. IQ tests seem to be socioculturally ________________, as evidenced by the fact that middle- to upper-socioeconomic-level households have an advantage because they are regularly exposed to the same kinds of tasks that the test measure.

d. IQ tests do not measure "street sense" which requires intellectual ability.

e. IQ tests are often given in a ________________ in which many cultural minorities are not fluent, resulting in artificially deflated IQ scores.

4. Diagnosticians use a cutoff score of 70 for mental retardation because people below that score tend to be deficient in their ________________ functioning.

5. Since adaptive behavior scales are not always accurate, clinicians must ________________ and judge the functioning level of each individual, and take into account the person's ________________ and community standards.

6. The most important, consistent difference between retarded and non-retarded people is that retarded people ________________ more slowly; the other differences relate to attention, ________________ memory, and language.

7. In this table, give the DSM-IV and the AAMR terms for levels of mental retardation based on IQ range. The AAMR identifications are based on the level of support needed.

IQ	DSM-IV	AAMR
50–70	*mild*	*intermittent*
35–69		
20–34		
below 20		

8. Complete this summary table by giving the percentages and characteristics of each listed group of mentally retarded individuals.

Group	Percentage	Characteristics
Moderate retardation (IQ 35–49)	*10% of retarded population*	
Severe retardation (IQ 20–34)		
Profound retardation (IQ under 20)		

9. Complete the statements about Down syndrome, the most common chromosomal disorder that leads to mental retardation.

a. About one in every __________ children are born with Down syndrome.

b. Children born to women over the age of _______, the incidence rises to 1 in 100.

c. Many older mothers undergo ______________________ to detect the presence of Down syndrome and other chromosomal abnormalities.

10. One of the three types of chromosomal abnormalities which may cause Down syndrome is named "trisomy 21." First describe trisomy 21 (a), and then list the other two types of chromosomal abnormalities linked to Down syndrome (b).

a. ____

b. ____

11. Complete these statements relating to other characteristics of Down syndrome.

a. IQ scores of people with the syndrome range from 35 to _______.

b. The __________________ process seems to occur more rapidly in people with Down syndrome; most show signs of __________________ as they approach age 40.

c. The "Down syndrome gene" is located on chromosome ______, the same one often associated with early __________________.

12. Fragile X syndrome is the second leading chromosomal cause of mental retardation, and occurs primarily in males. List three of its characteristics.

____

____

13. Metabolic disorders that result in retardation are caused by the pairing of two ____________ genes.

14. ____________ (PKU), the leading metabolic cause of retardation, is a result of an inability to convert phenylalanine into ____________, leading to accumulations of phenylalanine that convert into substances that poison the system, causing severe retardation.

15. Infants screened for PKU can develop normal ____________, as long as they are started on a low-phenylalanine diet before 3 months of age.

16. Complete these questions about Tay-Sachs disease.

a. It is most common in people of Eastern European ____________ ancestry.

b. It is caused by excessive accumulation of ____________ due to a missing enzyme in an infant's nerve cells.

17. Complete this table, by describing each prenatal cause of retardation and characteristics of children born with each problem.

Problem	Cause	Characteristics
Cretinism		
Fetal alcohol syndrome	*mother abuses alcohol during pregnancy*	
Rubella (German measles)		*mental retardation, heart disease, deafness, and other abnormalities*
Syphilis	*infection to mother during pregnancy*	
Birth-related causes	*a. anoxia (loss of oxygen)* *b. extreme prematurity*	*a.* *b.*

18. Serious head injuries, a result of an accident or abuse, can result in mental retardation. List other injury-related causes of mental retardation in children.

____

19. Complete the following statements about infections and multiple biological factors that can lead to mental retardation.

a. Effects such as brain damage and mental retardation caused by meningitis and ________________ can be prevented with early treatment.

b. Microcephaly, characterized by a small, ________________ shaped head, can be caused by a combination of hereditary, prenatal, birth, and postnatal factors.

c. Hydrocephalus is caused by an increase in cerebrospinal fluids resulting in head enlargement.

20. In this table, provide descriptions and supporting arguments for each of the two education environments/approaches for mentally retarded children,

Environment/ approach	*Description*	*Supporting argument*
Special education		
Mainstreaming		

I. Disorders of Later Life

A: Mood, Anxiety, and Substance Related Disorders

Complete these statements regarding the prevalence of depression in older adults.

________ percent of older adults meet the diagnostic criteria for depression.

Older people who have suffered the loss of a __________ (or some similar trauma) and who have serious ______________ illnesses have the highest rates of depression.

Older adults can be helped through a combination of __________ therapy and __________ medications.

Studies of older adults have found high correlations between measures of anxiety and __________ in this population, making differential diagnosis somewhat difficult for clinicians.

The prevalence rates for various anxiety disorders among the elderly are as follows: generalized anxiety disorders - 7 percent, __________ - up to 5 percent, __________ phobias - up to 12 percent, panic disorder - less than one percent, and obsessive-compulsive disorder - 3 percent.

B: Delirium and Dementia

1. Complete these questions about delirium, a condition often confused with dementia.

a. Delirium is a clouding of consciousness in which a person's awareness of the ______ becomes less clear and he or she experiences great difficulty ______, focusing attention, and maintaining a clear stream of thought.

b. One cause of delirium is substance intoxication. List three more.

______

2. Dementia is defined as a highly disruptive syndrome characterized by ______ impairment and other cognitive dysfunctions.

3. The prevalence of dementia increases with age, affecting from only 1 to 2 percent of those around age 65, and more than ______ percent of those over age 80.

Practice multiple-choice questions for this chapter begin on page 298.

Chapter 20

Law, Society, and the Mental Health Profession

Chapter Organization

In the previous ninteen chapters, you have learned about how psychologists describe and explain a vast array of mental disorders. You have also studied the techniques clinical practitioners use to treat people who suffer from psychological problems. In this final chapter of the textbook you will be examining the field of abnormal psychology from a different perspective. Specifically, the first three sections of Chapter 20 deal with the relationships between the mental health system—including clinical practitioners—and the legal system. The bulk of this chapter is focused on topics such as the insanity plea, criminal and civil commitment, and jury selection. Section IV takes a close look at ethical issues in clinical practice, and Section V explores the field of abnormal psychology in the context of business and economics. The final section of the textbook considers the human aspect of working in abnormal psychology.

Be sure to read through each section before completing the exercises for that section.

Exercises

I: Clinical Influences on the Criminal Justice System

United States courts hand out punishment on the assumption that individuals are responsible for their crimes and are capable of defending themselves in court.

1. If either part of the assumption described in the statement above cannot be made, then our courts will not find these individuals ____________________, nor will they incarcerate them in the ____________________ manner.

2. An individual brought before a U.S. court who is deemed mentally ____________________ does not meet the assumption described above.

3. There are two potential outcomes for people who are found guilty of a crime and who are deemed mentally unstable. Both involve "criminal commitment" in which the person is sent to a mental institution for treatment. Complete these questions regarding the two types of this kind of commitment.

a. When a person is deemed "mentally unstable at the time of their ____________________," the court finds them not guilty by reason of ____________________.

b. When a person is deemed "mentally unstable at the time of their ____________________," it is because they are not capable of understanding court procedures, or participating in their own defense.

A: Criminal Commitment and Insanity During the Commission of a Crime

1. Largely in reaction to the verdict of not guilty by reason of insanity in the trial of the would-be assassin of Ronald Reagan, federal law was shifted with regard to an insanity defense. What was the key change in the law?

____

2. Our tradition of a jury being able to acquit a defendant based on "insanity" goes back to sixteenth century Britain, with several important changes in that key definition coming along the way. Complete the following table which summarizes the tests of the insanity defense that have contributed to the current legal definition of "insanity."

• TEST	M'Naughten rule
Change in Criteria	*in addition to mental disorder, defendant must have been able to know right from wrong at the time of the crime*
• TEST	Irresistible impulse test
Change in Criteria	
• TEST	Durham test
Change in Criteria	
Criticisms or problems	*definition was too broad; it could include virtually any problem listed in DSM, and relied on contradictory opinions of clinicians*
• TEST	American Law Institute (ALI) guidlines
Change in Criteria	
Criticisms or problems	*in light of verdict in case of Reagan's would-be assassin, guidelines were seen as too lenient*

3. In 1983, the APA recommended that legal definitions of insanity retain only the ________________ criterion, essentially a return to the ________________ rule.

4. About two-thirds of defendants who are acquitted by reason of insanity qualify for a diagnosis of schizophrenia. Describe some of the characteristics of the typical person acquitted by reason of insanity.

____

One interesting criticism of the insanity defense lies in the seeming incompatibility between the assumptions, goals, and philosophy of the legal system and those of the behavioral sciences. Read this material closely and think very carefully about what the criticism is saying. Do you agree with it?

5. Other critics suggest that contradictory clinical testimony during trials points to a lack of professional consensus about mental health. What is one of the recent efforts to correct this impression that might be cited to counter this argument?

____

6. The widespread fear that the insanity defense systematically allows dangerous criminals to escape, would seem to be belied by the fact that less than one in ______ defendants in the U.S. is actually found not guilty by reason of insanity.

When defendants use the insanity plea, juries can find the defendant not guilty, acquit on the grounds of insanity, or they can find the defendant guilty. In some states, juries have another option—a verdict of "guilty but mentally ill." By rendering this verdict, juries are essentially saying, "We believe that you had a mental illness at the time of the crime, but we do not feel that this illness was sufficiently related to or responsible for the crime."

7. Complete the questions relating to the "guilty but mentally ill" verdict.

a. The verdict allows juries to ______________ a defendant, while trying to ensure that the person gets necessary mental health services.

b. Research findings indicate that juries who opt for this verdict deliver insanity acquittals less often.

c. Critics say that prisoners already have a right to mental health services, and that in truth, the verdict is no different than a ______________ verdict.

8. In what two circumstances do jurors seem to accept the "guilty with diminished capacity" defense

____

____

9. Complete these statements relating to "sex offender" statutes.

a. Sex offender statutes traditionally presume that people who ______________ commit certain sex crimes are mentally ill, and are thus labeled "mentally disordered sex offenders."

b. Give an important difference between the way the legal system views and deals with disordered sex offenders and those found not guilty by reason of insanity.

____

c. Give an important similarity between the way the legal system views and deals with disordered sex offenders and those found not guilty by reason of insanity.

____

3: Criminal Commitment and Incompetence to Stand Trial

. In order for a defendant to be found mentally competent to stand trial, they must demonstrate the following:

. An understanding of the ________________ and proceedings they are facing.

. Sufficient ability to ________________ with their attorney in preparing and conducting an adequate ________________.

. To ensure due process, all parties in a trial (including the judge) may recommend a ________________ ________________ for any defendant who exhibits signs of mental dysfunction.

. If a court rules that a defendant is not competent to stand trial at the present time, what happens to the defendant?

____

When a defendant is criminally committed, it is usually because he or she was deemed mentally incompetent, rather than found "not guilty by reason of insanity."

. What is the greatest inherent risk of competence provisions?

____

____

. Currently, incompetent defendants might be treated on an ________________ basis, particularly if the charge against him or her is a minor one.

I: Legal Influences on the Mental Health System

A: Civil Commitment

. Generally, individuals can be involuntarily committed if they are considered to be both in ________________ of treatment, and ________________ to themselves or to others.

. Complete the statements concerning the two principles upon which the state's authority to commit disturbed individuals rests.

. The principle of parens patriae allows the state to make decisions that promote the individual's best interests and protects him or her from ________________ or ________________.

. Police power enables the state to protect ________________ from harm that may be inflicted by a person who is homicidal or otherwise violent.

3. Apply the Supreme Court procedures set forth in *Parham v. J. R.* (1979) to the following situations. In each situation, describe the process the parents will have to follow in having their child committed.

a. *A mother and father become increasingly concerned about the bizarre behavior of their daughter who is a high school sophomore. Concerned that she might pose a danger to others, they seek to have her involuntarily committed.*

____

____

b. *The situation is the same as in Exercise a., except that the daughter is a 24-year-old woman, living on her own.*

____

____

4. Study and then complete this diagram describing how the current "minimum standard of proof" necessary for the commitment of adults was arrived at in the U.S. Supreme Court Case *Addington v. Texas.*

Background:

Before this case, every state had it's own standard of proof for commitment. The Texas standard was much more strict than many other states, (i.e., Texas required more proof of mental instability before commitment was permitted than most states).

The Case:

Addington's mother successfully petitioned to have her son committed by the state of Texas.

Addington appealed to the U.S. Supreme Court, arguing that the texas judgement should be overturned with a court mandate that the "beyond reasonable doubt" standard used in criminal cases should be applied to civil commitment cases.

Addington lost his appeal—the Supreme Court felt that because of "fallible psychiatric diagnoses," the criminal standard of "beyond a reasonable doubt" was too strict for civil commitment decisions.

The Minimum Standard of Proof:

With its ruling, the court established the "minimum standard of proof" for commitment cases based on the Texas standard.

Describe the "new" minimum standard of proof

5. In what instance might an emergency commitment (without due process) occur?

____

6. What is a "2-PCs" certification?

____

____

7. After researching the topic of violent behavior and people with mental disorders, John Monahan concluded that the rate of violent behavior among persons with ________________ mental disorders, particularly ____________________ disorders, is at least somewhat higher than in people without mental disorders.

8. One criticism of civil commitment is that the legal definitions of "mental illness" and "dangerous" are so vague that they could be applied to people simply deemed undesirable in some way. What is another criticism?

____

____

Since the Robinson v. California decision in 1962, civil commitment rates have declined. In part, this has been the result of the application of more specific criteria to commitment decisions. Read through the section on textbook pages 647 and consider the following question: "Do you think that the narrowing of civil commitment criteria ultimately benefits society or not?"

B: Protecting Patients' Rights

1. In *Wyatt v. Stickney* (1972) a federal court decision ordered Alabama to provide "adequate treatment" to all persons who had been involuntarily committed. In the ruling, specific services that Alabama was compelled to provide were spelled out. They included more therapists and better living conditions. List three more.

____

____

2. Complete the statements regarding two U.S. Supreme Court rulings regarding the right to treatment for those in mental health institutions.

a. *O'Conner v. Donaldson* (1975) established that the institutions must engage in periodic reviews of patients' cases, and that the state cannot confine a ________________ person who is capable of living successfully in the community.

b. In *Youngberg v. Romeo* (1982), the court again broadened the rights of mental patients by ruling that the involuntarily committed have a right to "reasonably ____________________ confinement conditions" and "reasonable care and safety."

c. However, the *Youngberg* ruling also cautioned courts against becoming too involved in the daily affairs of mental health institutions.

3. In order to ensure that mental health patients maintained their rights, Congress passed the ____________________ and ____________________ for Mentally Ill Individuals Act in 1986, which established systems with power to __________________ and legally pursue possible cases of patient abuse and neglect.

4. Most of the "right to refuse treatment" rulings have involved ________________ treatments such as psychosurgery, that are viewed as more intrusive, aversive, and ________________ than psychotherapy.

5. Some states have recognized a patient's right to refuse ____________, although the extent to which states allow such refusals varies greatly.

6. Complete the statements about court rulings regarding other rights of patients.

a. *Sounder v. Brennan* (1973) ruled that patients who perform work in mental institutions have a right to minimum wage (a right later narrowed to just patients in ________________ mental institutions).

b. *Stoner v. Miller* (1974) said that patients released from ________________ mental hospitals have a right to live in community "adult homes."

c. *Dixon v. Weinberger* (1975) said that individuals whose mental dysfunction was not severe enough to require ________________ in a mental institution have a right to treatment in less ________________ facilities.

The court decisions and legislative acts that you have studied represent some necessary safeguards against the violation of patients' rights. However, these guaranteed rights can also lead to undesirable outcomes for some patients.

7. Complete this exercise by summarizing the potential problems posed by each of these two patient rights.

a. *The mental patient's right to refuse medication*

____

____

b. *The mental patient's right to a minimum wage*

____

____

III: Other Clinical-Legal Interactions

All three subsections of this brief section will be covered in this part of the Workbook.

1. About ______ percent of psychiatrists have been sued; fewer ________________ and social workers are sued.

2. Lawsuits are filed against clinicians for many alleged acts of negligence or wrongdoing, including sexual activity with a client, improper termination of treatment, and negligence regarding a client who commits suicide. List three events that can precipitate claims against clinicians.

____

____

3. Read over the textbook description of the 1985 case involving an ultimately unsuccessful suit against an Alabama state hospital and its release of a patient who went on to commit a murder. What did investigators who later studied the hospital's release records conclude?

____

4. Clinicians known as "jury _______________" advise lawyers on juror selection and strategies on winning over jurors during trials.

5. In recent years, the legislative and judicial systems have given greater authority to psychologists—oftentimes authority that was once reserved for psychiatrists. Complete the statements regarding the increased privileges being given to psychologists.

a. Psychologists can receive reimbursements from _______________ for treating elderly and disabled people.

b. In some states psychologists can _______________ patients to state hospitals.

c. The authority of psychologists to _______________ _______________ is being examined by the Department of Defense and others.

IV: Self-Regulation: Ethics and the Mental Health Field

1. In your own words, complete the following list of obstacles or problems in clinicians' attempts to balance the goal of helping clients with the goal of respecting clients' rights.

a. Individual clients and therapists may have very different ideas about what constitutes "proper care" and how to best ensure client rights.

b. _______________

____

c. _______________

____

Mental health professionals regulate practices within their own profession by developing and enforcing ethical guidelines. The APA has developed extensive guidelines that promote the ethical practice of psychologists and calls for psychologists to guard against "factors that might lead to misuse of their influence."

2. Imagine that you are a member of an ethics board that fields questions posed by psychologists. Write responses based on APA ethical guidelines to the following questions.

> I have been ordered to testify in a legal case involving a client that I evaluated one year ago. What are the ethical guidelines I should attend to?

a. ______________________________

____

> I completed treatment with a client two months ago, and now I would like to ask her out for a date. Is this okay?

b. ______________________________

____

> Even though I don't know much about homosexuality, or about the issues that gay and lesbian people deal with, I would like to begin a therapy group for people who are in the process of "coming out" to friends and family. Any problem with me doing that?

c. ______________________________

____

> I was asked to appear on the Donahue show to help couples negotiate some areas of conflict. Am I allowed to do that?

d. ______________________________

____

> I am interested in what the APA says about ethical guidelines for the publication of research. What can you tell me?

e. ______________________________

____

3. Studies of therapists suggest that sexual misconduct among them is declining. What are two potential sources for this trend?

____

____

4. Confidentiality in therapy means that clinicians are obligated to refrain from disclosing information about their clients to other people. However, there are certain circumstances under which confidentiality might be compromised. List two of them below.

____

____

5. In an important 1967 case called *Tarasoff v. Regents of the University of California*, the California Supreme court declared that "the protective [client-therapist] privilege ends where the __________ __________ begins."

6. Surveys indicate that more than _____ percent of psychologists believe that breaking confidentiality is ethical in cases involving __________________, child abuse, or __________.

V: Mental Health, Business, and Economics

The two subsections of this section will be covered together in the Workbook.

1. Businesses often pay for programs conducted in occupational settings that are designed to help prevent and remedy psychological disorders in the workplace such as employee __________ programs and stress-reduction and __________ seminars.

2. The reason businesses pay for these programs is because they believe that they will save them money in the long run by preventing psychological problems from interfering with work performance. List some of the ways that untreated problems have cost businesses.

____

____

3. Although the number of people who need psychological services has increased __________, funding for services has increased only __________.

4. The growing economic role of private insurance companies has a significant effect on the way clinicians go about their work. Complete the following questions regarding ways in which that interaction has occurred.

a. Many insurance companies have developed __________ care systems which the insurance company often determines which therapists clients may use, as well as the __________ and the __________ of sessions.

b. Peer review systems have been instituted in which a panel of clinicians who work for the insurers may review a therapist's report of a client's treatment and recommend that ________________________ either be continued or terminated.

c. Many therapists and clients dislike peer reviews. List one of their criticisms.

____

VI: The Person Within the Profession

The main purpose of this final section of the textbook is to be to get you to think about how we view mental health care professionals. Keep in mind that the work clinicians do is influenced by their own personal strengths and weaknesses. As you will read in the textbook, many of them have themselves sought treatment for the same problems they are treating in others. (This may have something to do with the fact that so many therapists feel like "fakes" occasionally.) This is why it is important to consider the words of the textbook relating to the human context in which the study and practice of psychology exists: "Mental health researchers and clinicians are human beings, within a society of human beings, working to serve human beings."

Practice multiple-choice questions for this chapter begin on page 299.

Multiple-Choice Questions

Chapter 1

1. Mary dresses exclusively in men's clothes (including the underwear). This is an example of the feature of the definition of abnormality called
   a. distress
   b. deviance
   c. dysfunction
   d. danger to self or others

2. Rae, who is running for public office, seems to be developing a fear of crowds. To which aspect of the definition of abnormality is this example most relevant?
   a. distress
   b. deviance
   c. dysfunction
   d. danger to self or others

3. An eccentric person is likely to display all of the following except
   a. intelligence
   b. nonconformity
   c. noncompetitiveness
   d. disordered thinking

4. Some ancient societies practiced trephination, which consisted of
   a. blood letting
   b. removing a part of a patient's skull
   c. imposing social isolation on a sufferer
   d. a kind of exorcism practice by a shaman

5. During the middle ages, the dominant model of explanation for abnormal behavior was
   a. scientific
   b. humanistic
   c. philosophical
   d. demonological

6. The person now believed to be the founder of the modern study of psychopathology was
   a. Hippocrates
   b. Johann Weyer
   c. Philippe Pinel
   d. Sigmund Freud

7. The real beginning of the humane treatment of people with mental disorders began in
   a. Spain
   b. France
   c. England
   d. the United States

8. Which of the following is most consistent with the somatogenic view of mental illness
   a. hypnosis
   b. psychological disturbances can cause bodily ailments
   c. the symptoms of mental illness can be described and classified
   d. hysterical symptoms such as partial paralysis can be induced with hypnosis

9. The original developer of psychoanalysis was
   a. Josef Breuer
   b. Emil Kraepelin
   c. Sigmund Freud
   d. Ambroise-Auguste Liébault

10. Since the beginning of the deinstitutionalization movement in the 1950s
   a. the prescription of psychotropic drugs has significantly decreased
   b. the daily patient population in American mental hospitals has increased
   c. the number of violent crimes committed by mentally ill persons has doubled
   d. outpatient care has become the primary treatment for persons with psychological problems

Chapter 2

1. A psychologist doing research on anxiety studies a large and diversified group of anxious individuals in the hopes of understanding the phenomenon and developing a treatment. He is doing __________ research.
   a. case study
   b. nomothetic
   c. idiographic
   d. experimental

2. The data that Freud used to develop psychoanalysis came from the use of
   a. correlational studies
   b. experimental studies
   c. the case study method
   d. the nomothetic approach

3. Specifying abstract variables in terms of the procedures used to measure them is called
   a. measurement
   b. experimentation
   c. hypothesis testing
   d. operationalization

4. If a difference is judged statistically significant, that means that the
   a. result has external validity
   b. probability of a chance result is small
   c. difference was experimentally determined
   d. probability of the result being due to change is zero

5. Which of the following is a characteristic of longitudinal studies in general?
   a. There are repeated measurement of the participants.
   b. There is manipulation of a variable by the researcher.
   c. There is the use of blind or double-blind control procedures.
   d. There is the ability of repeated observations to allow the conclusion of causality.

6. Dr. Ramirez required half of a group of healthy volunteers to study a passage for 1 hour. The other half of the group read the passage once (5 minutes). When both groups were finished she administered a memory test to the participants who had studied for an hour and then to the participants who had just read the passage. She found that the participants who studied more remembered more. Which of the following was true?
   a. The results of the memory test were confounded.
   b. Study time and recall interval were confounded.
   c. She found that increased studying increased memory.
   d. The independent and dependent variables were confounded.

7. The principle behind random assignment is that
   a. placebo effects are eliminated from the study results
   b. every person in the population is equally likely to be selected
   c. it guarantees that the two groups will contain the same kinds of participants
   d. a participant is as likely to be in the control group as the experimental group

8. Which of the following is true of quasi-experiments?
   a. They allow a clear conclusion of causality.
   b. They employ random selection of subjects.
   c. They employ random assignment of subjects.
   d. The experimenters do not use random assignment.

9. One limitation of analogue studies is a potential lack of
   a. control
   b. external validity
   c. the placebo effect
   d. the design makes it difficult to rule out alternative explanations

10. Which of the following is not necessarily among the eight basic issues on which participants should be well informed?
    a. potential risks of the experiment
    b. the specific goals of the experiment
    c. what procedures will be used during the experiments
    d. that they are voluntarily participating in an experiment

Chapter 3

1. A paradigm is
    a. a specific law of behavior
    b. another name for a theory
    c. a set of the basic assumptions that organize ones's approach to an area under study
    d. a research study that determines the fundamental causes of a specific mental disorder

2. The originator of psychoanalysis was
    a. Jung
    b. Freud
    c. Breuer
    d. Charcot

3. Primary process thinking is characteristic of the
    a. id
    b. ego
    c. superego
    d. conscience

4. According to Freud's psychodynamic theory, the process of incorporating society's prohibitions into the personality is called
    a. learning
    b. catharsis
    c. introjection
    d. sublimation

5. According to Freud's psychodynamic theory, which of the following is an adult behavior that is characteristic of fixation at the phallic stage?
    a. aggression
    b. fear of intimacy
    c. extreme dependence
    d. extreme stubbornness

6. Focusing on past traumatic events, particularly from childhood, as causes of one's abnormal behavior is a major part of treatment in
   a. psychoanalysis
   b. cognitive therapy
   c. behavioral therapy
   d. biological treatment

7. Short-term psychodynamic therapies usually
   a. work well with alcoholics
   b. are best for severely disturbed patients
   c. require the therapist to be more confrontational
   d. demonstrate better outcome than longer traditional therapy

8. If you close your eyes and imagine biting into a big juicy sour lemon you are likely to salivate. The image of the lemon is the
   a. conditioned stimulus
   b. conditioned response
   c. unconditioned stimulus
   d. unconditioned response

9. Which of the following is a cognitive concept?
   a. behavior
   b. self-efficacy
   c. reinforcement
   d. unconditional positive regard

10. Carl Rogers is considered the pioneer of the
    a. behavioral model
    b. cognitive model
    c. existential theory
    d. humanistic theory

Chapter 4

1. In the past, psychological disorders with a known biological cause were called __________ mental disorders.
   a. organic
   b. physical
   c. structural
   d. functional

2. A part of the brain that is involved in memory is the
   a. amygdala
   b. basal ganglia
   c. hippocampus
   d. corpus callosum

3. Neural information gets from one neuron to another via
   a. a chemical messenger
   b. an electrical nerve impulse
   c. the movement of receptors across the synapse
   d. direct contact between an axon and a dendrite

4. When researchers look to see how many members of a family have a particular disorder they do a
   a. risk study
   b. case history
   c. longitudinal study
   d. family pedigree study

5. MAO inhibitors and the tricyclic drugs are used to treat
   a. anxiety
   b. depression
   c. schizophrenia
   d. antisocial personality

6. Which of the following is an antipsychotic drug?
   a. Xanax
   b. Prozac
   c. diazepam
   d. chlorpromazine

7. The point of describing mental disorders like windigo, susto, koro, and latah is that
   a. most culture-specific disorders have psychological causes
   b. abnormalities related to sexual issues are more prevalent in primitive cultures
   c. some patterns of abnormality are uniquely tied to a society's particular culture
   d. demonological treatments of abnormality are prevalent in non-Western cultures

8. What is the type of therapy in which a psychologist treats several unrelated clients together?
   a. psychodrama
   b. group therapy
   c. couple therapy
   d. a self-help group

9. The divorce rate in the United States and Canada is about
   a. 10%
   b. 25%
   c. 50%
   d. 75%

10. Which of the following would be an example of tertiary prevention of mental health problems?
    a. establishing a suicide hot line
    b. building a sheltered workshop where psychiatric outpatients can work
    c. advocating for establishing a day care center for neighborhood children
    d. consulting with teachers to identify children who may benefit from services

Chapter 5

1. In order to understand a client's problems, a clinician uses a process that includes
    a. assessment and diagnosis
    b. projective testing and interviewing
    c. structured observation and classification
    d. behavioral analysis and functional analysis

2. If a test accurately measures what it claims to measure, that test is said to have
    a. validity
    b. reliability
    c. concurrence
    d. standardization

3. A clinician who looks for information concerning assumptions, interpretations, and coping skills during an interview probably takes the __________ approach.
    a. cognitive
    b. biological
    c. behavioral
    d. humanistic

4. Current users of the Rorschach now pay attention mostly to the
    a. style of the response
    b. affect of the responder
    c. thematic content of the response
    d. symbolic meaning of the response

5. Simone is afraid of people and not at all assertive. Which MMPI-2 scale would she most likely score high on?
    a. schizophrenia
    b. psychasthenia
    c. social introversion
    d. psychopathic deviate

6. The PET scan makes a picture of the brain
    a. using X-rays that are projected at several different angles
    b. that reflects the degree of activity of the various areas scanned
    c. that reflects the magnetic properties of the atoms in the cells scanned
    d. using a recording of the electrical impulses produced by the neurons in the brain

7. One of the drawbacks of clinical observation is that the very presence of an observer might influence the behavior of the subject being observed. This is called
   a. reactivity
   b. observer bias
   c. observer drift
   d. external validity

8. Who developed the first influential classification system for abnormal behavior?
   a. Sigmund Freud
   b. Emil Kraepelin
   c. the American Psychiatric Association
   d. the American Psychological Association

9. What does Axis V include?
   a. a global assessment of functioning
   b. any relevant general medical condition
   c. any relevant psychosocial or environmental problem
   d. vivid clinical syndromes that typically cause significant impairment

10. What disorder would most likely be treated by both a psychotherapist and a pharmacotherapist?
   a. depression
   b. anorexia nervosa
   c. premature ejaculation
   d. borderline personality

Chapter 6

1. The most common mental disorders in the United States are the
   a. anxiety disorders
   b. conversion disorders
   c. personality disorders
   d. dissociative disorders

2. The aspect of response to stress that is cognitive is
   a. the fear
   b. the stressor
   c. the stress response
   d. primary appraisal

3. Megan loves the roller coaster, bungee jumping, skiing, and hang gliding. These activities scare her husband silly. This difference reflects a difference in
   a. trait anxiety
   b. state anxiety
   c. personality anxiety
   d. generalized anxiety

4. The Freudian view is that generalized anxiety disorder appears when a person is overwhelmed by
   a. realistic anxiety
   b. neurotic anxiety
   c. disintegration anxiety
   d. an ego defense mechanism

5. Anxiety disorders develop as a consequence of irrational or maladaptive assumptions or automatic thoughts that influence a person's understanding of life events. This illustrates which perspective?
   a. cognitive
   b. existential
   c. behavioral
   d. psychodynamic

6. The benzodiazepines seem to exert their anti-anxiety effect by
   a. facilitating GABA at receptor sites
   b. blocking serotonin at receptor sites
   c. blocking acetylcholine at receptor sites
   d. facilitating norepinephrine at receptor sites

7. TJ is terrified of going into crowded stores or anywhere else, unless she is accompanied by her sister. A diagnostician would probably diagnose her behavior as
   a. agoraphobia
   b. a social phobia
   c. a general phobia
   d. generalized anxiety disorder

8. According to the behavioral view, phobias may develop when a person learns a fear response to a specific object by the process of
   a. repression
   b. reinforcement
   c. operant conditioning
   d. classical conditioning

9. The most effective treatment of specific phobias seems to be
   a. cognitive therapy
   b. biological therapy
   c. behavioral therapy
   d. psychodynamic therapy

0. Participant modeling has been found to be most effective in treating
   a. agoraphobia
   b. social phobias
   c. specific phobias
   d. generalized anxiety disorder

Chapter 7

1. Mitral valve prolapse and thyroid disease are occasionally mistaken for
   a. agoraphobia
   b. panic attack
   c. a specific phobia
   d. generalized anxiety disorder

2. The apparent mechanism of action of the drugs useful in treating panic attacks is their ability to
   a. block norepinephrine
   b. block the action of serotonin
   c. mimic the action of serotonin
   d. restore the activity of norepinephrine

3. Max's physician had him breathe deeply and often until he was lightheaded. Max became very anxious. This procedure describes
   a. meditation
   b. anxiety sensitivity
   c. systematic desensitization
   d. a biological challenge test

4. Most studies on obsessions and compulsions indicate that
   a. obsessions and compulsions generally occur together
   b. there is no relation between obsessions and compulsions
   c. obsessions generally occur in the absence of compulsions
   d. compulsions generally occur in the absence of obsessions

5. Psychodynamic theorists believe that the ego defense mechanisms of isolation, undoing, and reaction formation are particularly common in people with
   a. mood disorders
   b. personality disorders
   c. dissociative disorders
   d. obsessive-compulsive disorders

6. According to the cognitive explanation of obsessive-compulsive disorder, the elimination or avoidance of repulsive and stressful thoughts is known as
   a. neutralizing
   b. ego defense reactions
   c. covert-response prevention
   d. constructing a strict code of acceptability

7. The placebo effect in drug studies of obsessive-compulsive disorder is about
   a. 0
   b. 5 %
   c. 25 %
   d. 60 %

8. The age of a female most likely to be raped is
   a. under 11 years
   b. between 11 and 17 years old
   c. between 17 and 29 years old
   d. over 29 years old

9. The rage and guilt that is part of the post-traumatic stress syndrome exhibited by many Vietnam veterans has been successfully treated with
   a. antianxiety drugs
   b. antidepressant drugs
   c. a form of group therapy
   d. the exposure and response prevention procedure

10. What is the first aim of disaster mental health professional?
   a. survival
   b. dealing with acute stress disorder
   c. normalizing people's response to the disaster
   d. diffusing anxiety, anger, and frustration regarding the disaster

Chapter 8

1. What role does gender play in the incidence of depression?
   a. Gender is unrelated to the incidence of depression.
   b. Men are twice as likely to suffer from depression as women.
   c. Women are twice as likely to suffer from depression as men.
   d. Depression is more frequent in women but more severe in men.

2. Which of the following would be a cognitive symptom of depression?
   a. lack of desire to eat
   b. a negative view of oneself
   c. experiences of sadness and anger
   d. staying in bed for hours during the day

3. To receive a diagnosis of major depressive episode, seasonal, the individual must display
   a. repeated episodes of depression
   b. mood fluctuation during the year
   c. motor immobility or excessive activity
   d. onset within four weeks of giving birth

4. What structure is responsible for secreting cortisol?
   a. pineal gland
   b. hypothalamus
   c. adrenal glands
   d. pituitary gland

5. Which theoretical perspective employs the concept of "symbolic loss" to explain depression?
   a. cognitive
   b. humanistic
   c. existential
   d. psychoanalytic

6. Who is the person who developed a behavioral theory of depression based on insufficient positive reinforcement?
   a. Beck
   b. Freud
   c. Seligman
   d. Lewinsohn

7. Which of the following statements illustrates Beck's concept of overgeneralization?
   a. I'm not popular. I'm not popular. I'm not popular.
   b. I couldn't remember the capital of New York, I'm really stupid.
   c. If I take the test, I might fail and my parents would not love me.
   d. My life is a real downer, I am miserable and it won't get any better ever.

8. Every time Sophie's homework is not done her teacher punishes her. When she does it she gets a low grade. If she complains about never being recognized for trying she is given detention. This is an example of a set of conditions that, over the long haul, is most likely to lead to
   a. depression
   b. schizophrenia
   c. anxiety disorder
   d. bipolar disorder

9. What critical feature does bipolar II have that is different from bipolar I?
   a. hypomania
   b. mild depression
   c. major depression
   d. full manic episodes

10. Some researchers believe that symptoms of mania can be due to
    a. excessive serotonin
    b. depleted levels of norepinephrine
    c. sodium ions increasing a neuron's resistance to firing
    d. abnormal function of proteins that transport sodium ions

Chapter 9

1. What disorder do psychodynamic therapists believe that unconscious grieving over real or imagined loss produces?
   a. conversion disorder
   b. unipolar depression
   c. counter-transference
   d. schizotypal personality disorder

2. Research with college students found that these students
   a. overestimate the happiness of others
   b. expect that most elderly people are generally happy
   c. overestimate the number of people who are unhappy
   d. have a generally accurate impression of the degree of happiness of others

3. Which of the following is most like the application of reinforcement and extinction techniques to the treatment of depression?
   a. psychoanalysis
   b. interpersonal psychotherapy
   c. personal effectiveness training
   d. the contingency management approach

4. George is depressed and has sought therapy. His cognitive therapist is most likely to
   a. test the reality behind his thoughts
   b. smile at him only when he says positive things
   c. ask him to describe how he talks to his wife and friends
   d. ask him how he felt when his mother did not hold him any more

5. Johnny has recently entered a large university and lately has been feeling depressed. He came from a very small high school with 35 seniors in his graduating class. He knew everyone and was a class leader. He feels lost amid the crowds here. According to the premises of interpersonal psychotherapy his depression stems from
   a. a grief reaction
   b. an interpersonal conflict
   c. an interpersonal role transition
   d. unrealistic expectations regarding his place in his new school

6. Why was the use of insulin, camphor, or metrazol to induce convulsions or comas in mentally ill people discontinued?
   a. It did not work.
   b. It was expensive.
   c. It was dangerous.
   d. The treatment was too difficult to manage.

7. What disorders are monoamine oxidase (MAO) inhibitors and tricyclics most effective in treating?
   a. agoraphobia
   b. schizophrenia
   c. bipolar disorders
   d. unipolar depression

8. There is some evidence that tricyclic antidepressant medications help depressed people feel bette by
   a. raising monoamine oxidase (MAO) activity
   b. lowering norepinephrine and serotonin activity
   c. increasing the level of norepinephrine and serotonin synthesis
   d. increasing the availability of norepinephrine and serotonin in the synapse

9. Which therapy appears to produce the longest-lasting improvements in depressed patients?
   a. cognitive therapy
   b. biological therapy
   c. behavioral therapy
   d. psychodynamic therapy

10. Which intervention is the single most effective current treatment for bipolar depression?
   a. ECT
   b. lithium
   c. tranquillizers
   d. antidepressant medication

Chapter 10

1. Self-destructive behavior is seen in animals other than humans. Theorists suggest that
   a. the human act of suicide is not the only example of beings knowingly ending their ow lives
   b. animals perform self-destructive behavior for reasons similar to those that motivat human suicide
   c. animals sometimes perform self-destructive behaviors that help the species survive in th long run
   d. there are few, if any, instances of animals that perform behaviors that lead directly to thei own deaths

2. A suicide note expresses hostility directed at the self and interpersonal problems. The writer i most likely
   a. younger than 40
   b. 40 to 49 years old
   c. 50 to 59 years old
   d. over 60 years of age

In Edwin Shneidman's taxonomy of people who end their own lives intentionally, those who do not believe that their self-inflicted death will mean the end of their existence are called
a. death darers
b. death seekers
c. death ignorers
d. death initiators

About what percent of people who successfully commit suicide leave suicide notes?
a. 5%-10%
b. 20%-30%
c. 40%-45%
d. 55%-60%

Why do more men than women commit suicide?
a. men use more lethal means
b. men make more attempts at suicide
c. men are more likely to be death initiators
d. women are more likely to be death ignorers

An important social factor that correlates with suicide rate is
a. death rate
b. divorce rate
c. unemployment rate
d. teenage pregnancy rate

What is the term for the belief that a current negative mood and situation cannot be changed?
a. anxiety
b. sadness
c. hopelessness
d. dichotomous thinking

The arguments in favor of a person's right to commit suicide generally focus on the issue of
a. role conflict
b. serious illness
c. occupational stress
d. abusive environment

According to Durkheim's sociological theory of suicide, egoistic suicide occurs when
a. persons sacrifice themselves for their society
b. persons have a close friend who commits suicide
c. persons have a history of few ties to their society
d. individuals experience a sudden change in their relationship to society

Which neurotransmitter has been linked to suicidal behavior when levels are low?
a. GABA
b. serotonin
c. dopamine
d. norepinephrine

Chapter 11

1. People who feign illness because they like "being sick" are diagnosed with a __________ disorde
   a. factitious
   b. somatoform
   c. psychogenic
   d. psychophysiological

2. The psychogenic disorders called hysterical disorders include
   a. malingering
   b. factitious disorder
   c. conversion disorder
   d. Munchausen syndrome

3. Which of the following is a correct pairing?
   a. conversion disorder -- heart disease
   b. factitious disorder -- somatization disorder
   c. somatoform disorder -- conversion disorder
   d. psychophysiological disorder -- "glove anesthesia"

4. A person who interprets minimal symptoms as signs of serious physical problems and suffers sig nificant anxiety and depression as a result, might be diagnosed with a
   a. conversion disorder
   b. somatoform pain disorder
   c. hysterical somatoform disorder
   d. preoccupation somatoform disorder

5. Preoccupation somatoform disorders are usually explained by theorists in the same way that the explain
   a. simple phobias
   b. anxiety disorders
   c. personality disorders
   d. dissociative disorders

6. Teresa was examined for her arm paralysis (conversion disorder). Her physician brought her in his consultation room and carefully explained the etiology of her paralysis (he made it up). H told her that this serious disorder would run its course and "heal itself" in about a month. Th therapy was based on
   a. insight
   b. suggestion
   c. confrontation
   d. reinforcement

7. What is angina pectoris?
   a. a heart problem
   b. a headache problem
   c. a breathing problem
   d. a blood pressure problem

8. What are the characteristics of someone with a Type A personality?
   a. calm, patient, and tolerant
   b. cold, withdrawn, and intolerant
   c. impatient, easily frustrated, and aggressive
   d. warm, outgoing, with high frustration tolerance

9. What did Hans Selye describe as a way of understanding the body's response to stressors?
   a. behavioral medicine
   b. the Type A personality
   c. the disregulation model
   d. the general adaptation syndrome

10. The white blood cells that produce protein molecules that bind to a specific antigen and prevent it from causing infection are called
    a. B-cells
    b. antibodies
    c. killer T-cells
    d. helper T-cells

Chapter 12

1. The relentless pursuit of thinness by starving to lose weight is called
   a. obesity
   b. obsession
   c. anorexia nervosa
   d. bulimia nervosa

2. The person who will be anorexic usually starts out
   a. underweight
   b. quite a bit overweight
   c. just to lose a little weight
   d. always with normal weight

3. One reason men are less likely to suffer from anorexia than women is the cultural stereotype that the "perfect" male body is
   a. thin
   b. tall
   c. muscular
   d. much more variable than for women

4. People who display anorexia nervosa usually display
   a. mania
   b. a clinical depression
   c. a preoccupation with food
   d. generalized anxiety disorder

5. For people with bulimia nervosa, binge episodes are often preceded by feelings of
   a. mania
   b. control
   c. high tension
   d. guilt and depression

6. In contrast to people suffering from anorexia nervosa, individuals suffering from bulimia nervosa are
   a. less concerned with food
   b. less likely to realize that they have a problem
   c. more likely to realize that they have a problem
   d. equally likely to realize that they have a problem

7. According to a survey of women in sports, the weight-control method that is most likely to be used/abused by female athletes in general is
   a. using diet pills
   b. using a diuretic
   c. using a laxative
   d. induce vomiting

8. Activation of the ____________ appears to produce hunger.
   a. thalamus
   b. lateral hypothalamus
   c. anterior hypothalamus
   d. ventromedial hypothalamus

9. Every time that Janie eats a reasonable meal she gets access to a telephone in her room to talk to her friends. If she eats poorly or not at all there is no phone. This procedure in the treatment of anorexia patients illustrates
   a. cognitive therapy
   b. operant conditioning
   c. sociocultural therapy
   d. changing interactions within the family

10. The prognosis for recovery from anorexia nervosa is worse as a function of
   a. the length of time in treatment
   b. amount of weight lost before treatment
   c. the weight of the patient at the onset of treatment
   d. the amount of weight gained by the patient during treatment

Chapter 13

1. Which of the following is not a characteristic of simple substance abuse?
   a. excessive reliance on a drug
   b. physical dependence on a drug
   c. excessive and chronic use of a drug
   d. the possibility of damage to family and social relationships

2. The legal limit for blood alcohol in the operator of a motor vehicle is .10 in most states. How many cans of beer would a 100 lb. female need to consume in an hour to be legally drunk (for purposes of driving)?
   a. a little over 1
   b. a little over 2
   c. a little over 4
   d. at least 4

3. How long does it take to fully sober up, that is to get all the alcohol out of your body, after a single beer?
   a. about 1 hour
   b. about 3 hours
   c. about 5 hours
   d. about 8 hours

4. Guessing to fill in memory lapses is a symptom of the condition called
   a. delirium tremens
   b. alcohol intoxication
   c. Korsakoff's syndrome
   d. withdrawal from opioids

5. Death by heroin overdose is often due to
   a. respiratory failure
   b. neuronal breakdown
   c. cirrhosis of the liver
   d. a drop in blood sugar levels

6. Which of the following are associated with the action of cocaine?
   a. endorphins and dopamine
   b. GABA and norepinephrine
   c. endorphins and norepinephrine
   d. dopamine, norepinephrine, and serotonin

7. Gina was sitting in her living room when she suddenly began experiencing the same pretty wavy visions as she did in her last trip two years ago. This is an example of
   a. a memory
   b. a flashback
   c. LSD psychosis
   d. a withdrawal symptom

8. According to psychodynamic theory, substance abuse develops when parents fail to fulfill a child's need for
   a. discipline
   b. nurturance
   c. dependence
   d. independence

9. Research on the efficacy of psychodynamic therapy for substance use disorders has found it to be
   a. detrimental to patients
   b. not particularly effective
   c. more effective than Alcoholics Anonymous
   d. effective in encouraging alternatives to drug taking

10. The reason there has been a reawakening of interest in methadone maintenance as a means of managing heroin addiction is
   a. that nothing else seems to work
   b. fear of AIDS from shared needles
   c. the development of a new "less addictive" substitute drug
   d. the increase in support for such programs because of federal grants

Chapter 14

1. Sexual dysfunction can occur during all of the following phases except
   a. desire
   b. orgasm
   c. arousal
   d. resolution

2. In females, the uterus lowers during which phase of the sexual response cycle?
   a. desire
   b. arousal
   c. orgasm
   d. resolution

3. Which of the following is the most common female sexual dysfunction?
   a. vaginismus
   b. dyspareunia
   c. sexual aversion
   d. hypoactive sexual desire

4. Which of the following drugs increases sexual drive at a low level and decreases it at higher levels?
   a. alcohol
   b. antidepressants
   c. antianxiety drugs
   d. antipsychotic drugs

5. Samuel experienced a period of high stress during which he was unable to perform sexually. Thereafter, he was detached and apprehensive during sexual activity and unable to perform. Samuel is displaying
   a. sexual frustration
   b. performance anxiety
   c. hypoactive sexual desire
   d. organically induced male erectile disorder

6. In a study on female orgasm, women who had higher rates of orgasm
   a. were more aggressive than other women
   b. behaved in a stereotypically "feminine" way
   c. had more affectionate parents than other women
   d. were more passive in their behavior than other women

7. A major component of sex therapy is
   a. hormone therapy
   b. elimination of performance anxiety
   c. relieving depression about the symptoms
   d. identifying who is responsible for the problem

8. Paraphiliacs treated by clinicians are usually
   a. male
   b. young
   c. female
   d. ordered into treatment by the court

9. During which period does frotteurism typically develop?
   a. adolescence
   b. early adulthood
   c. middle adulthood
   d. late adulthood

10. One characteristic of transsexuals is that they often feel
   a. heterosexuality is abnormal
   b. angry and exploited by others
   c. they were born the wrong sex
   d. they underwent a sex-change operation during childhood

Chapter 15

1. The term dementia preaecox what we now call schizophrenia, was coined by
   a. Eugen Bleuler
   b. Emil Kraepelin
   c. Benedict Morel
   d. Sigmund Freud

2. A person with the disorder called congenital generalized hypertrichosis would be characterized as
   a. psychotic
   b. animal like
   c. schizophrenic
   d. covered with hair

3. Neologisms may be displayed by people suffering from
   a. depression
   b. schizophrenia
   c. Korsakoff's syndrome
   d. anxiety-based disorders

4. The area of the brain that is most involved in language production is
   a. Broca's area
   b. Wernicke's area
   c. the left temporal lobe
   d. inactive during auditory hallucinations

5. Premorbid functioning refers to a schizophrenic person's functioning
   a. just prior to death
   b. during early childhood
   c. prior to recovery from the disorder
   d. prior to the appearance of the disorder

6. Type I schizophrenia is associated with
   a. structural abnormalities in the brain
   b. biochemical abnormalities in the brain
   c. poorer prior adjustment and premorbid functioning
   d. both structural and biochemical brain abnormalities

7. Chromosomal mapping studies on families in Iceland and England found abnormalities on which chromosome(s)?
   a. 5
   b. 9
   c. 18
   d. X & Y

8. Donald has a terribly flat affect. He does not move, smile, or want anything. His schizophrenia is most likely related to
   a. serotonin
   b. dopamine
   c. acetylcholine
   d. norepinephrine

9. According to the __________ perspective, schizophrenia is a result of extreme regression and attempts by the ego to reassert control.
   a. cognitive
   b. existential
   c. behavioral
   d. psychodynamic

10. According to the double-bind hypothesis, a person who is repeatedly exposed to internally contradicting messages may develop schizophrenia if he or she adopts a strategy of
   a. ignoring the primary communication
   b. responding only to congruent communications
   c. asking for clarification about the communication
   d. alternating attention to the primary communication and to the metacommunication

Chapter 16

1. What French physician is credited for beginning the movement toward more humane and moral treatment of mental patients?
   a. Henri Laborit
   b. Phillippe Pinel
   c. Pierre Deniker
   d. Maxwell Jones

2. The creation of a therapeutic community was a feature of
   a. moral therapy
   b. milieu therapy
   c. a token economy
   d. sociocultural therapy

3. What is the purpose of a leveled token economy?
   a. to keep patients interested in tasks
   b. to constantly upgrade the skills of the patient
   c. to make the patients more manageable for hospital staff
   d. to match the level of requirements to the capabilities of the patient

4. Which of the following are antipsychotic medications?
   a. tricyclics
   b. phenothiazines
   c. benzodiazepines
   d. MAO inhibitors

5. Which of the following is least likely to be relieved by an antipsychotic drug?
   a. delusions
   b. flat affect
   c. hallucinations
   d. bizarre behavior

6. The neuroleptic side effect characterized by involuntary muscular contractions and bizarre and uncontrollable movements is called
   a. dystonia
   b. akathisia
   c. tardive dyskinesia
   d. neuroleptic malignant syndrome

7. All other things being equal, which of the following patients appears most likely to develop tardive dyskinesia from taking a neuroleptic?
   a. a male
   b. a female
   c. a person who displays flatness of affect
   d. almost all patients who take neuroleptics for an extended period

8. Which of the following is most likely to help patients with schizophrenia?
   a. Haldol
   b. Clozapine
   c. psychotherapy
   d. the phenothiazines

9. Which symptom makes a schizophrenic person an unsuitable patient for conventional psychotherapy?
   a. flat affect
   b. loss of volition
   c. tardive dyskinesia
   d. formal thought disorders

10. The trend in treatment for people with schizophrenia since the 1960s has been towards
    a. more inpatient psychotherapy
    b. short-term hospitalization and community based services
    c. an increase in the hospital's use of medication to manage schizophrenia
    d. using more individual psychotherapy with medicated patients prior to release from the hospital

Chapter 17

1. Karen experienced a mugging and robbery in which her prized Siamese cat was kidnapped. Eventually the cat was found and returned. However, she was able to recall only certain events that occurred between the attack and the safe return of her cat, such as conversations with friends and phone calls from the police. This is a classic example of
   a. selective amnesia
   b. localized amnesia
   c. continuous amnesia
   d. generalized amnesia

Cameron had the traumatic experience of seeing his wife run over by a truck. Two days later, he neither remembers this event nor who he is. He ends up in another town working in a fast-food restaurant under a new name and identity. His overall reaction would probably be diagnosed as

a. amnesia
b. displacement
c. dissociative fugue
d. multiple personality

What event most often precipitates the onset of dissociative identity disorder?

a. sexual abuse
b. physical abuse
c. personal stress
d. natural disasters

What has been found out about the subpersonalities of people with multiple personalities?

a. They have similar abilities to one another.
b. They differ in age and family history but not gender or race.
c. They rarely exhibit a unique pattern of physiological responses.
d. They differ from one another in age, sex, race, and family history.

Glenda experiences a horrifying event. She lets her mind drift to other subjects, reducing her anxiety. She does this more often, and each time the behavior is reinforced by the reduction in anxiety. This pattern may be used by behaviorists to describe the development of

a. mood disorders
b. anxiety disorders
c. personality disorders
d. dissociative disorders

Self-hypnosis has been offered as an explanation for

a. personality disorders
b. dissociative disorders
c. schizophrenic disorders
d. impulse control disorders

Which class of drugs have been used to treat dissociative amnesia and fugue?

a. barbiturates
b. antipsychotics
c. antidepressants
d. antianxiety drugs

Which of the following structures is embedded under the temporal lobes?

a. thalamus
b. hippocampus
c. hypothalamus
d. mammillary bodies

9. Symptoms of the middle stage of Alzheimer's disease include
   a. denial of symptoms
   b. anger about symptoms
   c. indifference to symptoms
   d. anxiety or depression about symptoms

10. On autopsy a brain is seen to have an extraordinary number of neurofibrillary tangles and senil plaques. What did the person most likely have?
   a. presenile delirium
   b. Alzheimer's disease
   c. multiple-infarct dementia
   d. Jakob-Creutzfeldt disease

Chapter 18

1. An inflexible pattern of inner experience and outward behavior that deviates markedly from th expectations of one's culture is called a
   a. neurosis
   b. fugue state
   c. personality trait
   d. personality disorder

2. In a study of role-playing, subjects with paranoid personality disorder generally responded tc ambiguous behavior with
   a. anger
   b. confusion
   c. withdrawal
   d. confrontation

3. A lack of interest in sexual behavior is likely to be a feature of the
   a. schizoid personality disorder
   b. paranoid personality disorder
   c. antisocial personality disorder
   d. dependent personality disorder

4. The symptom of illusions displayed by many schizotypal patients involves
   a. loose associations
   b. sensing an external force or presence
   c. the belief that unrelated events pertain to them
   d. conversing in a vague manner and making inappropriately elaborate statements

5. What childhood disorder places a person at risk for developing antisocial personality disorder as an adult?
   a. autism
   b. conduct disorder
   c. childhood depression
   d. generalized anxiety disorder

6. Which disorder is most likely to accompany borderline personality disorder in a woman?
   a. a mood disorder
   b. conduct disorder
   c. attention deficit disorder
   d. antisocial personality disorder

7. People who are diagnosable with histrionic personality disorder are somewhat unusual compared to those with other personality disorders in that they
   a. are unhappy
   b. tend to seek treatment
   c. display strange behavior
   d. behavior in a maladaptive way

8. The avoidant personality disorder is one of the
   a. odd personality disorders
   b. Axis I personality disorders
   c. anxious personality disorders
   d. dramatic personality disorders

9. Decision making is a particular problem for the person who suffers from
   a. borderline personality disorder
   b. dependent personality disorder
   c. narcissistic personality disorder
   d. obsessive-compulsive personality disorder

10. Max spends so much time organizing his attack on the problem that he never gets to work on the problem. This is a habitual pattern with him. His behavior is a symptom of
   a. avoidant personality disorder
   b. antisocial personality disorder
   c. dependent personality disorder
   d. obsessive-compulsive personality disorder

Chapter 19

1. Compared to men, women are
   a. less likely to be well adjusted
   b. much more likely to commit suicide
   c. more likely to have a diagnosable psychological disorder
   d. somewhat less likely to have a diagnosable psychological disorder

2. Threats of suicide are most common in children suffering from
   a. depression
   b. generalized anxiety
   c. disruptive behavior disorder
   d. attention-deficit disorder with hyperactivity

3. The development of juvenile delinquency appears to be closely tied to problems in
   a. socioeconomic class
   b. attention deficit disorder
   c. parent-child relationships
   d. parental monitoring of child behaviors

4. The drugs that are sometimes helpful for children with attention-deficit hyperactivity disorder are
   a. stimulant drugs
   b. antianxiety drugs
   c. antipsychotic drugs
   d. antidepressant drugs

5. Dyslexia is a language disorder that applies to
   a. reading
   b. writing
   c. listening
   d. speaking

6. Tara often says "me" when she apparently means "you." She just can not seem to get this part of speech correct. This error is called
   a. echolalia
   b. neologism
   c. nominal aphasia
   d. pronominal reversal

7. The diagnosis of profound mental retardation is given when the IQ score is
   a. 50-70
   b. 35-49
   c. 20-34
   d. below 20

8. Melissa's baby was born looking a bit dwarf-like. Early testing revealed a thyroid gland deficiency. The diagnosis of the baby's condition is likely to be
   a. cretinism
   b. Tay-Sachs disease
   c. fragile X syndrome
   d. phenylketonuria (PKU)

9. The most common mental health problem of older adults is
   a. dementia
   b. depression
   c. schizophrenia
   d. substance abuse

10. Mr. Mathews is 85 years old. He is in the emergency room because he is confused. He can not seem to concentrate and is not apparently aware of his immediate surroundings. He can not think straight. This happened over the last several hours. He is displaying
   a. delirium
   b. dementia
   c. depression
   d. an anxiety attack

Chapter 20

1. Mario has been accused of a killing. Just as the court date arrives he starts displaying the symptoms of schizophrenia. In a couple of days he is essentially not functional any more. What is likely to happen in court?
   a. He is likely to be tried for the crime.
   b. He is likely to be committed indefinitely.
   c. He is likely to get off because he is not competent.
   d. He is likely to be committed until he is competent to stand trial.

2. John Hinckley was found not guilty of shooting President Ronald Reagan in 1981. The basis for the finding was that
   a. he had a mental disorder
   b. no crime was committed
   c. he was mentally unstable at the time of the crime
   d. he was mentally unstable at the time of the trial and unable to defend himself

3. According to the criteria of the American Law Institute, a person is judged not criminally responsible if he or she has functioned
   a. under a mental disease or mental defect
   b. under a compulsion or an irresistible impulse to act
   c. without the knowledge of the nature of the act he was doing or that what he was doing was wrong
   d. without appreciation for the wrongfulness of his conduct, or lacking the ability to conform his conduct to the requirements of law, as a result of mental disease or defect

4. What percent of defendants who use the insanity plea are actually found not guilty?
   a. 1 %
   b. 10%
   c. 25%
   d. 30 %

5. In Jackson v. Indiana, the U. S. Supreme Court ruled that when a person is judged not competent to stand trial
   a. prison confinement is an option
   b. indefinite commitment is not legal
   c. a person must be release from custody
   d. a person may be committed indefinitely under criminal status

6. One of the justifications for civil commitment is that a person
   a. needs treatment
   b. has been found guilty but mentally ill
   c. has been found not competent to stand trial
   d. has been found not guilty by reason of insanity

7. What is the function of the two-physician certificate ("2 PC") commitment procedure?
   a. It is used for the commitment of a child.
   b. It is only used in cases of criminal commitment.
   c. It allows family members to order civil commitment.
   d. It allows quick commitment in an emergency situation.

8. In the case of Robinson v. California, the U. S. Supreme Court ruled that
   a. involuntarily committed people had a right to treatment or release.
   b. committing drug addicts to treatment facilities may violate the Constitution.
   c. sending drug addicts to prison for being addicts may violate the Constitution.
   d. when one is ruled legally not competent, he or she gives up all constitutional rights.

9. What form of therapy are patients most likely to be granted the right to refuse?
   a. ECT
   b. medications
   c. psychosurgery
   d. psychotherapy

10. The Department of Defense is conducting a pilot program designed to evaluate the possibility that psychologists should be given the power to
   a. prescribe drugs
   b. do psychoanalysis
   c. admit patients to hospitals
   d. perform ECT and other forms of biological treatments of mental disorders

Multiple Choice Answer Key

Look up correct answers by chapter and question number. Immediately following the correct answer is the page reference for the textbook, the difficulty level of the question, and if the question is factual (Fa) or applied (Ap).

Chapter 1
1. b, p. 3, D1, Ap
2. c, p. 4, D2, Ap
3. d, p. 7, D2, Fa
4. b, p. 9, D1, Fa
5. d, p. 11, D1, Fa
6. b, p. 14, D2, Fa
7. b, p. 15, D2 Fa
8. b, p. 18, D2, Ap
9. c, p. 20, D1, Fa
10. d, p. 22, D2, Fa

Chapter 2
1 b, p. 30, D2, Ap
2 c, p. 31, D1, Fa
3 d, p. 34, D1, Ap
4 b, p. 36, D1, Fa
5 a, p. 38, D2, Ap
6 b, p. 38, D2, Ap
7 d, p. 39, D1, Fa
8 d, p. 41, D1, Fa
9 b, p. 44, D2, Ap
10 b, p. 47, D1, Fa

Chapter 3
1 c, p. 53, D1, Fa
2 b, p. 54, D1, Fa
3 a, p. 55, D1, Fa
4 c, p. 55, D2, Fa
5 b, p. 58, D2, Fa
6 a, p. 59, D1, Fa
7 c, p. 61 , D1, Fa
8 a, p. 66, D2, Ap
9 b, p. 71, D2, Ap
10 d, p. 79, D1, Fa

Chapter 4
1 a, p. 90, D1, Fa
2 c, p. 91, D1, Fa
3 a, p. 92, D2, Ap
4 d, p. 93, D2, Fa
5 b, p. 95, D1, Fa
6 d, p. 96, D1, Fa
7 c, p. 100, D2, Ap
8 b, p. 105, D2, Fa
9 c, p. 111, D1, Fa
10 b, p. 114, D2, Ap

Chapter 5
1 a, p. 120, D1, Fa
2 a, p. 121, D1, Fa
3 a, p. 124, D1, Fa
4 a, p. 126, D1, Fa
5 c, p. 129, D2, Ap
6 b, p. 133, D1, Fa
7 a, p. 137, D1, Fa
8 b, p. 138, D1, Fa
9 a, p. 142, D1, Fa
10 a, p. 151, D1, Fa

Chapter 6
1 a, p. 156, D1, Fa
2 d, p. 157, D2, Ap
3 b, p. 159, D2, Ap
4 b, p. 164, D2, Fa
5 a, p. 168, D1, Fa
6 a, p. 173, D1, Fa
7 a, p. 178, D2, Ap
8 d, p. 183, D1, Fa
9 c, p. 186, D1, Fa
10 c, p. 189, D1, Fa

Chapter 7
1 b, p. 198, D2, Fa
2 d, p.200, D2, Fa
3 d, p. 202, D2, Ap
4 a, p. 204, D1, Fa
5 d, p. 208, Fa
6 a, p. 211, D1, Fa
7 a, p. 214, D1, Fa
8 b, p. 219, D1, Fa
9 c, p. 227, D1, Fa
10 a, p. 229, D1, Fa

Chapter 8
1 c, p. 236, D1, Fa
2 b, p. 241, D1, Fa
3 b, p. 242, D1, Fa
4 c, p. 246, D2, Fa
5 d, p. 250, D1, Fa
6 d, p. 253, D1, fa
7 b, p. 255, D2, Ap
8 a, p. 257, D2, Ap
9 a, p. 265, D2, Fa
10 d, p. 267, D2, Fa

Chapter 9
1 b, p. 274, D2, Fa
2 c, p. 276, D1, Fa
3 d, p. 278, D2, Ap
4 a, p. 281, D2, Ap
5 c, p. 283, D2, Ap
6 c, p. 287, D1, Fa
7 d, p. 288, D1, Fa
8 d, p. 291, D1, Fa
9 a, p. 293, D1, Fa
10 b, p. 296, D1, Fa

Chapter 10
1 c, p. 304, D2, Fa
2 a, p. 305, D2, Fa
3 c, p. 309, D2, Fa
4 b, p. 310, D2, Fa
5 a, p. 311, D1, Fa
6 c, p. 313, D1, Fa
7 c, p. 315, D1, Fa
8 b, p. 318, D1, Fa
9 c, p. 322, D2, Fa
10 b, p. 323, D2, Fa

Chapter 11
1 a, p. 338, D1, Fa
2 c, p. 340, D2, Fa
3 c, p. 340, D2, Ap
4 d, p. 343, D1, Fa
5 b, p. 345, D1, Fa
6 b, p. 348, D2, Ap
7 a, p. 350, D1, Fa
8 c, p. 351, D1, Fa
9 d, p. 352, D1, Fa
10 a, p. 355, D1, Fa

Chapter 12
1 c, p. 371, D1, Fa
2 c, p. 373, D1, Fa
3 c, p. 374, D1, Fa
4 c, p. 377, D1, Fa
5 c, p. 379, D1, Fa
6 c, p. 382, D2, Fa
7 a, p. 386, D2, Fa
8 b, p. 390, D1, Fa
9 b, p. 393, D2, Ap
10 b, p. 397, D1, Fa

Chapter 13
1 b, p. 404, D1, Fa
2 b, p. 406, D2, Fa
3 d, p. 407, D2, Ap
4 c, p. 410, D1, Fa
5 a, p. 414, D1, Fa
6 d, p. 416, D1, Fa
7 b, p. 422, D1, Ap
8 b, p. 427, D1, Fa
9 b, p. 431, D1, Fa
10 b, p. 436, D1, Fa

Chapter 14
1 d, p. 444, D1, Fa
2 d, p. 445, D1, Fa
3 d, p. 447, D2, Fa
4 a, p. 448, D1, Fa
5 b, p. 452, D1, Ap
6 c, p. 456, D2, Fa
7 b, p. 460, D2, Fa
8 a, p. 465, D1, Fa
9 a, p. 469, D1, Fa
10 c, p. 471, D1, Fa

Chapter 15
1 b, p. 480, D1, Fa
2 d, p. 482, D1, Fa
3 b, p. 486, D1, Fa
4 a, p. 487, D2, Fa
5 d, p. 490, D1, Fa
6 b, p. 492, D2, Fa
7 a, p. 495, D2, Fa
8 a, p. 497, D2, Ap
9 d, p. 500, D1, Fa
10 a, p. 503, D2, Fa

Chapter 16
1 b, p. 510, D1, Fa
2 a, p. 511, Dl, Fa
3 b, p. 512, D2, Fa
4 b, p. 515, D1, Fa
5 b, p. 516, D2, Ap
6 a, p. 517, D2, Fa
7 c, p. 518, D2, Ap
8 b, p. 519, D1, Fa
9 d, p. 519, D2, Ap
10 b, p. 524, D1, Fa

Chapter 17
1 a, p. 537, D2, Ap
2 c, p. 537, D1, Ap
3 b, p. 541, D1, Fa
4 d, p. 542, D1, Fa
5 d, p. 545, D2, Ap
6 b, p. 547, D1, Fa
7 a, p. 548, D1, Fa
8 b, p. 550, D2, Fa
9 d, p. 557, D2, Fa
10 b, p. 558, D2, Fa

Chapter 18
1 d, p. 567, D1, Fa
2 a, p. 570, D1, Fa
3 a, p. 571, D2, Fa
4 b, p. 572, D2, Fa
5 b, p. 576, D1, Fa
6 a, p. 582, D2, Fa
7 b, p. 585, D1, Fa
8 c, p. 588, D1, Fa
9 d, p. 592, D2, Ap
10 b, p. 589, D1, Fa

Chapter 19
1 c, p. 600, D1, Fa
2 a, p. 603, D2, Ap
3 d, p. 605, D2, Fa
4 a, p. 608, D1, Fa
5 a, p. 611, D1, Fa
6 d, p. 613, D1, Ap
7 d, p. 621, D1, Fa
8 a, p. 623, D2, Ap
9 b, p. 626, D2, Fa
10 a, p. 627, D2, Ap

Chapter 20
1 d, p. 636, D2, Ap
2 c, p. 636, D1, Fa
3 d, p. 638, D1, Fa
4 c, p. 639, D2, Fa
5 b, p. 643, D1, Fa
6 a, p. 644, D2, Fa
7 d, p. 646, D1, Fa
8 c, p. 647, D2, Fa
9 c, p. 650, D2, Fa
10 a, p. 653, D1, Fa